Apple Pro Training Series

# Motion 4

Mark Spencer

Apple
Certified

Apple Pro Training Series: Motion 4
Mark Spencer
Copyright © 2010 by Mark Spencer

Published by Peachpit Press. For information on Peachpit Press books, contact:

Peachpit Press
1249 Eighth Street
Berkeley, CA 94710
(510) 524-2178
Fax: (510) 524-2221
http://www.peachpit.com
To report errors, please send a note to errata@peachpit.com.
Peachpit Press is a division of Pearson Education.

**Apple Series Editor:** Serena Herr
**Editor:** Bob Lindstrom
**Production Coordinator:** Kim Wimpsett, Happenstance Type-O-Rama
**Technical Editors:** Dion Scoppettuolo, Charles Meyer
**Technical Reviewer:** Brendan Boykin
**Copy Editor and Proofreader:** Elissa Rabellino
**Compositor:** Chris Gillespie, Happenstance Type-O-Rama
**Indexer:** Jack Lewis
**Media Reviewer:** Eric Geoffroy
**Cover Illustration:** Kent Oberheu
**Cover Production:** Happenstance Type-O-Rama

ISBN 10: 0-321-63529-9
ISBN 13: 978-0-321-63529-7
9 8 7 6 5 4 3 2 1
Printed and bound in the United States of America

**Acknowledgments** Thanks to the following individuals and organizations for contributing projects and/or footage for this book:

Kent Oberheu and the band The Eyes/Pale Divine

Overture Films, LLC, and Billy Fox, A.C.E.

One Trick Pony Film Co.

Steve Martin and the entire Ripple Training crew

Alex Lindsay and the good folks in the Pixel Corps

Steve Szabo

Charles Meyer at Apple, Inc.

# Contents at a Glance

# Table of Contents

# Getting Started

Welcome to the official Apple Pro training course for Motion 4, Apple's revolutionary real-time motion graphics application. This book is a comprehensive guide to designing with Motion. It covers the use of behaviors, keyframes, particle dynamics, text, audio, keying, paint, tracking, round-tripping with other Final Cut Studio applications, and working in 3D.

Whether you've been creating motion graphics for years or are encountering these techniques for the first time, Motion's design approach is different from anything you've used before. The real-time design engine and behavior system are easy to learn, yet they open the door to expansive creativity.

## The Methodology

This book takes a hands-on approach to learning the software. It's divided into projects that methodically introduce the interface elements and ways of working with them, building progressively until you can comfortably grasp the entire application and its standard workflows.

Each lesson in this book is self-contained, so you can jump to any lesson at any time. However, each lesson is designed to support the concepts learned in the preceding lesson, and newcomers to motion graphics should go through the book from start to finish. The first five lessons, in particular, teach basic concepts and are best completed in order.

### Course Structure

The lessons are project based and designed to teach you real-world techniques for completing the types of motion graphics projects most commonly encountered in a professional setting. As you progress through the book, you will learn Motion's features and capabilities while you create a high definition (HD) show promo, a television ad, an HD web advertisement, a DVD motion menu, an HD greenscreen composite, and a visual effects shot.

The lessons are organized into the following sections:

▶  Lessons 1–5: Fundamentals

In Lesson 1, you build a project while becoming familiar with Motion's user interface: You learn how to import video files, transform them, and add filters, behaviors, and masks; apply blend modes; and create and animate text. Lesson 2 explores compositing in depth, including working with layers and groups, blend modes and filters, and masks and clones; as well as editing in the Timeline. Lesson 3 details Motion's templates, how to create them, and how to use them in Final Cut Pro. Lesson 4 focuses on the workflow between Final Cut Pro and Motion; and in Lesson 5, you learn several ways to share your completed project.

▶  Lessons 6–7: Animation

After mastering the basics, you are now ready to try animation. Lesson 6 focuses on using behaviors, and Lesson 7 is devoted to keyframing.

▶  Lessons 8–11: Motion Graphics Design

Having acquired basic skills in compositing and animation, you turn your attention to designing motion graphics using Motion's tool set. In Lesson 8, generators, shapes, and paint strokes are used to create animated content. Lesson 9 covers text styling and animation. Lesson 10 examines particle emitters and replicators, and Lesson 11 covers multiple ways to work with audio.

▶ Lessons 12–14: Visual Effects Design

This section explores visual effects design. In Lesson 12, you create speed changes; in Lesson 13, you create a visual effects shot for a Hollywood film; and in Lesson 14, you composite a greenscreen shot.

▶ Lessons 15–16: An Introduction to 3D

The final section provides an overview of Motion's 3D capabilities. In Lesson 15, you build a 3D scene; and in Lesson 16, you animate a camera through the scene, adding lights, reflections, depth of field, and shadows.

Because this book is project based, earlier lessons sometimes call on you to use features and techniques that aren't explained in detail until later lessons. When this occurs, you'll see a note indicating that the technique is covered in more detail in a later lesson.

## Some Terminology

Here are two key terms used throughout the book:

▶ Composite—Most often this refers to your final work: the image you see on the screen. You could also think of this as a *composition*. The term is occasionally used as a verb: You *composite* several objects together to create the final product.

▶ Objects—This is the word used by Motion to describe the individual elements of a composite. *Objects* can include QuickTime movies, image sequences, still images, and text. The objects are layered together to create the composite.

For a full list of motion graphics–related terms, a glossary is included at the end of the book.

## System Requirements

All systems are not created equal, and the more power you have in your hardware, the more you'll be able to do in real time (that is, without rendering) in Motion.

Here's a brief explanation of how Motion leverages your hardware. If you're thinking of upgrading your system to run Motion, it might help you to decide what configuration will give you the best results.

The following sections are a little technical, so if you start to lose track, don't panic. Just remember: Faster equals better, more RAM equals better, and a more powerful graphics card equals better.

### System Memory

Motion uses system RAM to cache all the objects that make up your composite throughout your preview range (see the Glossary if these terms are new to you).

Here's an example. Let's say you have three QuickTime movies you're combining in Motion to create a final, single image—your composite. Imagine that you have a moving fractal background clip (Element 1), a rotating web (Element 2), and some random boxes (Element 3).

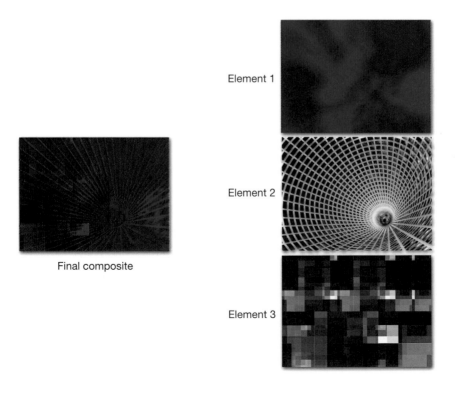

Element 1

Element 2

Element 3

Final composite

Each frame of 8-bit NTSC video contains 720 pixels horizontally and 486 pixels vertically (480 for DV). When you add up the memory required to store every one of those pixels in the computer's memory, it works out to about 1.3 MB (including an alpha channel). A full raster 8-bit 1920 x 1080 HD video requires about 8.3 MB for each frame.

So if you wanted Motion to generate a real-time preview of your three-layer composite that lasted for 120 frames (about 4 seconds), you'd need to multiply the memory requirement for a single frame by the number of objects onscreen at the same time, and then multiply that by the number of frames you wished to play back in real time: 1.3 x 3 x 120 = 468 MB. For HD video, the memory requirement would be about 3 GB.

To make real-time adjustments to the three clips in our hypothetical composite, you'd need to have at least 468 MB of free RAM, or 3 GB for HD. And that's beyond the RAM used by the operating system, Motion, and other background applications. So for this scenario to work well, you'd need at least 1 GB of system RAM for NTSC, or 4 GB for HD. (PAL format video requires essentially the same amount of RAM as NTSC video: Although the images are 720 x 576, there are only 25 of them each second.)

Have I lost you in geek speak? That's OK. All you really need to know is that if you have more system RAM, you can play back more objects in real time and watch a longer preview of your composite than you could with minimal RAM. Hang in there, though, as this is only part of the story.

### Video Card Memory (VRAM)

In addition to your system RAM, your Macintosh has memory on the graphics card itself. This memory is known as *VRAM* (*video RAM*) and is used by the graphics card while it's performing calculations to draw an image to your computer monitor. Your graphics card also has its own processor, called a *GPU* (*graphics processing unit*), which calculates how things should get drawn.

Every time Motion draws a frame of your composite on the monitor, it sends one frame of each object in your composite to the VRAM of the graphics card, along with a set of instructions telling the processor on the graphics card what it's supposed to do with each image. The processor might be told to scale down an image, blur another, or color-correct another, before combining them all into a single image. This is where the real-time part of Motion takes place.

Since the graphics card's processor can render only what's been put into its VRAM, the number of layers that can be processed in real time is going to be limited by how much VRAM you have.

Now, in our NTSC example, we have only three layers of video, each layer taking up 1.3 MB of memory per frame. In theory, we need only 3.9 MB of VRAM to draw a frame, but in reality, overhead is created by other processes, and certain filters and effects will use VRAM over and above that used for the video layers themselves.

Once a single frame is drawn, the VRAM is free to load up the objects for the next frame. So the amount of VRAM affects how many layers and effects can be combined at *one frame* of the sequence, not the whole sequence. In other words, the number of frames being previewed is not affected by how much VRAM you have—it only affects the number of objects that can be composited in a single frame.

Finally, even when you reach your VRAM limits, Motion has a clever RAM-caching feature that allows you to render a real-time preview and still manipulate individual objects in real time via a soloing feature.

### CPU Speed

You've always been told that a faster CPU is better. That's also true for Motion, but not in the way you might think. Since the processor in your graphics card is doing all the heavy lifting, the CPU doesn't really have much to do with the actual construction of the composite.

Where the main system CPU comes into play is in calculating Motion's behaviors, particle trajectories, motion paths, and curves before sending them to the graphics card. So if you're using a lot of complex behaviors in your project, you'll definitely benefit from a faster processor.

### Summarizing Hardware Requirements

The good news from the preceding technobabble is that if your system meets the minimum system requirements, improving Motion's performance doesn't necessarily mean buying a faster computer; upgrading your graphics card may be all that's required.

Here's the story in a nutshell:

▶ System RAM determines how many frames of animation you can preview in real time (and to some degree, how many objects in a composite can be viewed in real time before you have to perform a RAM Preview render).

▶ VRAM (video RAM on the graphics card) determines how many objects in a composite can be rendered in real time before a RAM Preview render is required. If you want more objects on the screen with more filters and effects, you'll need more VRAM.

▶ CPU speed determines how many complex behaviors and simulations can be applied to the composite objects in real time. It has less impact on the number of layers that can be drawn to screen; the amount of VRAM is more important in determining this.

Visit www.apple.com/finalcutstudio/motion for a current list of system requirements and supported hardware. In addition, be sure to install any Apple updates to the Motion 4 software.

## Using Motion on a Laptop

Some of the keystrokes identified in this book for desktop use work differently if you are using a MacBook Pro. Specifically, you'll need to hold down the Function key (fn) at the bottom left of the keyboard when pressing any of the F keys (F1 through F8) along the top of the keyboard. To avoid this, you open the Keyboard & Mouse section of System Preferences (in the Apple menu), and in the Keyboard pane, select the "Use all F1, F2, etc. keys as standard function keys" checkbox.

Even with this checkbox selected, however, you will still need to press the fn key when using the Home and End keys, located at the lower right of the keyboard.

## Gestures

Motion supports two types of gestures: gestures that you perform on the Multi-Touch trackpad of a MacBook Pro; and Motion's own gestures language, which is a set of patterns that you draw using a Wacom Intuos tablet and pen. (Motion gestures are available exclusively for tablets in the Wacom Intuos family.)

### Multi-Touch Gesture Support

You can use two-finger scrolls, three-finger swipes, pinches, and rotation movements on the Multi-Touch trackpad of a MacBook Pro to perform actions such as scrolling through a list of files, resizing icons, opening the Project or Timing pane, and moving the playhead.

### Gestures

Unlike gestures performed on a Multi-Touch trackpad, Motion's gestures are movements that you make using a pen and graphics tablet to address a larger variety of tasks, such as playback control, Timeline navigation, editing, and executing general commands.

To use gestures, you need to enable Handwriting Recognition in Mac OS X Ink preferences, which can be accessed through Motion's Gestures preferences pane.

For information on how to enable and use gestures, and to view a table of all available gestures, see Appendix F in the Motion 4 User Manual, which you can open by choosing Help > Motion Help.

## Copying the Motion Lesson Files

*Apple Pro Training Series: Motion 4* comes with a DVD containing all the files you need to complete each lesson. The project and media files are contained within the Motion4_Book_Files folder.

### Installing the Lesson Files

1    Insert the *Apple Pro Training Series: Motion 4* DVD into your computer's DVD drive.

2    For best results, drag the entire Motion4_Book_Files folder from the DVD to the top level of your computer's hard drive or to an attached media drive.

The disc contains approximately 2 GB of data.

It is important that you put this folder on the top level of your hard drive as described; this will ensure that the Motion project files correctly link with their media.

## Reconnecting Broken Media Links

For any number of reasons, you may need to separate the lesson files from the media files when you install and use them. For instance, you may choose to keep the project files in a user home directory and the media files on a dedicated media drive. In this case, when you open a project file, a window will appear asking you to reconnect the project files to their source media files.

Reconnecting files is a simple process. Just follow these steps:

**1** When you open a lesson's project file, a dialog may appear listing one or more files as missing. Click the Reconnect button.

**2** In the window that appears, navigate to Motion4_Book_Files > Media, and open the appropriate project folder.

**3** Select the highlighted file and click Open.

**4** Continue to connect files as necessary until the window closes.

**5** Be sure to save the newly reconnected project file, or you will have to perform the reconnect operation every time you open the project.

## About the Apple Pro Training Series

*Apple Pro Training Series: Motion 4* is both a self-paced learning tool and the official curriculum of the Apple Pro Training and Certification Program. Developed by experts in the field and certified by Apple, the series is used by Apple Authorized Training Centers worldwide and offers complete training in all Apple Pro products. The lessons are designed to let you learn at your own pace. Each lesson concludes with review questions and answers summarizing what you've learned, which can be used to help you prepare for the Apple Pro Certification Exam.

For a complete list of Apple Pro Training Series books, see the ad at the back of this book, or visit www.peachpit.com/apts.

## Apple Pro Certification Program

The Apple Pro Training and Certification Program is designed to keep you at the forefront of Apple's digital media technology while giving you a competitive edge in today's ever-changing job market. Whether you're an editor, graphic designer, sound designer, special-effects artist, or teacher, these training tools are meant to help you expand your skills.

Upon completing the course material in this book, you can become a certified Apple Pro by taking the certification exam at an Apple Authorized Training Center. Successful certification as an Apple Pro gives you official recognition of your knowledge of Apple's professional applications while allowing you to market yourself to employers and clients as a skilled, pro-level user of Apple products.

For those who prefer to learn in an instructor-led setting, Apple offers training courses at Apple Authorized Training Centers worldwide. These courses, which use the Apple Pro Training Series books as their curriculum, are taught by Apple Certified Trainers, and they balance concepts and lectures with hands-on labs and exercises. Apple Authorized Training Centers have been carefully selected and have met Apple's highest standards in all areas, including facilities, instructors, course delivery, and infrastructure. The goal of the program is to offer Apple customers, from beginners to the most seasoned professionals, the highest-quality training experience.

For more information, please see the ad at the back of this book; or to find an Authorized Training Center near you, go to training.apple.com.

## Resources

*Apple Pro Training Series: Motion 4* is not intended as a comprehensive reference manual, nor does it replace the documentation that comes with the application. For more information about Motion, refer to these sources:

▶ Motion User Manual—Accessed through the Motion Help menu, the User Manual contains a complete description of all the features.

▶ Apple's website—www.apple.com.

▶ Peachpit's website—As Motion 4 is updated, Peachpit may choose to update lessons or post additional exercises as necessary on this book's companion webpage: www.peachpit.com/apts.motion4.

# Fundamentals

# 1

| | |
|---|---|
| Lesson Files | Motion4_Book_Files > Lessons > Lesson_01 |
| Media | Motion4_Book_Files > Media > Intro |
| Time | This lesson takes approximately 60 minutes to complete. |
| Goals | Create a new project |
| | Navigate the Motion interface |
| | Add video to a project |
| | Duplicate elements |
| | Set a play range |
| | Make transformations |
| | Add and modify effects |
| | Apply blend modes |
| | Use Library content |
| | Create and animate text |

# Lesson 1
# Getting Around in Motion

With its intuitive interface, Motion lets you immediately start combining video and graphics, animating text, or creating dazzling particle effects. But don't confuse clean design with simplicity—Motion is a deep application that can help you realize your creative vision, no matter how intricate or complex.

In this first lesson, you won't focus too much on what things are or why they work the way they do. That will all come in the lessons that follow. Instead, you'll jump right in and start building a new project from scratch. This way, you'll get a feel for what's unique about Motion— and what makes it so much fun to work with.

## Following a New Paradigm

With Motion, you can do something on a desktop or portable computer that was unthinkable only a few short years ago: create compelling, professional-looking motion graphics and visual effects in a real-time design environment. What used to require a million-dollar suite in a swank post-production facility can now be accomplished in a home office, high school lab, or campus dorm room.

Whether you answer to a director, producer, agency, or corporate client—or to your own unencumbered creative muse—you can design motion graphics in a fluid, interactive way that is natural and downright addictive.

Motion is designed to make it easy to perform the tasks of the motion graphics artist: *compositing* and *animating*. Compositing involves designing an image using multiple elements that are layered together. Animating involves changing properties of those layers over time so that they fly, drift, grow, fade, spin, or wriggle. Motion's real-time design engine and unique *behaviors* allow you to design and animate interactively—meaning you can add and adjust elements as your project plays.

And with Motion's intuitive 3D design tools, you can spread out your elements in 3D space; add lights, reflections, and shadows; and fly virtual cameras around a 3D world.

Using Motion's integration with Final Cut Studio, you can edit and create basic motion graphics and effects in Final Cut Pro, and then efficiently move the results to Motion for further polish and refinement.

Whether you're designing an opening title sequence, producing a series of lower thirds, or building a DVD motion menu, Motion makes designing motion graphics and visual effects more accessible, more interactive, and more enjoyable.

## Opening Motion

Let's start by opening Motion and creating a new project.

1   Navigate to the Applications folder in your home folder, and double-click the Motion icon.

    **NOTE ▶** You can also drag the Motion application to the Dock and open it from there.

    When Motion opens, it greets you with the Welcome screen, where you can choose to view web-based tours, follow a tutorial, open a template, or start with a new project. In this exercise, you'll choose the last option, which is already selected.

**TIP** ▶ If you want to bypass the Welcome screen, click the "Show Welcome Screen at startup" checkbox to deselect it. If you change your mind, you can restore the Welcome screen in Motion's Preferences, which you'll work with in later lessons.

**2** Verify that "Start with a New Project" is selected and click Continue.

Motion prompts you to select a project preset.

**3** In this lesson, you'll be working with a video clip that was shot with a Sony XDCAM EX video camera in HD (high definition) at 23.98 frames per second (fps). So, from the Preset pop-up menu, choose XDCAM EX 720p24.

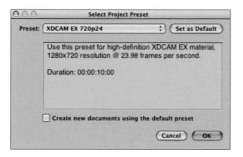

**NOTE** ▶ Whenever a preset name includes *24*, it's shorthand for 23.98 fps; *30* is short for 29.97, and *60* is short for 59.94. These fractional frame rates are leftovers from the NTSC television standard's conversion from black and white to color back in the 1950s.

**TIP** You usually choose a project preset based on the format of the video material you are working with and your final output specifications—you would choose one preset to create a spot for standard definition television and another for HDTV content. If you plan to use the same preset repeatedly, click "Set as Default" to automatically select the preset the next time you create a project. If you want to bypass the Select Project Preset dialog altogether and immediately create a project using your default preset, select the "Create new documents using the default preset" checkbox.

**4**  Click OK.

A new, empty Motion project opens.

## Importing a Video Clip

The Motion interface, called the *workspace*, consists of several windows that can be arranged in various layouts. The large window to the right, dominated by a black rectangle, is the *Canvas*. Here you build and view your project. The tall, skinny window to the left is the *utility window*, where you find content to add to your project. You'll also use the utility window to change elements already placed in your project. Motion's workspace has other interface elements that are hidden by default—you'll open them as you need them.

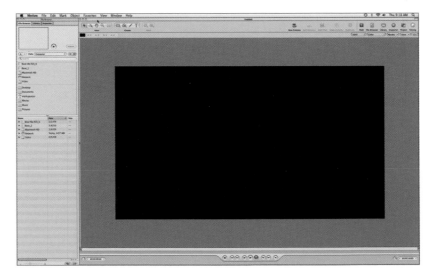

At the top of the utility window are three tabs. The first one, File Browser, is in front. The File Browser is where you locate, preview, and import media into your project. Media includes graphics, video, and audio files that are located on your computer or connected storage devices.

Let's bring a video clip into the project.

**1**   In the middle of the File Browser, click the Macintosh HD icon. This section of the File Browser is called the *sidebar*.

**NOTE ▸** If you renamed your main hard drive, you'll see that name in the sidebar.

The contents of the hard disk are now displayed in the lower section of the File Browser, called the *stack*.

**2**   Double-click the Motion4_Book_Files folder.

**3**   Double-click the Media folder, and then double-click the Intro folder.

Inside this folder is a single video clip.

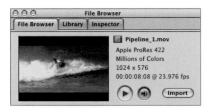

**4**   Click the file and look at the top of the File Browser.

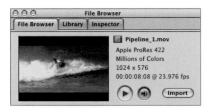

This is the *Preview area*, in which you can preview a video clip and also find important information about that clip, including its resolution, codec, and frame rate.

Now that you've confirmed that this is the clip you want to use, you can add it to your project by simply dragging it in.

5    Drag the clip from the File Browser stack (not from the Preview area) to the Canvas—but don't release the mouse button just yet.

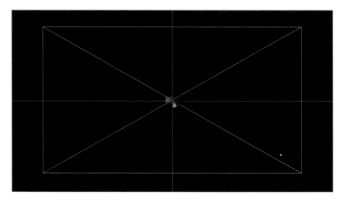

Yellow lines appear as you move the clip near the vertical and horizontal center of the Canvas, and you'll feel the clip *snap* to those lines when it approaches them. These lines are the *dynamic guides*, and they help you center an element in the Canvas and align multiple elements.

6    Snap the clip to the center of the Canvas and release the mouse button.

**NOTE ►** If the dynamic guides don't appear, choose View > Snap or press N to turn on snapping.

Before you go any further, it's a good idea to save your project.

7    Choose File > Save, or press Command-S.

8    Navigate to Macintosh HD > Motion4_Book_Files > Lessons > Lesson_01 > Student_Saves.

9    Name your project *Lesson_01_practice* and click Save.

When you added the clip, you may have noticed a translucent gray window that appeared above the Canvas. It's called the *heads-up display*, or *HUD*. You'll use it later in this lesson. For now, you can turn it on and off by clicking the HUD icon at the top right of the Canvas or by pressing F7.

## Setting a Play Range

Now for the fun part: building your project while it plays back. First you'll set a play range to focus your efforts.

1    At the bottom of the Canvas are the transport controls. Click the Play button or press the Spacebar to start playback.

> **TIP** If you pause playback before moving the play range In or Out point, the playhead will temporarily jump to the new Out point and the Canvas will display the frame you are on, making it easier to choose a play range based on a specific frame.

The video clip plays. It was shot in slow motion, so it appears to be playing more slowly than real time, but at the top left of the Canvas in the Status Bar, you'll see an indicator that shows the current playback speed in frames per second (FPS).

You'll notice a few seconds of black that plays after the end of the clip. This is because the clip is shorter than the duration of your project. At the bottom of the Canvas, notice the blue bar that doesn't quite extend to the end of the project.

The area that contains the blue bar titled *Pipeline_1* and the yellow playhead above it is called the *mini-Timeline*. It shows the currently selected element and is handy for moving and trimming elements in your project.

To play just a section of the video clip, you'll adjust the *play range*, the area identified by blue triangles that can loop, or repeat, during playback. Changing the play range is a great way to focus on a specific part of your project.

2   With the project playing, drag the play range Out Point (the rightmost blue triangle) to 5:00 (5 seconds).

At 5 seconds, the surfer in the clip has just landed in the water, a good point at which to stop.

**NOTE** ▶ To start at this point in the lesson, open Lesson_01_A.

A tooltip appears that shows the new location of the Out point, displayed in either timecode or frames.

**NOTE** ▸ To switch between timecode and frame displays, click one of the watch icons at the bottom left or right of the Canvas. The icon on the left is the current frame icon, and the icon on the right is the duration icon.

3    Review the results of the new play range, and then press Command-S to save your work.

## Transforming and Duplicating a Clip

Every element you add to a Motion project can be manipulated or *transformed*, whether it's a video clip, a graphic, or a Motion object such as a text or shape layer. Transformations include changing an element's position, scale, rotation, and other properties.

1    Notice the thin white line around the edge of the clip. This is called a *bounding box* and appears around any selected element. Click in the black area outside the video clip to deselect it. The bounding box and the blue bar in the mini-Timeline disappear.

2    Click the clip to select it again. Now click anywhere inside the clip and drag it around. You can change the position of a selected element just by dragging it.

3    Choose Edit > Undo Move or press Command-Z to return the clip to the center of the Canvas. The clip doesn't fill the Canvas, but you can easily scale it up to do so. You'll use one copy of the clip as a full-screen background and another copy as the main foreground element.

The small circles at the corners and midpoints of the bounding box are called *transform handles*. You can use them to manipulate the clip size.

4   Drag the top right transform handle up and to the right, then down and to the left.

The clip changes size *nonproportionally*—that is, you can make it skinny or fat— which is something you often want to avoid. Second, it doesn't stay centered as you scale—rather, the opposite control handle at the bottom left stays locked in place as the center of the clip moves around.

Often you'll want to scale an element proportionally *and* around its center. To do so, you can press modifier keys when dragging a transform handle.

5   Press Command-Z to undo the scale change.

6   Shift-drag the top right transform handle; then press Command-Z to undo. The clip now scales proportionally, but the center is still moving.

7   With the Shift key held down, also hold down the Option key. Now Shift-Option-drag the top right transform handle again. The clip scales both proportionally and around its center.

8   Scale up the clip to fill the black area of the Canvas. Use the tooltip as a guide to make it about 127 percent of its original size.

NOTE ▶ Normally you want to avoid scaling a graphic or video over 100 percent in size because the image can start to look soft or pixilated, but in this case you are using the clip as a background design element, so its clarity is not critical.

TIP ▶ The "x" in the center of the clip represents the element's *anchor point*, which can be repositioned. You'll work with anchor points in a later lesson.

In a moment you'll add some filters to this clip to make it into a more appropriate background design. But first, you'll duplicate it and scale down the copy for the foreground.

**9**   With the clip still selected, choose Edit > Duplicate or press Command-D. Nothing seems to have happened, but if you look at the mini-Timeline, you'll see that the currently selected clip is called *Pipeline_1 copy*.

**10**   Shift-Option-drag any transform handle to scale down the duplicate clip to 100 percent size. Because you are scaling proportionally and around the center, you can use any transform handle to get the same result.

**11**   Press Command-S to save your work.

## Adding Effects

You'll now use some effects to make your project come to life. Motion has three categories of effects: *filters*, *behaviors*, and *masks*. You'll use at least one of each for this project to get a feel for the ways they work. You'll also try out a powerful technique for changing how overlapping elements interact with each other, called *blend modes*. But first, it's time to introduce one of the hidden parts of Motion's interface: the Project pane.

**NOTE** ▶ If you want to start from this point, open *Lesson_01_B*.

### Displaying the Project Pane

While you can work exclusively in the Canvas, you'll eventually find it helpful to view a list of all the elements in your project when you want to select, rename, or reorganize them.

Motion calls this view the *Project pane*. You'll open it using an icon in the *Toolbar*, which is at the top of the Canvas.

**1**   At the top right of the Toolbar, click the Project icon, or press F5.

The Project pane slides open. It contains three tabs, but the tab in front, the Layers tab, is the one you'll use the most. It displays all the elements in your project as layers stacked inside groups.

Notice that when the Project pane is open, part of the video may be cut off.

2  In the Toolbar, click the Zoom Level pop-up menu and choose Fit In Window. The video scales to fit in the available space, and even adjusts its size dynamically as you open and close the Project pane.

> **TIP** Shift-Z is the keyboard shortcut for Fit In Window, the same as it is in Final Cut Pro. Using this command can cause the Canvas to scale larger than 100 percent if you have a large screen. To scale to exactly 100 percent, press Option-Z.

3  In the Layers tab, deselect the checkbox for the upper, foreground clip, `Pipeline_1 copy`. This *activation checkbox* toggles the visibility of the layer. With the foreground clip hidden, you can focus on the background clip.

4  In the Canvas, click the larger, background clip. Notice that the selected clip has a bounding box in the Canvas, is darkened in the Layers tab, and appears in the mini-Timeline.

## Stylizing with Filters

You use filters to change the look of an element in your project. For example, you can use filters to color-correct a video clip that is too dark, turn a flat map into a sphere, or remove a greenscreen background to composite one clip on top of another.

You'll find the filters in the second tab of the utility window: the Library.

1  In the utility window, click the Library tab, or press Command-2.

> **TIP** If you press Command-2 when the Library is already open, the entire utility pane closes. Press Command-2 again to open it again.

The Library is organized like the File Browser: a Preview area at the top, a sidebar in the middle, and a stack at the bottom. But rather than containing files from your hard drive, the Library contains all the elements that are installed with Motion.

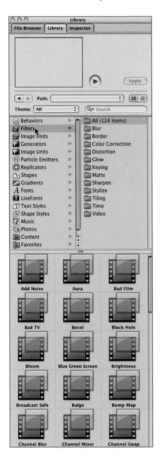

2   Choose the Filters category.

Let's use a blur filter to soften this background clip—that way, it won't distract the viewer's attention from the foreground.

**NOTE** ▶ Your filter icons in the stack will not resemble the previous figure if you are viewing the Library contents as a list. To toggle between View as Icons and View as List, click the buttons to the right of the Path pop-up menu.

3   Choose the Blur folder.

**4**   In the Library stack below, locate the Gaussian Blur filter.

**5**   With the project continuing to play, drag the filter onto the video in the Canvas. The video immediately blurs while continuing to play.

Now let's add another filter to further stylize this background.

**6**   Choose the Glow folder, locate the Light Rays filter, and then drag it onto the Canvas.

Notice that the filters appear in the Layers tab under the layer you applied them to. The Light Rays filter really blows out the bright areas of the ocean spray, so let's adjust it.

**7**   If the HUD is not visible, click the HUD icon in the Toolbar or press F7.

**8**   Reduce Glow to about 1.08 and increase Amount to 90. Those adjustments bring the whites back down and accentuate the rays.

Finally, let's darken the clip so that it doesn't compete too much with the foreground.

**9**   In the Library, choose the Color Correction folder, and then drag the Gamma filter onto the Canvas.

**10**   In the HUD, adjust Gamma to .72. The filter darkens the midtones nicely, leaving the whites bright and not crushing the blacks.

With the background element stylized, you'll now turn your attention to the foreground clip.

## Framing with a Mask

Masks allow you to hide parts of a layer based on a shape or a characteristic of another layer. With Motion, you can create a myriad of complex masking effects.

For this exercise, you'll add a simple shape mask to the foreground video clip and adjust it to create a more interesting framing.

**NOTE ▶** To start at this point in the lesson, open Lesson_01_C.

**1**   Stop playback and press the Home key to return the playhead to the first frame of the video.

To draw a mask, it will be easier to work on a single frame of the video. The first frame is a good place to start.

**2**   In the Layers tab, click the *Pipeline_1 copy* layer to select it.

**3**   Select the activation checkbox for the layer to make it visible in the Canvas.

**4**   In the Toolbar, click the Rectangle Mask tool.

**5**   Starting Starting above and to the left of the surfer, draw a rectangle that encompasses the surfer and includes some room to the right to reveal his direction of travel. The video now appears inside this rectangle only. Notice that the mask appears in the Layers tab and is selected.

You may want to adjust the size and position of the mask once you've drawn it. You adjust the mask the same way that you transformed the video clip earlier.

**6**   With the mask selected, drag inside the clip to reposition the mask.

**7**   Drag a transform handle on the bounding box to change the shape and size of the mask.

Let's soften and round the edges of the mask a bit.

**8**   In the HUD, increase Feather to 25 and Roundness to 20.

To distinguish the foreground clip from the background clip, you can add a drop shadow.

**9**   In the Layers tab, select Pipeline_1 copy.

**10**  In the HUD, select the Drop Shadow checkbox.

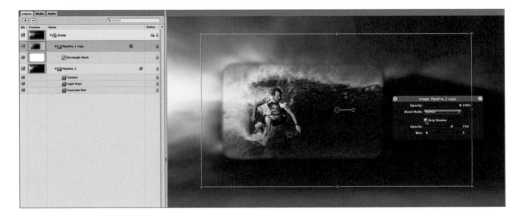

**11**  Save your work.

**12**  Start playback.

You've given a single video clip some pizzazz by transforming it, duplicating it, and adding a few filters and a mask. But if you watch the clip as it plays, the surfer flies up and out of the mask. So let's put that mask into motion.

## Animating with Behaviors

Behaviors are a type of effect in Motion that lets you create animation with drag-and-drop simplicity. To make something move, grow, spin, wriggle, oscillate, speed up, or slow down, you just apply a behavior and adjust it to suit the situation.

In this exercise, you'll use behaviors to animate the mask applied to the foreground video layer.

**NOTE ▶** To start from this point in the lesson, open *Lesson_01_D*.

1   With the foreground layer *Pipeline_1 copy* selected and the project playing, go to the Library and choose the Behaviors category.

2   Choose the Basic Motion folder.

3   Select the Throw behavior and watch the preview. The Preview area shows an animation of what the behavior does, and also displays an explanation.

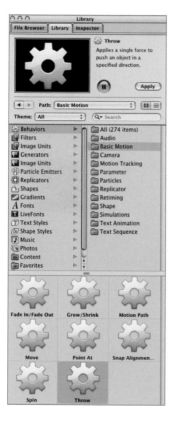

4   Drag the Throw behavior onto the Rectangle Mask in the Layers tab.

You want to animate the mask only, not the video, so you must drag the behavior onto the mask. If you were to drag the behavior onto the Canvas, the behavior would be applied to the video clip along with the mask, which would move the entire video clip.

5    In the HUD, drag from the center of the circle out to the right and up while watching the project play, to make the mask follow the surfer and keep him in the frame.

The mask now moves with the surfer, up and to the right. Make sure you don't throw the mask too high or it will reveal the hard edge of the video frame. It's OK if the surfer goes out of the mask at the top of the jump.

To add more movement, you'll rotate the mask as it moves.

6    Drag the Spin behavior from the Library to the Rectangle Mask in the Layers tab.

7    In the HUD, drag clockwise from the top of the circle to give the mask a slight clockwise rotation.

8    Drag the rotation handle that extends out of the center of the video clip to rotate the clip slightly counterclockwise, so that it starts on an angle. You may find it easier to rotate the clip if you stop playback.

**NOTE** ▶ You may need to adjust the Throw behavior so that the mask doesn't move off the edge of the video. To do so, first select the Throw behavior in the Layers tab.

The mask now follows the surfer up and across the screen, and the Spin behavior makes the move a little more dynamic.

## Compositing with a Blend Mode

Blend modes are a compositor's best friend: They alter how text, image, or video layers interact with other layers based on the color and/or luminance of the layers. In this exercise, a blend mode will add some punch to the foreground video.

**NOTE** ▶ To start at this point in the lesson, open *Lesson_01_E*.

1    In the Layers tab, select the foreground layer, *Pipeline_1 copy*.

2    In the HUD, click the Blend Mode pop-up menu.

You can choose from many blend modes. In later lessons, you'll learn more about how they are organized and when certain modes are best used.

3    From the Blend Mode pop-up menu, choose Screen.

The clip is still a bit dark because of the drop shadow behind the video clip.

4   In the HUD, deselect the Drop Shadow checkbox to turn off the shadow.

The Screen blend mode lightens the combined pixels, making the foreground clip really pop.

With the video clips now composited, masked, filtered, and animated, you'll turn your attention to adding some new elements to round out the project: animated text to describe the scene, and an animated graphic to draw attention to the text. For this animated graphic, you'll dive once more into Motion's Library.

## Using Library Content

While you can create graphics from scratch, Motion gives you a head start with a massive repository of graphical elements, many of them already animated. These elements are stored in the Content category of Motion's Library.

For this exercise, you'll add an animated graphic on the bottom third of the video that leads the viewer's eye to a title.

> **NOTE** ▶ You may have noticed a trend here. You started with the background video element, then added the foreground copy; and now you are adding graphics. Finally, you'll place text on top of those graphics. In other words, you are working from the bottom upward, building up layers as you create your composition. No hard and fast rule applies to compositing with this workflow, but building from the bottom up is often the most effective strategy.

**1**    In the Library, choose the Content category. As you can see, this folder includes over 1,400 elements.

**NOTE** ▶ To start at this point in the lesson, open Lesson_01_F.

**2**    Choose the Lines folder; then scroll down through the icons, select Curl 31, and view the preview. This blue, wavelike animated graphic is a great complement to the surfing video clip.

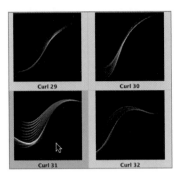

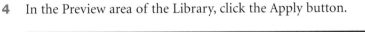

**TIP** ▶ You choose to view these elements as a list or as icons by clicking the appropriate button near the top of the Library. When viewing as icons, you can change the size of the icons by dragging the slider at the bottom of the Library.

3    Make sure that the foreground video clip, **Pipeline_1 copy**, is selected and that the project is playing.

4    In the Preview area of the Library, click the Apply button.

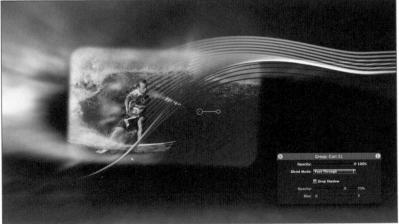

The animated graphic is added to the center of the Canvas, on top of the other layers. It needs to be lower on the screen and smaller, and should animate in the opposite direction, moving from left to right. That's the same direction that the surfer is moving in and the direction in which you want the viewer to look before the text comes on.

**5**  Stop playback and move the playhead to a frame where most of the animated wave graphic is visible.

**6**  In the center of the Canvas, drag the rotation handle to rotate the graphic 180 degrees.

> **TIP** If you Shift-drag, the rotation will snap to 45-degree increments, making it easier to stop at exactly 180 degrees.

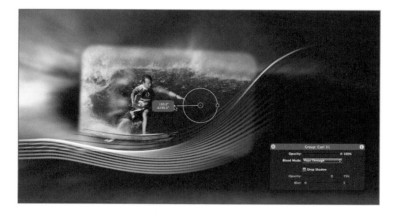

**7**  Option-drag the top middle transform handle to vertically scale down the graphic around its anchor point. Watch the tooltip to stop at about 75%.

When you hold down the Option key, both the top and bottom of the graphic scale toward the center at the same time, keeping the graphic in its new location.

**8**  Drag the graphic down to the lower part of the Canvas.

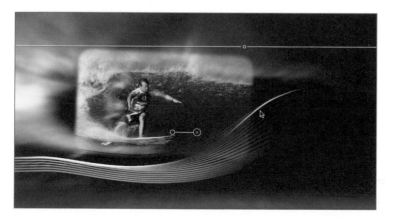

That's better, but the graphic comes in too early. You want your viewers to watch the surfer for the first few seconds, and then move their eyes to the text.

**9**   In the mini-Timeline, drag the Curl 31 bar to the right, using the tooltip to stop when the In point reaches 1 second (1:00).

**10**   Play the project.

The flow of the graphic animation now nicely mimics the movement of the surfboard. However, the graphic animates off the screen before the end of the project, leaving a lot of open space. Let's add a copy of this graphic and move it a little later in time.

**11**   Press Command-D to duplicate the graphic.

**12**   In the mini-Timeline, drag the copy to the right until the Out point of the blue bar meets the play range Out point.

In just a few short steps, you've added a nice animated graphical element that complements the footage and will lead the viewer's eye to the text—the final element of this project.

## Adding and Animating Text

Our surfer is doing his thing at the Pipeline surf break on the Hawaiian island of Oahu. You'll communicate this information to your viewers by adding text and animating it onto the screen with a behavior.

> **NOTE ▸** To start at this point in the lesson, open Lesson_01_G and press F5 to open the Project pane.

**1**   In the Layers tab, select the top group, named *Group*, and then press F5 to close the Project pane.

**2**   Click in the gray area of the Canvas to deselect everything, or choose Edit > Deselect All.

**3**   Press the Spacebar to start playback, if necessary.

> **TIP** ▸ Depending on your hardware configuration, your playback performance may decrease as you add more elements to your project. One way to improve performance is to turn off layers and/or groups temporarily. For example, as you work on creating text, you don't need to see the background **Pipeline_1** video—so you could turn it off by deselecting its activation checkbox in the Layers tab of the Project pane.

You'll add the text while the project is playing so that you can manipulate it interactively.

**4**   In the Toolbar, click the Text tool.

**5**   Click near the center of the Canvas, a little below and to the right, and type *Pipeline Surf Break*.

**6**   Press the Esc key to return to the Select/Transform tool. The Select/Transform tool is the default tool, and looks like an arrow.

**7**   In the HUD, click the Font pop-up menu. Drag down to scroll through the fonts, and choose Impact.

As you drag, the Canvas updates in real time to show you each selected font.

**8**   Drag the HUD's Size slider to change the font size to 56 points.

**9**   Drag the text to position it over the animated wave.

If this project were intended for broadcast, you'd need to make sure that the text stayed within the title safe region, so let's turn on the safe guides.

**NOTE** ▸ *Title safe* and *action safe* refer to regions in the frame that are 10 percent and 5 percent from the edge, respectively. Analog television sets overscan the image and also have bevels that cover part of the cathode ray tube to hold it in place, and the combination can cut off part of the picture. By keeping your content within the safe regions, you're guaranteed that all the key content of your project will be visible on analog televisions. Although digital TVs frequently show the entire raster, or video frame, it's still a good idea to use the title safe and action safe guides to ensure that you don't crowd the edges of the screen.

**10**   At the top right of the Canvas, from the View pop-up menu, choose Safe Zones.

**11**   Position the text inside the inner blue rectangle.

Currently, the text is onscreen from the very first frame of the project. It would be more effective if the text appeared after the animated wave passed by.

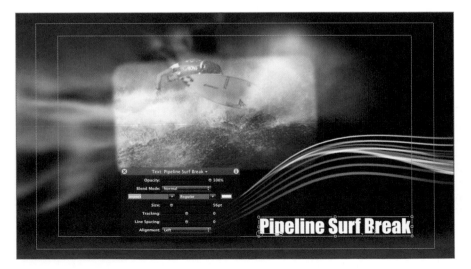

**12** In the mini-Timeline, move the pointer over the left edge of the blue bar until it changes to a resize pointer.

**13** Drag right until the tooltip indicates that the In point is at 2 seconds (00:00:02:00).

To animate the text, you will apply a behavior from the shortcut menu.

**14** In the Toolbar, click the Add Behavior icon, and choose Text-Basic > Blur In.

The text now fades in, letter by letter, as the wave passes by. You can make the text a little more dynamic by animating the entire layer with a Throw behavior.

**15** In the Toolbar, click the Add Behavior icon and choose Basic Motion > Throw.

**16** In the HUD, drag the center of the circle directly left to add a slow drift to the text.

**TIP** Shift-drag in the HUD to constrain the direction horizontally or vertically.

Terrific! You've created your very first Motion project and have become familiar with Motion's interface and many of its key features, including real-time playback; importing and transforming media; filters, masks, and behaviors; blend modes; Library content; and working with text.

## Using the Function Keys

You have now worked briefly with two of the tabs in the utility window: the File Browser and the Library. You've also looked at one tab in the Project pane, the Layers tab.

But more tabs are here to explore: a third tab in the utility window, two more tabs in the Project pane, and an entire pane you haven't yet opened that contains three tabs of its own. While Toolbar icons are available for each of these panes and tabs, it's much quicker to use their keyboard shortcuts.

**NOTE** ▸ To start at this point in the lesson, open Lesson_01_H.

1   Press F5 to open the Project pane.

2   Click the Media tab.

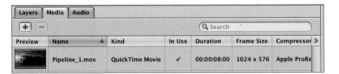

The Media tab displays a list of all your media—video and graphics—that is included in the project. Notice that the text and the wave graphic aren't included here because they are elements that came from Motion's Library.

3   Click the Audio tab. If you have any audio in your project, you can see it, select it, and adjust it here.

4   Click the Layers tab again and select the *Pipeline_1 copy* layer.

5   If the HUD isn't visible, press F7.

As you've seen, the HUD gives you quick access to a few key parameters for the selected element. But it doesn't show you everything you can change. For that, you'll use the Inspector.

**6**    In the utility window, click the Inspector tab.

The Inspector contains four tabs of its own. In the first one, the Properties tab, you can make precise adjustments and set keyframes for parameters that are common to any kind of layer—such as a graphic, video, text, a particle emitter, or even a group itself. You'll work with the Properties tab extensively in later lessons.

**7**    Press the F2 key to open the Behaviors tab. This tab is empty because no behaviors are applied to the selected layer.

**8**    In the Layers tab, select the Rectangle Mask. Now the two behaviors that are applied to the Mask, Spin and Throw, appear in the Behaviors tab.

**9** Press F3 to bring the Filters tab forward, and then in the Layers tab, select the *Pipeline_1* layer. You can adjust all the parameters for any applied filters in this tab.

**10** Note that the last tab currently says "Image." In the Layers tab, click below all the layers to deselect everything. The tab name changes to "Object."

**11** Press F4 to bring the Object tab forward. The Object tab is context sensitive. Its name and contents change depending on what is selected.

> **NOTE ▶** You'll work in all these Inspector tabs in later lessons.

**12** Press F1 to return to the Properties tab. Notice that you can navigate to these four tabs by pressing the function keys F1, F2, F3, and F4.

You already know that F5 opens and closes the Project pane. Leave it open for now.

**13** Press F6 to open the Timing pane. The Timing pane contains three tabs: the Timeline, the Keyframe Editor, and the Audio Editor. The Timeline tab is selected by default.

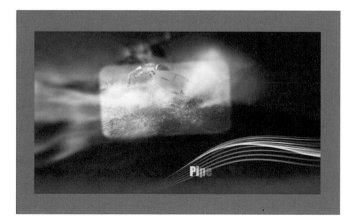

You already know that F7 toggles the visibility of the HUD.

**14** Press F7 to hide the HUD. Click in the bottom of the Layers tab to deselect everything, and then press F8 to open Full Screen mode.

**NOTE ▶** Full Screen mode is not available if you have more than one project open in Motion.

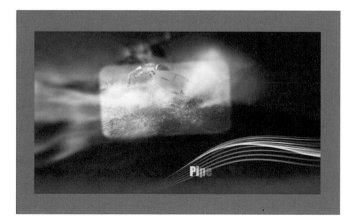

In Full Screen mode, you can view just your project without seeing any of Motion's interface. However, you can still apply changes to the project in this mode.

**TIP ▶** In Full Screen mode, you may want to press Option-Z to make your zoom level exactly 100 percent.

**15** Press F8 to exit Full Screen mode.

**16** Save your work.

Additional keyboard shortcuts are available that allow you to go directly to each of the nine tabs and to execute a variety of Motion commands. You'll explore these in later lessons. If you have a graphics tablet, you can use a special set of commands called *gestures* to navigate the interface and perform many other tasks. For more information, see the Motion Help documentation under the Help menu.

## Lesson Review

1. After the Welcome screen, what must you select to open a new Motion project?
2. Identify the two main windows that are visible in a new project.
3. How can you precisely center a clip in the Canvas?
4. What part of the Motion interface do you use to change the play range or adjust the selected layer without opening the Timing pane?
5. Do you have to stop playback to change the scale of a video clip?
6. How do you change the scale of a layer in the Canvas without changing its proportions?
7. Name the three kinds of effects you can add to a layer.
8. How can you change the way the pixels of one layer combine with pixels of a layer underneath?
9. Where is all of the content that ships with Motion located?
10. In what part of Motion's interface can you interactively view fonts for a text layer without going to the Inspector?
11. Identify the keyboard shortcut that opens Full Screen mode.

### Answers

1. A project preset.
2. The utility window and the Canvas.
3. Drag the clip and use the dynamic guides with snapping enabled, or click the Import button in the File Browser.
4. The mini-Timeline.
5. No. You can build an entire Motion project while the project is playing, although it's sometimes easier to accomplish certain tasks when the playhead is stopped.

6. Shift-drag a transform handle.

7. Filters, masks, and behaviors.

8. Change the blend mode.

9. In the Library.

10. In the heads-up display, or HUD.

11. F8.

## Keyboard Shortcuts

---

### File Commands

**Command-S**     Save the project

### Windowing Keys

**F1**              Open the Properties tab of the Inspector

**F2**              Open the Behaviors tab of the Inspector

**F3**              Open the Filters tab of the Inspector

**F4**              Open the Object tab of the Inspector (this tab changes titles depending on the selected object)

**F5**              Open and close the Project pane (which opens to its Layers tab by default)

**F6**              Open and close the Timing pane (which opens to its Timeline tab by default)

**F7**              Turn the HUD on and off

### Navigation

**Option-Z**        Zoom Canvas to 100 percent

**Shift-Z**         Set the Canvas to Fit in Window zoom mode

### Play Range Commands

**Home**            Place the playhead at the beginning of the project

**Spacebar**        Turn playback on and off

### Miscellaneous

**Command-Z**     Undo the previous action

---

# 2

| | |
|---:|:---|
| Lesson Files | Motion4_Book_Files > Lessons > Lesson_02 |
| Media | Motion4_Book_Files > Media > Rockumentary |
| Time | This lesson takes approximately 90 minutes to complete. |
| Goals | Apply blend modes and combine with filters |
| | Import layered Photoshop files |
| | Copy layers and filters |
| | Expand image sequences |
| | Perform Timeline edits |
| | Change preferences |
| | Make clone layers |
| | Transform and add masks to groups |

# Lesson 2
# Building a Composite

Creating motion graphics involves both compositing and animating. Before diving into animation, it's useful to gain a good grasp of compositing.

To build a composite image, you combine often disparate elements to create a visually striking, integrated look that makes the whole much greater than the sum of its parts.

In this lesson, you'll build part of a DVD menu animation and work in the Layers tab to organize your composite. You'll use image sequences and Motion's Timeline to employ various editing options; and you'll combine blend modes, opacity changes, and filters to build up textures from different graphical elements to create a cohesive overall design.

## Setting Up the Project

The rock group Pale Divine has asked you to create the DVD menu for their new "rockumentary" project, called *One—to Document the Years*. All they have given you are a handful of publicity and performance shots of the band and their logo. You'll combine the pictures with some ink and paper graphics to create an organic, gritty look. First, let's preview the completed project.

**1**   In the Finder, navigate to Motion4_Book_Files > Lessons > Lesson_02, open **Rockumentary_Menu.mov**, and play the movie file.

The movie has two distinct sections: the opening, with the photos and other graphics appearing to fall through space, and the rest of the movie, which has only subtle movements.

This design is typical of an animated, or *motion*, menu for a DVD. The menu elements animate onto the screen and then land into position. When the end of the menu is reached, it starts playing again, but not from the beginning. It resumes with the frame at which all the menu elements have arrived in their final resting positions, so that the DVD highlights can clearly indicate which item you wish to play. This frame is called the *loop point*.

> **NOTE ▸** You can start the movie at the loop point by choosing MenuLoopPoint from the chapter index menu at the bottom right of the QuickTime Player window.

**2**   Close the QuickTime Player and open Motion (or, if Motion is already open, choose File > New). Then, in the Select Project Preset window, from the Preset menu, choose NTSC DV.

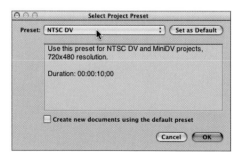

This preset has a resolution of 720 x 480 pixels, which is required to make a standard definition DVD for NTSC-based countries such as the United States and Japan.

**NOTE ▶** If you wanted to make a PAL DVD to play in PAL countries such as those in Europe and much of Asia, you would choose the PAL DV preset.

The project defaults to a 10-second duration, which is a little short for the looping section of the DVD menu. Viewers probably will see it loop before making a selection.

**3** Click in the project duration field at the bottom right of the Canvas, type *20.* (20 followed by a period), and press Enter.

Now the menu will play for 20 seconds before looping. However, the play range, indicated by the blue In and Out point arrows in the mini-Timeline, remains at the original 10-second duration.

**4** Choose Mark > Reset Play Range or press Option-X to reset the play range to the full duration of the project.

**TIP ▶** In Final Cut Pro, pressing Option-X does almost the same thing: It clears In and Out points from the Timeline.

You should always perform one more step when building DVD menus in Motion: create a solid background. One way to accomplish this is to change the way Motion treats transparent areas of your composition.

Right now, the Canvas for this new project is empty. It appears to be black, but Motion is just using that color to show that the area is empty. The background is actually transparent.

At the top of the Canvas, just below the Toolbar on the right side, is a set of View options: Zoom Level, Channels, Render, View and Overlay, and View Layouts. You use these menus to change the appearance of the Canvas.

**5** From the Channels pop-up menu, choose Transparent. A gray and white checkerboard pattern now appears, to indicate that the background is transparent.

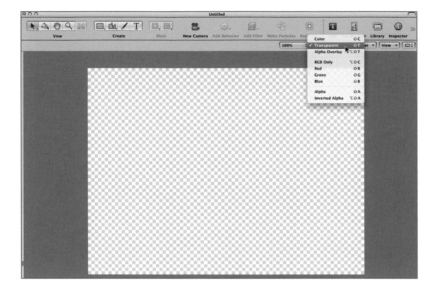

Any areas of transparency in your final project will appear gray in your final DVD menu, not black as you might assume. Therefore, it's a good idea to fill your background with a solid color that will render as part of the final project. You can do this in the Project Properties window.

**6**  Choose Edit > Project Properties or press Command-J.

The General tab of the Project Properties window contains information about project settings such as resolution, bit depth, aspect ratio, and frame rate—all the settings that you chose when you selected a preset to create the project. In this window, you can change and customize that preset, or change the background.

**7**    From the Background pop-up menu, choose Solid. The description under the menu explains that the background will now create a solid alpha channel. In other words, a black "layer" will exist under all the layers you add to your project.

**8**    Click OK. Notice that the Canvas turns black, even though the Channels menu is still set to Transparent.

**9**    Choose File > Save or press Command-S. Navigate to Motion4_Book_Files > Lessons > Lesson_02 > Student_Saves, name the project *My Rockumentary DVD menu*, and click Save.

With the technical considerations addressed, you can now turn your attention to the creative process of building your composition.

## Creating a Background: Using the Inspector

You'll be compositing many layers for this project, and you'll be using blend modes to make layers interact. To see the interactions between shapes and colors, it can be helpful to start from the bottom layer and build up. Therefore, your first step is to create a background. You'll use a single graphic placed in its own group to keep the project organized, and you'll apply a filter to modify the graphic.

**1**    Press F5 to open the Project pane, and rename the default group to *Background*.

**2**    In the utility window, open the File Browser, navigate to Motion4_Book_Files > Media > Rockumentary, and select **radial_gradient.psd**.

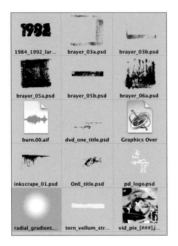

In the Preview pane, notice that the white blurred circle is displayed against a gray background and that the bit depth is described as "Millions of Colors+." The + (plus) symbol indicates that this graphic file includes an alpha channel, or transparency information. In other words, the graphic is composited over a transparent background.

**3**   Near the top of the File Browser, click the Import button to import **radial_gradient.psd** into the *Background* group. The blurred circle appears in the Canvas over a black background. By previously setting the background to Solid, you ensured that no transparent areas would appear in the final project.

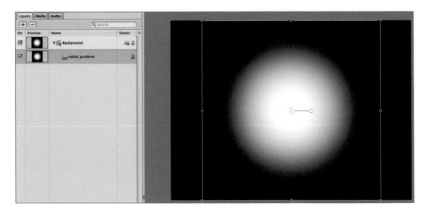

Notice that the layer's bounding box touches the top and bottom of the Canvas. By default, Motion automatically scales down still images to fit the Canvas. This resizing can be helpful, but in this case, you want to use the graphic at its original size to create a soft vignette effect.

**NOTE** ▶ To change this behavior, choose Motion > Preferences, select the Project icon, and then click the Large Stills pop-up menu. You can choose Scale to Canvas Size, Do Nothing, or Down-Res to Canvas Size. Down-Res is a great option if you are working with many large images, such as those taken with a digital camera. Their resolutions automatically will be reduced to match the Canvas size, improving Motion's playback performance. However, if you want to zoom in closely to the photos, it's best to keep them large enough to avoid going over 100 percent scale.

While you could directly transform the scale of the layer in the Canvas, there's a better option when you want to make precise adjustments, or when you want to change parameters that aren't available in the Canvas or the HUD (heads-up display). For these situations, you'll use the Inspector.

4   In the utility window, click the Inspector tab.

   **TIP** ▶ The keyboard shortcuts to select the three top tabs of the Inspector are Command-1 to open the File Browser, Command-2 to open the Library, and Command-3 to open the Inspector. If you press a keyboard shortcut for a tab that is already visible, the entire utility window will close, which can be quite alarming. Press the keyboard shortcut for any of the tabs to reopen the utility window.

The Inspector contains four tabs: Properties (which is visible by default), Behaviors, Filters, and the Object tab—a contextual tab that changes depending on the type of layer selected. Currently, it is the Image tab.

The Properties tab contains all the layer parameters that you can change directly in the Canvas—such as position, rotation, and scale—as well as parameters such as anchor point, blend mode, drop shadow, and crop. The parameters on the Properties tab apply for almost any type of layer—graphic, video, text, or other Motion object. Changes made in the Canvas are reflected in the Inspector and vice versa.

**5**    In the Canvas, drag the *radial_gradient* layer to change its position. Note how the Inspector's Position parameter changes as you drag.

**6**    Choose Edit > Undo Move or press Command-Z.

You can change values in the Inspector by using sliders, dials, and value fields.

**7**    To change the Scale parameter, try dragging the slider, clicking the arrows in the value field, typing a value in the value field, and dragging directly in the value field. Undo your alteration after each change.

Dragging directly in the value field is often the quickest way to make a change, and you can frequently enter a value that can't be achieved using the slider. For example, the Scale slider only goes to 400%, but you can drag or enter higher values in the value field.

**TIP** ▶ Shift-dragging in a value field changes the parameter ten times faster, which is great when you want to make an extreme change in the layer scale or to quickly move the layer far away. Option-dragging changes the parameter 100 times more slowly and is great for fine-tuning.

Sometimes you want to reset all of the basic properties of a layer. Rather than repeatedly typing a value in each value field, you can click the Reset buttons—the hooked arrows along the right side of the Inspector—to quickly reset groups of parameters.

**8**    Next to the Transform group of parameters, click the Reset button.

All the Transform parameters are reset to their default values, so Scale is now 100%, which makes the gradient nice and large in the Canvas and creates the vignette effect.

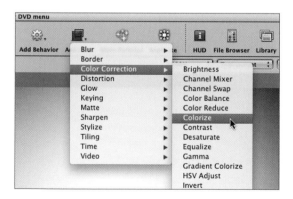

A filter can give the layer some color. In Lesson 1, you previewed filters in the Library before applying them to a layer. You can also use a shortcut method when applying filters.

9   In the Toolbar above the Canvas, click the Add Filter icon and choose Color Correction > Colorize. The filter appears underneath the layer it is applied to, and the white color in the Canvas changes to a pale off-white.

In the Inspector, the Filters tab automatically comes forward. The HUD contains some of the parameters that can be found in the Inspector. (Press F7 if the HUD is not visible.)

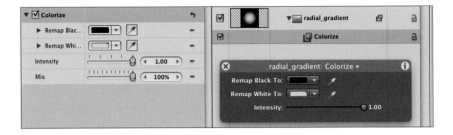

Sometimes the HUD contains all the parameters for a selected layer or effect, but the Inspector always contains every adjustable parameter. In this case, you can use the Inspector to input specific RGB values.

**NOTE ▶** A filter is an effect, which is always applied to a layer or group and appears underneath the element to which it is applied. Motion includes three types of effects: filters, behaviors, and masks.

**10** In the Inspector, next to the Remap White To parameter, click the disclosure triangle. Enter *0.63* for Red, *0.35* for Green, and *0.06* for Blue.

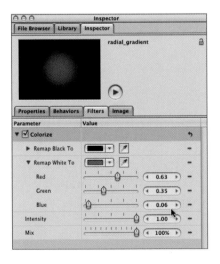

**NOTE ▶** Motion employs an RGB scale of 0 to 1, with 0 using none of that color channel and 1 using all of the color channel. You may have seen a range of 0 to 255 used in other applications. That range is based on an 8-bit color space, in which each color channel has 256 possible values. Because Motion can work in 8-, 16-, and 32-bit modes, its 0 to 1 scale works for any bit depth.

The background group is now complete. Next, you'll add the DVD title elements, which will appear on top of the composition.

## Using Photoshop Files

Instead of building this project strictly from the bottom up, you'll now add the very top elements. Why? Because the elements that sit on top of all other layers are the DVD titles and graphics, which can serve as guides as you composite the elements beneath them. You can think of this top group as a template that helps you align the entire composition.

The DVD title elements were created in Photoshop, using multiple layers and blend modes. Motion gives you several options for working with these Photoshop elements.

> **NOTE ▶** You do not need to have Photoshop installed on your system in order to use Photoshop files (.psd files) with Motion.

1　At the top of the Layers tab, with the Colorize filter selected, click the Add button (+) to create a new layer.

Notice that the new group is created inside the *Background* group. Groups are always added just above the selected layer (or selected effect). However, you want this new group to be outside and above the *Background* group.

> **NOTE ▶** In projects with 2D groups, such as this, the stacking order in the Layers tab always determines the stacking order in the Canvas. In 3D groups, which you will work with in later lessons, z-depth, rather than layer stacking order, determines which layer is on top in the Canvas.

**2**  Drag the new group above the *Background* group, wait for the insertion bar and the + symbol to appear, and then release the mouse button.

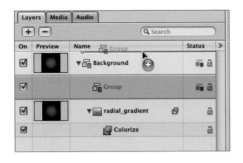

The new group is now above the *Background* group. Make sure that the insertion bar is visible before releasing the mouse button. If the *Background* group has a black out-line, it means you'll be dragging the selected group back inside the *Background* group.

**TIP** ▶ If nothing is selected when you create a new group, it is automatically placed at the top of the Layers tab.

**3**  Rename the new group to *DVD Titles*. Immediately naming new groups based on their intended contents will help organize your project.

**4**  Click the *Background* group disclosure triangle to collapse the group. Closing groups you aren't currently working on reduces Layers tab clutter and helps focus your attention.

**5**  Press Command-1 to open the File Browser, and select **dvd_one_title.psd**.

**TIP** ▶ To display more files or larger icons, drag the slider at the bottom of the File Browser to change icon size in the stack in icon view.

The Preview area description tells you that this is a Photoshop file. The "+" next to "Millions of Colors" tells you that it has transparency. This Photoshop file has a few other properties that aren't listed: It comprises seven layers, each with a blend mode applied.

**NOTE ▶** Blend modes are also referred to as *blending modes, composite modes,* and *transfer modes.*

**6** With the *DVD Titles* group selected, click the Import button in the File Browser. The file appears as a single layer in the Layers tab, and all of its elements appear in the Canvas.

Motion's default behavior is to combine all the Photoshop layers into a single layer. While this result is often useful, it has two disadvantages. First, any applied blend modes are lost; second, you cannot individually transform or animate the Photoshop layers. While you won't be animating the layers in this lesson, you will want to keep the blend modes intact. Fortunately, Motion provides an alternative to combining the layers.

**7** Press Command-Z to undo the media import.

**8** From the File Browser, drag **dvd_one_title.psd** to the *DVD Titles* group, but don't release the mouse button yet.

A drop menu appears. You can choose Import Merged Layers, which is the default, or Import All Layers; or you can select a specific layer to import. The layer names in the drop menu match the layer names in the Photoshop file.

9 Choose Import All Layers. A new group with the name of the Photoshop file appears within the *DVD Titles* group, and each Photoshop layer appears as a separate layer within that group.

Because you have already created a group for these layers, you don't need the *dvd_one_title* group. In fact, this group is not allowing the blend modes applied to its layers to pass through to the background layer. Therefore, you'll move all the layers and delete the group.

**NOTE ▶** When you import a layered .psd file to Motion, the group containing all the layers is set to fixed resolution by default. You can turn off this default in the Group tab of the Inspector. When a group is set to fixed resolution, any blend modes applied to layers within the group aren't passed through to the groups beneath it.

10 To select all the layers, click the uppermost, *lines* layer, and then Shift-click the lowest layer, *credit_chapter_back*.

11 Drag all the layers from the *dvd_one_title* group into the *DVD Titles* group, and release the mouse button when a black outline appears around the target group.

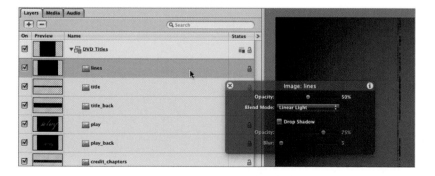

**12** Select and delete the now-empty *dvd_one_title* group.

> **TIP** An empty group doesn't have a disclosure triangle next to its name.

Notice that the text in the Canvas now has a red glow because the blend modes are enabled. How can you see the blend modes applied to each layer? One method is to use the HUD.

**13** Select the uppermost *lines* layer, and if the HUD is not already visible, press F7. The HUD indicates a Blend Mode of Linear Light.

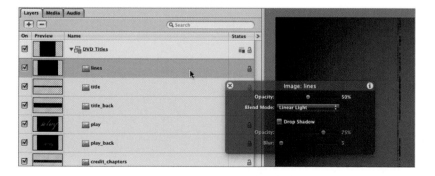

> **TIP** Blend modes for an individual layer can also be seen (and changed) in the Properties tab of the Inspector or by Control-clicking (or right-clicking) the layer in the Layers tab.

You could click each layer to inspect its blend mode, but there is a way to see the blend modes of all layers at once.

**14** At the top right of the Layers tab, click the right angle bracket next to the column headers, and from the pop-up menu, choose Blend. The blend mode for each layer now appears on the layer itself.

**NOTE ▶** You may need to adjust the Name column width, by dragging between the column headers, to see the full blend mode names. You can also make the Project pane wider by dragging the small vertical double line along the middle right edge of the pane.

**NOTE ▶** Certain Photoshop effects and elements, such as layer effects, layer masks, adjustment layers, paths, and shapes, will not appear in Motion unless the layers are first rasterized or converted to Smart Objects.

The two outer layers of your composition "sandwich"—a background and the DVD titles—are complete. You'll now turn your attention to the "meat" of the project: the graphics to give it mood and texture, the photos to give it life, and text to give it meaning.

## Compositing with Blend Modes and Filters

With the top elements in place, you'll return to the bottom-up construction process, adding graphics that will appear under the photographs to give your composition texture, color variation, and depth.

For source material, you'll start with still images of ink and ripped paper. You'll then scale, rotate, and position those elements to complement or frame the DVD title elements and the pictures that will appear on top. Finally, you'll use duplicates, blend modes, and filters to make these layers work together with the other layers in the project.

This is a creative, interpretive process, so feel free to deviate from the recommendations in the exercise and come up with your own unique look.

**1**  Close the *DVD Titles* group. You are finished with this group.

**2**  Select the Background group, and press Command-Shift-N to create a new group, which is placed above the selected group and sandwiched between the two current groups.

**3**  Name the new group *Graphics Under*. This group will contain all the graphics underneath the band pictures.

**4**  In the File Browser, locate **brayer_03a.psd** and drag it to the *Graphics Under* group. The image appears in the Canvas, automatically scaled down to fit.

**NOTE ▸** Although this is a Photoshop file, it contains only one layer, so holding it over a group will not open a drop menu.

A *brayer* is a hand roller used to spread ink for making prints. This image, and several others in the File Browser, is derived from the extra ink that is rolled onto a backing sheet after the print has been removed. It's organic, grungy, and real—a nice design element.

**5**   In the Canvas, rotate the image 90 degrees counterclockwise, scale it down to about 75%, and position it at the bottom right of the frame. It appears that you have obliterated the word "Play," but you'll fix that a little later.

**TIP ▸** Because exact values aren't necessary here, manipulating the layer directly in the Canvas is faster than using the Inspector. Holding down the Shift key while rotating a layer will constrain the rotation to 45-degree increments.

**6**   Drag **brayer_03b.psd** into the *Graphics Under* group. When dragged to a group, layers are added above any existing layers.

**7**   Scale the layer down to about 70%, and position it at the top left of the frame.

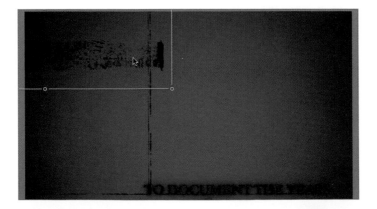

**8**  Choose Edit > Duplicate or press Command-D to make a copy of this layer. Then scale down, rotate, and reposition the copy near the red vertical line.

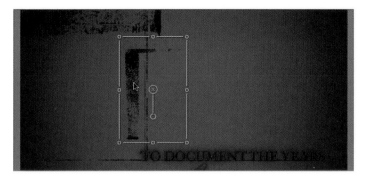

**TIP**  If the yellow dynamic guides appear as you drag, press N to turn off snapping.

**9**  Add **brayer_06a.psd**, rotate it 90 degrees clockwise, and then scale and reposition it to roughly fill the upper right square formed by the red lines. It's OK if it obscures the text. You'll fix that in the next few steps.

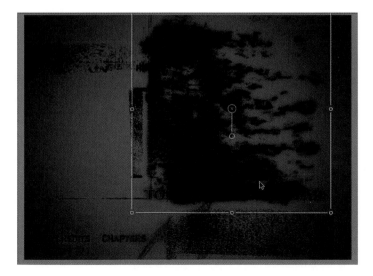

**10**  Click the Blend Mode column of the *brayer_06a* layer to display all the available blend modes.

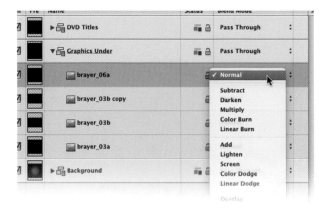

Each blend mode performs a mathematical operation that combines the pixels of the selected layer or group with the pixels of the underlying layer. The default blend mode, Normal, uses just the pixels of the selected layer, obscuring anything underneath.

The best way to determine a blend mode's impact is to try it out. Blend modes are organized into logical groups delineated by separator bars, and there are some general rules that often (but not always) apply to the groups:

▶   The first group of five blend modes, starting with Subtract, will generally darken the resulting image. Of these, Multiply is probably the most commonly used.

▶   The second group of five modes, starting with Add, will generally lighten the resulting image. Of these, Add and Screen are probably the most commonly used.

▶   The third group of seven modes will generally do both: make the light pixels lighter and the dark pixels darker to increase overall contrast. Of these, the first mode, Overlay, is probably the most commonly used.

The rest of the blend modes have more specialized functions.

Sometimes a blend mode's effect is too strong, too weak, or not quite what you expected. You can use a filter to change the impact of a blend mode, and you can adjust the opacity of a layer to moderate the intensity of a blend mode.

**11**  Choose the Linear Light blend mode. The image stays black, because this blend mode only affects pixels that aren't completely black or white. To see its impact, you'll add a filter.

**12** In the Toolbar, click the Add Filter icon and choose Color Correction > Colorize.

**13** In the HUD, click the disclosure triangle next to the Remap Black To color well and sample a dark yellow to make the graphic a brownish-orange color. Then in the HUD, lower the Opacity to about 20%.

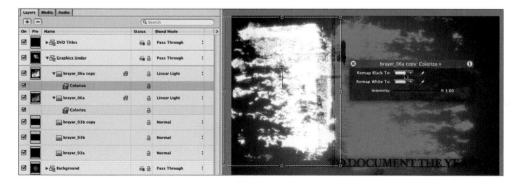

The combination of a blend mode and the Colorize filter allows for a great deal of creative control. You'll use this same layer and filter, with a few adjustments, in another part of the composition.

**14** Select the brayer_06a layer. Press Command-D to duplicate the layer; then, in the Canvas, rotate it 180 degrees and reposition it to cover the leftmost rectangle. Feel free to scale it nonproportionally (without holding down the Shift key) to fit the rectangle.

**15** On the copied layer, select the Colorize filter and remap black to a light gray.

By transforming a layer and changing the filter parameters, you can reuse the same elements multiple times in the same composition.

### Completing the Underlying Graphics

To finish the graphics that will sit underneath the images and text, you'll add a few more layers and apply both blend modes and filters.

As you complete these steps, feel free to experiment with the transformations, blend modes, and filter adjustments to create your own look.

**1**    From the File Browser, import **brayer_05a.psd** to the *Graphics Under* group.

**2**    Change the scale and position of the layer so that it covers the *brayer_06a copy* layer at the upper left of the Canvas.

This layer will add more texture to the composition. You'll use a blend mode to brighten it up and make the title you place on it stand out. Rather than applying the Colorize filter from the Add Filter icon, you can copy one of the existing filters.

**3**    Option-drag the Colorize filter from the *brayer_06a copy* layer onto the *brayer_05a* layer. Option-dragging copies any selected layer, group, or effect to the new location.

**4**    In the HUD, change the blend mode of the *brayer_05a* layer to Linear Light, and change the Colorize filter's Remap Black To parameter to a darker gray so that the image doesn't appear too bright.

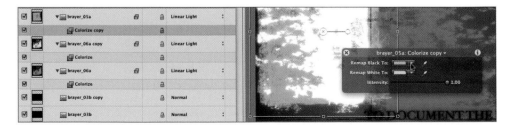

**NOTE** ▶ When applying blend modes, it's very easy to end up with brightness, or luminance, levels that are not broadcast legal. If your work is intended for broadcast distribution, you'll want to check the luminance values and adjust them, if necessary. One way to keep levels broadcast legal is to apply Motion's Broadcast Safe filter in the Video category, after all other filters have been applied. Another method is to import the Motion project (or exported video file) into Final Cut Pro and then use Final Cut's Video Scopes to check levels, and adjust them by applying a broadcast safe filter or the Color Corrector three-way filter.

To accent the vertical line separating the brayer graphics, you'll use another graphic.

5   Import the **brayer_05b.psd** file to the same group.

6   Rotate, scale, and position it to cover the vertical red line. You can see how the DVD Titles elements you already added allow you to position these underlying graphics.

7   Option-drag a Colorize filter from any of the other layers to this new layer.

8   Change the layer's blend mode to Multiply.

9   In the HUD, remap black to a red so that the graphic is a dark reddish brown. The Multiply blend mode in combination with the filter blends the graphic with the elements beneath it.

To finish, you'll add a graphic to highlight the DVD titles.

**10** Drag **torn_vellum_strip.psd** to the same group, wait a moment, and choose Import Merged Layers. This is a multilayered Photoshop file, but it has no blend modes applied, so you can bring it into the composition as a single file.

**11** Press F1 to open the Properties tab of the Inspector, and then, next to the Transform group, click the hooked arrow to reset the scale of the graphic to 100%. Because the graphic is larger than the Canvas, it was automatically scaled down, but it will work better at full size.

**12** Reposition the graphic underneath the lines of text, and lower its opacity in the HUD to about 60%. The lower opacity reveals the black brayer graphic underneath but makes the torn strip look a bit dingy.

**13** Choose Edit > Duplicate or press Command-D to make a copy of the layer.

**14** Change the blend mode of the copy to Overlay, and decrease the opacity to about 50%. These changes brighten up the strip and still allow the lower graphics to show through.

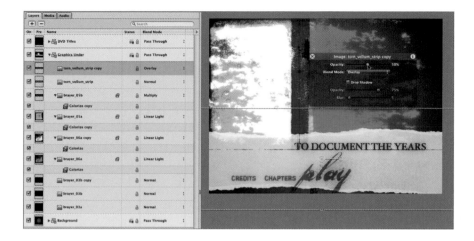

Good work! You've built a richly textured background that creates a mood, leads the eye to the DVD title elements, and leaves open spaces for the band pictures and logo.

## Editing in Motion

So far, you have built a static composite that does not change over time. Every layer lasts for the full project duration. Your next step is to add a series of photographs that will change as the project plays.

To add layers that start and stop at specific points in a project, you'll explore Motion's editing options, including composite edits, overwrite edits, and sequential edits.

### Working with Image Sequences

First, you'll look at the photos that you'll be editing into the composition.

1    Press Command-1 to open the File Browser. Select **vid_pix_[###].jpg:1:20**, and play it in the Preview area.

This file appears as a single icon in the stack and plays like a movie that contains a series of one-frame images. It is described as a "JPEG Sequence." A collection of still images with sequentially numbered filenames will appear in the File Browser as a single *image sequence*. You can use this image sequence as you would use any other QuickTime movie in Motion.

Sometimes you'll want to work with a series of images as an image sequence, but other times you'll want to work with the images individually. Motion lets you do both.

**2**  At the bottom of the File Browser is a button that toggles how image sequences are viewed. By default, the button is enabled. Click the "Show image sequences as collapsed" button to expand the image sequence. The individual images now appear in the stack. There are 20 images, which is why "1:20" appeared at the end of the sequence name.

**TIP** ▶ Digital cameras frequently save files with sequential numbers, so if you are looking for digital photos in the File Browser and see only one image, it may be multiple images collapsed as an image sequence.

For this project, you want to work with the individual images. Before adding those images to the project, you'll create a group to contain them.

**3**    Close the *Graphics Under* group. Select that group, create a new group above it, and name the new group *Stills*.

| On | Pre | Name | Status | Blend Mode | > |
|----|-----|------|--------|------------|---|
| ☑ | ▓ | ▶ 🎞 DVD Titles | 🎞 🔒 | Pass Through | : |
| ☑ |  | 🎞 Stills | 🎞 🔒 | Pass Through | : |
| ☑ | 🎞 | ▶ 🎞 Graphics Under | 🎞 🔒 | Pass Through | : |
| ☑ | ● | ▶ 🎞 Background | 🎞 🔒 | Pass Through | : |

You'll composite the photos on top of everything you've created so far except for the DVD title graphics.

There are 20 photos, and the project is 20 seconds long. So let's keep things simple and have each photo play for 1 second, one after the other. You have several options for editing the photos into the project.

**4**    With the Stills group selected, select **vid_pix_001.jpg** and click the Import button.

The layer appears in the Layers tab; the graphic appears in the Canvas; and in the mini-Timeline, the blue bar representing the graphic extends for the length of the project.

By default, elements that you add to a composition will start at the playhead and end at the end of the composition. This behavior was effective for all the background elements you previously worked with, but in this case, you want each picture to last just 1 second. One way to achieve this is to trim each layer to the correct duration and location in time. For the first photo, you want to set the Out point of the clip at 1 second.

5    In the mini-Timeline, move the pointer over the very end of the *vid_pix_001* bar and click to change the pointer to a resize icon.

6    Drag left until the tooltip indicates a duration of 1:00. The layer now lasts only 1 second, starting from the beginning of the project.

**TIP** ▶ You can also trim a clip's Out point by moving the playhead to the point at which you want to make the trim (at 1 second, in this case) and choosing Mark > Mark Out or pressing O.

Normally, when you import an element into a project, it is composited on top of the other existing layers, without changing those layers in any way. But you can choose other editing options when you are working in the Timeline.

### Editing in the Timeline

You can perform many editing operations in the mini-Timeline: trimming In and Out points, moving layers in time, and even slipping video clips. But when you want to see how layers and effects related to each other over time—or if you want access to additional editing options—you'll want to open the Timing pane and work in the Timeline.

1    Press Command-Z to undo the last trimming operation.

2    Press F6 to open the Timing pane, and if necessary, click the Timeline tab to open it. Close any open groups except for the *Stills* group.

In the Timeline, you can simultaneously see the duration of multiple layers. The left side shows the groups and layers—exactly like the Layers tab of the Project pane. The right section contains blue bars that indicate the duration of each layer. Currently, every layer lasts for the full duration of the project, including the *vid_pix_001* layer.

To perform editing options, you can drag clips directly into the Timeline. It can be helpful to first move the playhead to the desired In point.

3    In the Timeline tab, click in the current frame field. Type *1.* (1 period) and press Return to move the playhead to 1 second.

4    From the File Browser, drag **vid_pix_002.jpg** to just above the *vid_pix_001* layer in the Timeline. Snap it to the playhead and wait for the drop menu to appear.

**NOTE ▶** It is critical to position the pointer just above the layer, not below. If you position the pointer below the layer, different options will appear in the drop menu.

The vertical black line along the playhead indicates that the clip will start at the playhead location. The horizontal black line above the *vid_pix_001* layer indicates that the clip will be placed above this layer.

The drop menu offers three choices: the default Composite, Insert, and Overwrite. If you edit with Final Cut Pro, you are probably already familiar with the last two.

5   Choose Overwrite. The new layer overwrites the existing layer, trimming it to 1 second.

**NOTE ▶** An insert edit would split the *vid_pix_001* layer in two, with the second half on a new layer and its In point pushed forward in the Timeline to start after the Out point of the *vid_pix_002* layer.

This approach is clearly more efficient than manually trimming each layer. You could add all of the images this way, moving the playhead to 2 seconds, overwriting the next photo, and so on. But because you know that you want every photo to last for 1 second, you can tell Motion to make them last that long automatically.

6   Choose Motion > Preferences or press Command-, (comma), and click the Project icon at the top of the window.

You use the Preferences window to change Motion's default settings.

7   In the Still Images & Layers section, for Default Layer Duration, choose "Use custom duration," and in the value field enter *1.0*.

You may want to restore this to "Use project duration" later, but for now it will make the editing process much more efficient.

**NOTE ▶** Changes you make to Preferences remain in effect for all projects, so it's a good habit to review them when you create a new project or update an older project.

**8**   Close the Preferences window.

**9**   Move the playhead to 02;00.

**10**  From the File Browser, drag **vid_pix_003.jpg** to the playhead in the Timeline just above the *vid_pix_002* layer, and from the drop menu, choose Overwrite.

The new layer comes in already trimmed to 1:00. The overwrite edit causes the lower *vid_pix_002* layer to be divided into two pieces, and you'll delete the second piece.

**11**  Select and delete the *vid_pix_002 1* layer.

With all layers set to last just 1 second, you could now drag each photo to the end of the previous photo and use the default composite edit to edit the rest of the pictures into the sequence. But another edit type is perfect for adding a sequential set of images: the sequential edit.

**12** Near the top of the File Browser, click the List View button to see the files in the stack displayed as a list. This view will make it easier to select all the files in order.

**13** Click the Name column header to sort the files by name; then drag a marquee or Shift-select **vid_pix_004.jpg** and **vid_pix_020.jpg** to select the remaining 17 photos.

**14** Drag the photos from the File Browser to the Timeline, above the Out point of the *vid_pix_003* layer, and wait for the drop menu to appear. A new option appears underneath the default Composite edit: Sequential.

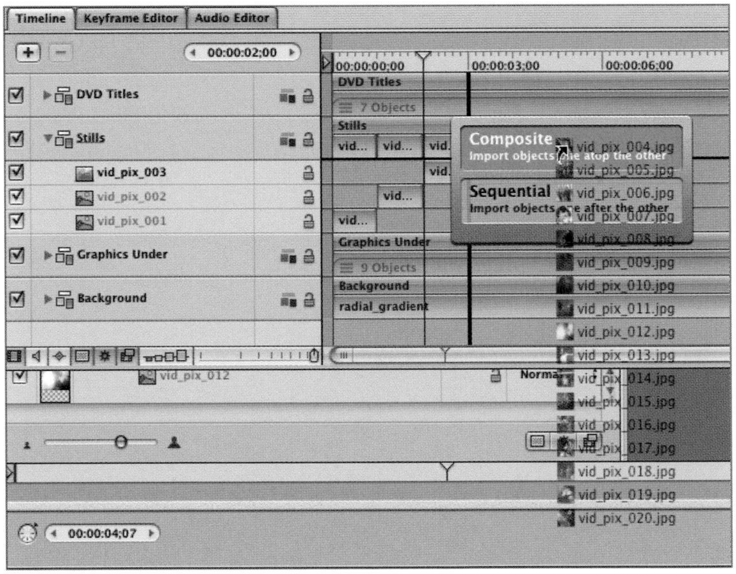

**NOTE** ▶ You did not relocate the playhead this time, so make sure that a solid black vertical line appears that aligns with the Out point of the *vid_pix_003* layer and a solid horizontal line appears above the same layer.

**15** Choose Sequential. All the selected images are laid into the Timeline one after the other, creating a staircase of clips that will play sequentially.

**TIP** ▶ The sequential edit works with any type of file, not just image sequences.

The files will be added in the order in which you select them in the File Browser. If you want to play them in a different order than they are numbered, you can Shift-click to select them in the order you desire.

**16** Press F6 to close the Timeline, choose Edit > Deselect All, save your work, and then play the project.

The photos now play in order, each lasting for 1 second. With the editing complete, you'll turn your attention to making the images blend in with the other elements.

## Applying Masks and Using Clones

The series of photographs look like they have been slapped on top of the other layers, with some in color, some in black and white. You will now use a combination of masks, clones, and blend modes to integrate the images into the composition.

**1** Stop playback, and press Home to return the playhead to the first frame.

**2** Close the *Stills* group and then select it. By transforming and applying effects to the group, you'll affect all the layers within the group in the same way.

3     In the Canvas, scale down the group to about 80%, and reposition it to fit roughly in the upper right rectangle. You will use a mask to blend the edges of the images into the background.

4     In the Toolbar, click and hold the Rectangle Mask tool to display the Circle Mask tool, and then choose it.

5     With the *Stills* group still selected, Shift-Option-drag a mask from the center of the photo in the Canvas and make it large enough to encompass the drummer.

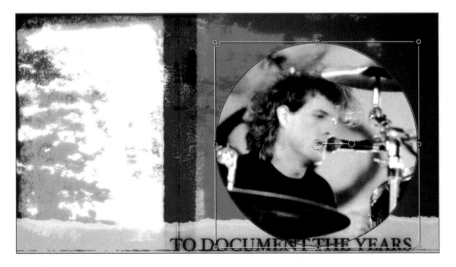

**TIP** ▶ The same modifier keys that work when transforming layers—Shift to constrain proportions and Option to scale around the anchor point—also work with masks.

6     In the HUD, increase the Feather amount all the way to 100. That's really not enough feathering. Remember, if you can't get the value you want from the HUD, try the Inspector.

**7**   Press F4 to go to the fourth tab of the Inspector. This is the context-sensitive tab that
changes its name depending on the selected element. It is now called Mask.

**8**   Increase the Feather amount to about 200. The increased feathering may reveal the
original edges of the photo.

**9**   In the Canvas, adjust the scale and position of the mask as necessary.

To further integrate the look of the photos into the overall look of the project, you'll
make a copy of them and add some filters to the copy.

Previously you copied layers by duplicating them. Motion provides an alternative to
duplicating called *cloning*. By cloning a layer or a group, you use less memory, and
changes made to certain properties of the source layer(s) will be passed through to
the clone.

**10**  Close and select the *Stills* group.

**11**  Choose Object > Make Clone Layer or press K. A new clone layer appears in a new
group above the *Stills* group. The clone is an exact copy of the *Stills* group, sitting on
top of it and covering it.

**12** Change the blend mode of the clone layer to Linear Light. That's not quite the look of the rest of the composition. You'll colorize the clone and blur it to make it blend in.

> **NOTE ▶** The position of a clone layer may be slightly different from the original. Drag the clone layer in the Canvas to align it with the original.

**13** Click the Add Filter icon and choose Color Correction > Colorize.

**14** Remap black to a dark gray and white to a light brown.

**15** Click the Add Filter icon and choose Blur > Gaussian Blur, and increase the blur amount to about 20.

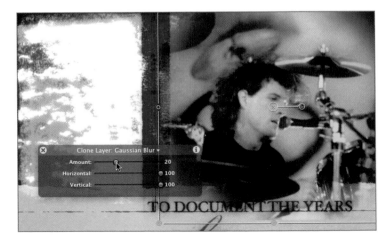

**16** Save your work, and then play through the project. You can reposition the clone layer or individual photos in the *Stills* group to suit yourself.

> **TIP** ▶ For photos of people facing toward the edge of the Canvas, consider adding a Flop filter from the Distortion category. Just make sure that text doesn't appear in the shot.

Excellent! The last step is to add the graphics on top of the photos.

## Importing Motion Projects

The graphics that you'll add on top of the photos include the band's logo, the title of the DVD (*One*), graphics that represent the years included in the DVD (1984 to 1992), and one more ink-based element to add a bit more grunge and tie everything together. Blend modes, colorize filters, and blur filters will help integrate these elements.

Because you have worked with these concepts, you'll add these elements "prebaked." They have been saved as a Motion project that you can just drop into the current project. But first, as usual, you will need to organize the Layers tab to make room for the new guests.

**1** Rename the group containing the clone layer to *Graphics and Stills*. This group will contain all the elements that are not in the *DVD Titles* group on the very top or in the *Background* group on the very bottom.

**2** Drag the *Stills* group on top of the *Graphics and Stills* group.

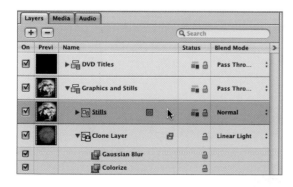

The Stills group is now on top of the clone layer, but it needs to be underneath for the clone to blend with it.

**3** Choose Object > Send to Back or press Command-Shift-[ (left bracket). The *Stills* group moves to the bottom of the *Graphics and Stills* group, and the Canvas looks correct again.

> **TIP** Using a menu command or a keyboard shortcut to move layers or groups within a group can be easier than dragging. For example, when dragging, it's possible to accidentally drag a group into another group.

**4** Drag the *Graphics Under* group on top of the *Graphics and Stills* group; then press Command-Shift-[ (left bracket) to move it to the bottom of the group.

**5** Open the File Browser, switch to Icon view, and locate **Graphics Over**.

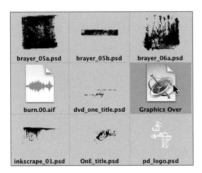

This file has the Motion application icon because it represents a group of layers from a Motion project saved by dragging the group from the completed project to the File Browser.

**6** With the playhead located at the first frame of the project, drag the **Graphics Over** file to the *Graphics and Stills* group. A new group, *Graphics Over*, appears at the top of the *Graphics and Stills* group.

**7** Open the *Graphics Over* group and all of its layers. The layers in this group all have blend modes and filters applied to help composite them into the project.

> **TIP** Depending on your screen size and resolution, you may not be able to see all the layers without scrolling. You can change the height of layers and groups by positioning the pointer between any two layers, waiting for it to change to a resize pointer, and dragging upward.

**8**   Select and deselect the activation checkboxes next to the layers and filters in the group to determine how they have been composited in the Canvas. Once again, feel free to try different blend modes and filter settings to customize the look.

**9**   Play through the project, and make any final adjustments to individual photos.

Applying a Flop filter makes the musician face the center of the Canvas instead of looking offscreen.

**10**   Save your work.

Congratulations. You now have a solid grasp of many of the compositing options in Motion using blend modes, opacity adjustments, and filters to create an integrated look. Along the way, you've learned how to make edits in the Timeline, use clones and masks, and work with the Layers tab—all critical skills for compositing motion graphics.

## Lesson Review

1. How can you ensure that transparent areas of your project will appear black when used as a menu in DVD Studio Pro?
2. You are using the HUD to change the brightness of a filter, but even at the maximum setting, it's not bright enough. Where can you enter a higher value?
3. Name two blend modes that will generally result in a lighter image.
4. Identify two ways to modify the impact of a blend mode.
5. When you want to make a copy of a layer or group, what is an alternative to duplicating?
6. Identify the three options for importing a multilayered Photoshop file.
7. A client gives you 50 digital photos to use in a Motion project. You put them in a folder on your desktop, but when you look in that folder using Motion's File Browser, all you see is a single icon. What's going on, and what can you do to see all the photos?
8. Name three types of edits you can perform in Motion.

### Answers

1. Choose Edit > Project Properties and set Background to Solid.
2. In the Inspector.
3. Add, Lighten, Screen, Color Dodge, Linear Dodge.
4. Lower the opacity of the layer, duplicate the layer, or add a colorize filter.
5. Use Make Clone Layer.
6. As merged layers, as all layers, or by selecting an individual layer.

7.  The photos are numbered sequentially and appear by default in the File Browser as a collapsed image sequence. Click the "Show image sequences as collapsed" button to see the individual files.

8.  Composite, overwrite, insert, sequential.

## Keyboard Shortcuts

| | |
|---|---|
| **K** | Clone a group or layer |
| **Command-1** | Open the File Browser |
| **Command-2** | Open the Library |
| **Command-3** | Open the Inspector |
| **Command-D** | Duplicate the selected layers(s) or group(s) |
| **Command-J** | Open Project Properties |
| **Command-Shift-N** | Create a new group |
| **Command-,** **(comma)** | Open Preferences |
| **Command-[** **(left bracket)** | Send the selected layer back (down) |
| **Command-]** **(right bracket)** | Move the selected layer forward (up) |
| **Command-Shift-[** **(left bracket)** | Send the selected layer to the back (bottom of the group) |
| **Command-Shift-]** **(right bracket)** | Bring the selected layer to the front (top of the group) |
| **Option-X** | Reset the play range |
| **Option-drag** | Create a copy in the Canvas, Layers tab, or Timeline |

# 3

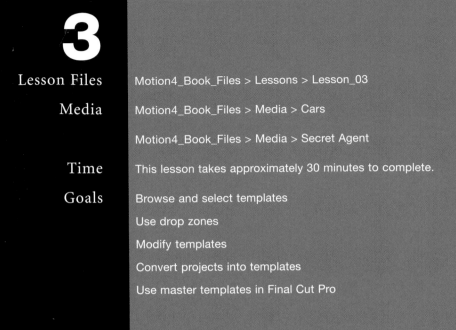

**Lesson Files**    Motion4_Book_Files > Lessons > Lesson_03

**Media**    Motion4_Book_Files > Media > Cars

    Motion4_Book_Files > Media > Secret Agent

**Time**    This lesson takes approximately 30 minutes to complete.

**Goals**    Browse and select templates

    Use drop zones

    Modify templates

    Convert projects into templates

    Use master templates in Final Cut Pro

Lesson **3**

# Working with Templates

One of the fastest ways to get started with Motion is to use a template. The application contains dozens of professionally designed templates in both standard definition and high definition formats. Some are designed around text elements, and others include drop zones that you can use to easily add your own graphics or video.

You can use the templates just as they are, changing only the text and the drop zone content, or you can modify their contents and add layers and effects.

You can even convert your Motion projects into templates. These templates become part of your Motion template collection, and you can also use them in Final Cut Pro without opening (or knowing anything about) Motion!

## Using the Template Browser

You select a template in the Template Browser, where you can filter and preview templates.

**1**   Choose File > Close to close any open projects.

**2**   Choose File > Open Template to open the Template Browser. Templates are organized into groups called *themes*. You select a theme to view all the templates contained in that theme.

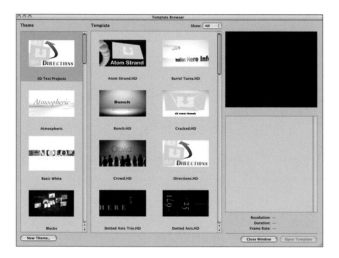

**3**   Select the Basic White theme. Eight templates in multiple formats appear in the Template pane. You can filter the templates to see only templates in a specific format.

**4**   From the Show pop-up menu, choose NTSC to view only the NTSC templates. When you select a template from a theme, a preview of the template plays in the Preview area.

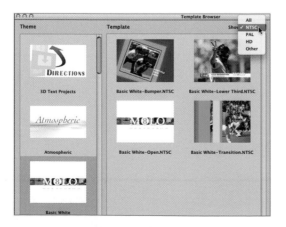

**5**  From the Show pop-up menu, choose All.

**6**  Scroll to the bottom of the Theme list and select the Vine theme.

**7**  In the Template pane, select the Vine-Open.HD template.

The template plays in the Preview area. In the lower right, the Template Browser displays the resolution, duration, and frame rate of the selected template to help you pick a template that is appropriate for your project.

**NOTE ▸** The themes installed with Motion contain high definition (HD) templates and standard definition (SD) templates. The 3D Text Projects theme contains HD projects with a resolution of 1280 x 720 pixels. All the other HD themes contain templates that are 1920 x 1080 pixels. The SD template themes include both NTSC (720 x 486) and PAL (720 x 576) versions.

The Vine theme includes templates with text and animated graphics. Other templates also include *drop zones*, which are a special type of layer in which you can add your own graphics or video.

**8**  Scroll to the middle of the Theme list and select the Light theme.

**9**  Select the Light-Open.NTSC template and watch the preview movie. This is an NTSC template—720 x 486 pixels, 29.97 frames per second (fps)—that lasts a little over 23 seconds and is appropriate for a U.S. broadcast television ad. You'll use it to create a promo for a show called *Classic Cars*.

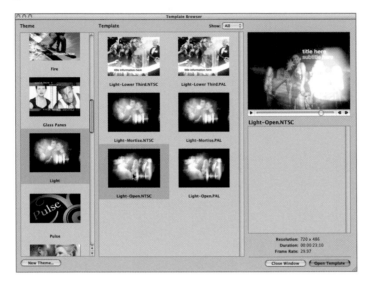

**10** Click the Open Template button. A new, untitled Motion project opens.

**11** Press Command-S; then navigate to Lesson_03 > Student_Saves, and save the project with the name *Classic Cars Promo*.

**12** Play the project.

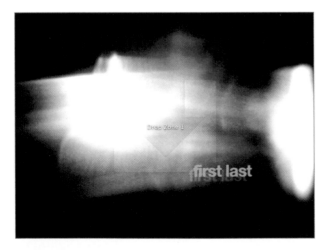

The project looks as it did in the preview, but each of the placeholder graphics has been replaced by a downward arrow graphic with the phrase "Drop Zone 1," "Drop Zone 2," or "Drop Zone 3." You'll replace these graphics with your own content.

## Working with Drop Zones and Text

To create a professional-looking animation with your own graphics or video, you need only to replace the drop zone content and change the text. You can drag graphics or video directly to a drop zone in the Canvas without even opening the Project pane.

**1**   Stop playback and press Home to return the playhead to the first frame. Drop Zone 1 is visible in the Canvas on this frame. You'll replace it with a video clip.

**2**   Press Command-1 to open the File Browser, and navigate to Motion4_Book_Files > Media > Cars. This folder contains three video clips of a vintage automobile. Notice that each clip has a different color balance.

**3**   Select **CarGrillCu.mov** and watch as the clip plays in the Preview area. The clip is high definition footage encoded with the Apple ProRes codec and runs at 23.976 fps. Although your Motion project has a different resolution and frame rate, you can still use this clip in your project.

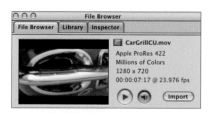

NOTE ▶ It's generally preferable to match the project frame rate to avoid duplicating or skipping frames; but for stylized shots such as these, the difference won't be noticeable.

4   Drag **CarGrillCU.mov** from the File Browser to the Canvas, wait for the hooked arrow pointer and a yellow outline to appear, and then release the mouse button.

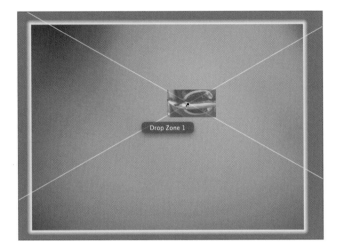

The yellow highlight tells you that your media is over the drop zone layer, and the hooked arrow pointer indicates that your clip will replace the arrow graphic in the layer.

NOTE ▶ You can also replace the content of a drop zone by dragging the new graphic or video to the drop zone layer in the Layers tab, waiting for the hooked arrow to appear, and releasing the mouse—this process is called an *exchange edit*. The advantage of using an exchange edit the Layers tab is that the procedure works on any graphic or movie layer, whether or not it is a drop zone.

5   Scrub the playhead forward to play the video in the project, and stop the playhead when you can see Drop Zone 2.

6   Drag **CarTrackMS.mov** from the File Browser onto Drop Zone 2.

7   Scrub the playhead to a frame where you can see Drop Zone 3, and then drag **CarShotWide.mov** onto it.

**8**   Save your work and play the project. The clips are now styled according to the look of the template and have a unified color balance.

> **TIP** ▶ The video clips you select must be long enough to play through the duration of each drop zone. If the video is too short, you can slow it down or hold the last frame. You'll explore these techniques in a later lesson.

The next step is to replace the text.

**9**   Stop playback and move the playhead to a point where you can clearly see the "first last" text over the first car clip.

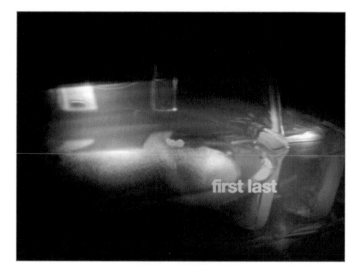

You need to select the text to change it. If you try to select the text by clicking in the Canvas, it's easy to accidentally select another element. You could open the Layers tab of the Project pane and look through the groups to find the text layer, but there's a faster way.

**10**   Press X to perform the Expose Active Layers command. Just as in Exposé in the Finder, all the overlapping layers spread out in the Canvas so that you can see and select any one of them.

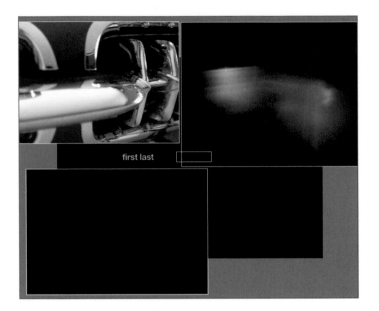

**TIP** ▶ Pressing X exposes active layers, which means the layers that exist at the current playhead location. Pressing Shift-X performs the Expose All Layers command, which will show you every layer in your project.

11 Move your pointer to the left of the words "first last" until the layer's name appears and the small rectangle is highlighted.

**NOTE** ▶ You select exposed images and video by moving the pointer over the anchor point of a layer. The anchor point of the text layer happens to be far to the left of the text itself. You can see this anchor point in the following figure. Depending on your screen size, you may need to move the pointer directly over the words to highlight the rectangle.

12 Click the layer name to select the text layer, and return the Canvas to its normal appearance.

**13** Double-click one of the letters to select the entire phrase, type *classic style* to replace the text, and then press Esc to exit the Text tool. You will apply the same technique to the rest of the text layers.

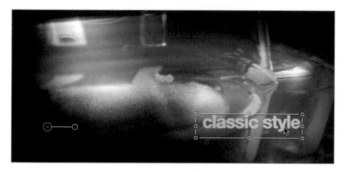

**14** Move the playhead to display each of the other text layers, changing the next one to read "classic curves" and the last one (which contains two text layers) to read "Classic Cars" and "Wednesdays 8pm."

**TIP** ▶ On the last line of the text "Wednesdays 8pm," you may want to use the HUD (heads-up display) to decrease the text size. From the View and Overlay pop-up menu, choose Safe Zones; then drag the HUD's Size slider until the text doesn't cross the inner blue line.

**15** Save your work and play the project.

## Modifying a Template

Because every template comprises the same layers and effects as any Motion project—text, shapes, graphics, video, blend modes, filters, behaviors, and masks—you can do more than just replace the drop zones and lines of text: You can customize the template any way you like.

When playing this project, you may notice that the first two video clips have some nice camera movement, but the last clip is stationary and a little dull. You can use a behavior to create a short dolly-type camera move to make this shot more dynamic.

1   Stop playback, press F5 to open the Project pane, and close any open groups.

> **NOTE** ▸ When you selected a text layer in the last exercise, the group that contained the layer automatically opened to display it, even when the Project pane was closed.

2   Open the *User Content* group, select the *Drop Zone 3* layer, and choose Mark > Go To > Selection In Point, or press Shift-I, to move the playhead to the layer's In point.

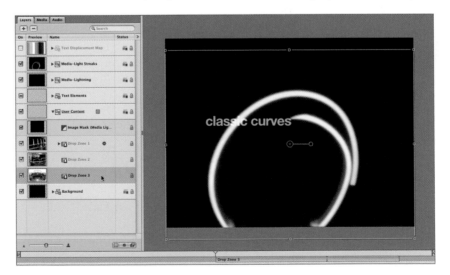

This is the first frame of the last video clip, the clip with no movement. You'll set a play range around it so that you can play it as you work and not waste time playing parts of the project you aren't working on.

3   Choose Mark > Mark Play Range In or press Command-Option-I.

**4**  Press Shift-O to move the playhead to the layer's Out point; then press Command-Option-O to set a play range Out point.

**5**  Start playback.

You will use a Grow/Shrink behavior to animate the video's scale over time so that the video appears to grow; but the headlights of the car are already at the edge of the screen, so you want it to start with the video scaled down.

**6**  In the Canvas, Shift-Option-drag a corner of the bounding box to resize the layer to about 80%.

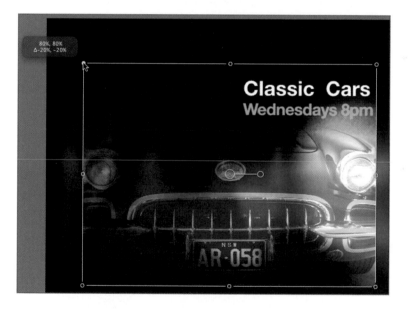

The Shift key keeps the scaling proportional, and the Option key scales around the anchor point, keeping the layer centered in the Canvas.

**7**  In the Toolbar, click the Add Behavior icon, and choose Basic Motion > Grow/Shrink.

**8**  In the HUD (press F7 if it isn't visible), drag outward on a corner of the outer box to grow the layer. Drag far enough so that the car fills the screen by the end of the behavior.

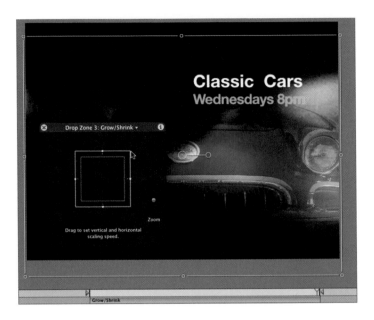

The movement looks good, but the video clip has a hard edge until it moves off the screen. You can see this more clearly if you temporarily turn off the bounding box overlay.

9   Stop playback near the start of the clip. Then, to turn off the overlays, from the View and Overlay pop-up menu choose Show Overlays, or press Command-/ (slash).

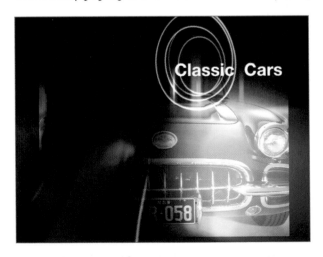

You can remove the hard edge by adding a feathered mask.

**10**  Press Command-/ (slash) to turn on the overlays.

**11**  In the Toolbar, choose the Rectangle Mask tool.

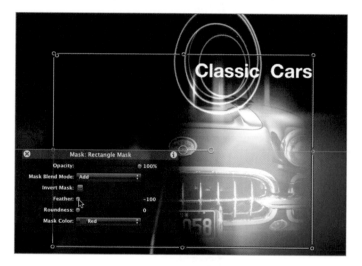

**12**  In the Canvas, draw a rectangle inside the bounding box of the layer.

**13**  In the HUD, drag the Feather slider all the way to the left.

**14**  Press Command-/ (slash) to turn off the overlays so that you can see the result of the mask more clearly. The car now blends in nicely with the background.

**15**  Turn on the overlays again, click in the gray area of the Canvas to deselect everything, and play the project to view your changes.

> **NOTE ▶** If you still see a hard edge at certain frames, you can reduce the size of the mask by selecting it in the Layers tab and then adjusting the scale of the bounding box.

**16**  Choose Mark > Reset Play Range, play the project to see how your changes look in the context of the full project, and save your work.

By using drop zones with Motion's Expose Active Layers command, you've seen that you can put your own content into a template directly in the Canvas. And if you want to modify the template, you can open up the groups and layers in the Layers tab and change anything you wish.

## Converting a Project to a Template

In addition to using the included templates, you can create your own templates from scratch. Or you can convert a project into a template.

In this exercise, you'll convert a project into a template by changing the video layers into drop zones and saving the project as a template. It will become available in the Template Browser in Motion and in the Master Template Browser in Final Cut Pro.

**1**    Close any open projects. Navigate to Lesson_03; then open and play the Show_Open project.

**TIP** ▶ This is a complex HD project with many layers and effects, so playback performance will depend upon your hardware configuration. You can create a RAM preview of the project (subject to your available RAM) by choosing Mark > RAM Preview > Play Range or pressing Command-R. The RAM preview should allow you to view at least part of the project in real time.

This 3D project incorporates many of the features you'll explore in upcoming lessons, so you may notice a few new interface elements in the Canvas. Your goal is to turn the project into a template so that the video and text elements can be easily replaced by a Final Cut Pro editor when he or she creates new show episodes.

To make a template, you use drop zones and save the project as a template. You can add new drop zones or convert any graphic or video layer into a drop zone. Since the video clips are already present in this project, you will convert each clip into a drop zone.

**TIP ▶** To add a new drop zone to a project, choose Object > New Drop Zone or press Command-Shift-D.

If you were given a project created by someone else, it could take some time to dig into all the groups and layers to locate the video layers, especially if the person didn't label the layers and groups. Once again, Motion's Expose Active Layers command allows you to select a layer right from the Canvas.

2   Stop playback and move the playhead to around 5:20, where you can see the first video clip.

3   Press X, and then locate and select the video clip. The video clip's layer name is *DROPZONE01* because the project was created with the intention of converting it into a template.

4   Press F4 to go to the context-sensitive Object tab of the Inspector, which is now called the Image tab.

To convert a graphic or video layer into a drop zone, select the Drop Zone checkbox. However, if you have scaled the layer, converting it to a drop zone can change the scale of the layer. You'll check the layer's properties before converting it.

5   Press F1 to go to the Properties tab of the Inspector. Note that the Scale value of this layer is 163%.

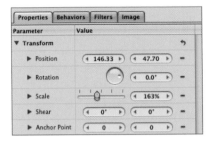

6   Press F4 to return to the Image tab, and select the Drop Zone checkbox. The video clip shrinks in the Canvas.

7   Press F1 to return to the Properties tab.

The Scale value is still 163%. This may seem counterintuitive, but when you convert a layer to a drop zone, the drop zone is created at 100% scale. However, the Scale value still indicates the scaling of the source image. All you need to do is rescale the drop zone.

8   In the Scale field, drag right until the bottom edge of the bounding box passes the bottom edge of the visible Canvas area, at about 321%. Because this is a template, you'll remove the current media to make the template more generic.

**9**  Press F4 to return to the Image tab, and click the Clear button. The video clip is replaced by the drop zone down-arrow graphic.

**NOTE ▶** In the Image tab, the Fit parameter lets you choose how content is handled when dragged into a drop zone that doesn't match the content's size or proportions. The default Fit parameter is usually the best choice because it will scale the new content without distorting it. Choosing Center will leave the new content at 100% size, centered in the drop zone. Choosing Stretch will force the content to fit the drop zone horizontally and vertically, even if it has to squeeze or stretch the content to do so.

You'll use this same method to convert the remaining two video clips into drop zones.

**10** Move the playhead forward until you see the man jumping from the airplane.

**11** Press X and select the *DROPZONE02* video layer.

**12** In the Image tab of the Inspector, select the Drop Zone checkbox.

**13** Click the Clear button to replace the video with the drop zone graphic.

**14** In the Properties tab or in the Canvas, scale up the layer until it fills the top and bottom of the screen, at about 310%.

> **NOTE ▶** If you drag a bounding box handle in the Canvas, remember to hold down Shift-Option to scale proportionally around the layer's anchor point.

**15** Move the playhead to a frame where you can see the running-man clip.

**16**  Press X to select the *DROPZONE03* video clip layer. In the Image tab, select the Drop Zone checkbox. Clear the drop zone, and scale up the clip.

That's all there is to setting up a project as a template.

## Saving Templates and Using Master Templates in Final Cut Pro

Now you just need to save your project as a template in order to access it in the Template Browser in Motion or Final Cut Pro.

**1**  From the File menu, choose Save As Template.

**2**  In the field that contains the text "New Template," type *Action Show Open*.

When you looked at the Template Browser earlier in this lesson, you saw that templates are arranged into themes. You need to pick a theme for this template. Rather than placing it in one of the default themes, you can create a new theme in which you can place other related templates. For example, a single theme might include a title sequence, a lower third, and a bumper graphic for a show package, all using the same design concept.

**3**  Click the New Theme button, name your theme *Action*, and click Create.

The new theme is added to the Theme pop-up menu and is selected. Next, you'll change the format, as this project is an HD project.

**TIP** ▶ Choose Edit > Project Properties or press Command-J to inspect the format of the project.

4   Click the Format pop-up menu and choose HD.

Since you may want to install the template on other Final Cut Studio workstations, it's a good idea to collect the media into a folder.

5   From the Collect Media pop-up menu, choose "Copy into Folder," and then deselect the Include Unused Media checkbox. There's no need to copy the video clips that you cleared from the drop zones.

6   Select the Create QuickTime Preview checkbox. The QuickTime preview is the small movie that appears in the Template Browser.

7   Click Save. The media is copied, the project is saved, and the Export dialog shows the rendering progress for the QuickTime preview movie.

**NOTE** ▶ When you save a project as a template, it is saved in your home folder in Library > Application Support > Final Cut Studio > Motion > Templates, in a folder with the theme's name—in this case, Action. If you copy this folder to another Final Cut Studio workstation, it will appear in the Template Browser. If the target workstation does not have any custom templates installed, you will need to create the Templates folder within the Motion folder.

Your new template is now available in both Motion and Final Cut Pro.

8   Press Command-Shift-O to open the Template Browser, choose the Action theme, and then select the Action Show Open.HD template.

The template preview plays, and the resolution, duration, and frame rate of the project are displayed. User-created template themes have a folder icon, and the themes themselves have a thumbnail that shows one frame of the project.

You can now open this template in Motion, replace the drop zones, change the text, and modify its elements. In addition, all the Motion templates in the Template Browser, including any you create, are also available in Final Cut Pro. So, a Final Cut Pro editor can apply a template and change the drop zone content and text without knowing a thing about Motion. In Final Cut Pro, Motion templates are called *master templates*.

**9**  In the Finder, navigate to Lesson_03 and open the Master_Templates Final Cut Pro project file.

This Final Cut Pro project contains a folder of still images from the Rockumentary project, a folder of video clips from the Pipeline project, and an empty Timeline that is set up for a 1280 x 720 pixel, 23.98 fps HD project, the same project settings as in the template you just created.

**10** Click in the Timeline to make it the active window; then choose Sequence > Add Master Template.

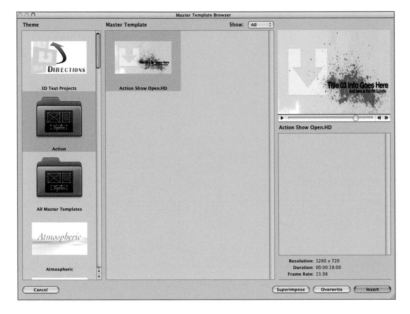

The same Template Browser as in Motion opens in Final Cut Pro. The only difference is that it's called the Master Template Browser and displays additional options at the lower right that provide ways to edit the template into the Timeline.

**NOTE ▶** Any audio contained in a Motion project will not become part of the master template. You can export the audio from Motion, import it to Final Cut Pro, and overwrite it below the template.

**11** Choose the Action theme, select the Action Show Open.HD template, and click Insert to perform an insert edit.

The Motion project appears in the Timeline and is also automatically loaded into the Viewer, with the Controls tab visible. In the Controls tab, you can replace the drop zone content and edit the text. To see the impact of your changes in the Canvas, you'll need to move the playhead.

**12** Move the playhead to about 5:21, where you can see the first title and drop zone.

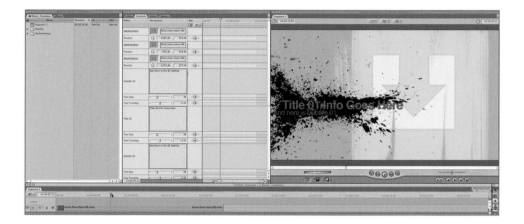

**13** In the Browser, open the Rockumentary bin, and then drag **vid_pix_006.jpg** into the DROPZONE01 well in the Controls tab of the Viewer.

> **TIP** ▶ For best results, use video clips that match the aspect ratio and frame rate of the Motion template. Also make sure that your video clip duration is at least as long as the duration of the drop zone.

**14** In the Controls tab, scroll down and highlight the "Title 01" text. Type *Pale Divine* to change that text, and then change the "Subtitle 01" text to "A Look Back."

In the Controls tab, you can also adjust the size and tracking of text.

**15** Move the playhead to the next drop zone, and experiment with adding different images or video clips, editing the text, and adjusting the text size and tracking.

**TIP** ▶ In Final Cut Pro, you are limited to changing just the drop zone content and the text. If you want to modify other elements of the template, you can Control-click (or right-click) the template and, in the shortcut menu, choose "Open in Editor" or "Open Copy in Editor" to make the changes in Motion. Those changes will automatically update in Final Cut Pro.

Well done. You can now use and modify Motion's built-in templates and create your own templates for use in Motion and Final Cut Pro.

## Lesson Review

1. How do you access Motion's templates?
2. What type of layer can be replaced with a different graphic or video directly in the Canvas?
3. How can you display all the layers that exist at the current playhead location?
4. True or false: In Motion, you can modify only a drop zone and the text of a Motion template.
5. Describe two ways to create a drop zone.
6. How do you open the Template Browser in Final Cut Pro?
7. True or false: In Final Cut Pro, you can modify only the drop zone content and the text of a Motion project.

### Answers

1. Choose File > Open Template Browser or press Command-Shift-O to open the Template Browser.
2. A drop zone layer.
3. Press the X key to perform the Expose Active Layers command.
4. False. You can modify any layer or effect just as in any Motion project.
5. Create a new drop zone by choosing Object > New Drop Zone (or pressing Command-Shift-D), or convert an existing graphic or video layer into a drop zone by selecting the Drop Zone checkbox in the Image tab of the Inspector.
6. Choose Sequence > Add Master Template.
7. True.

**Keyboard Shortcuts**

| | |
|---|---|
| **Command-Shift-D** | Create a new drop zone |
| **Command-Shift-O** | Open the Template Browser |
| **X** | Display all active layers |
| **Shift-X** | Display all layers in the project |

# 4

| | |
|---|---|
| Lesson Files | Motion4_Book_Files > Lessons > Lesson_04 |
| Media | Motion4_Book_Files > Media > Pipeline |
| Time | This lesson takes approximately 90 minutes to complete. |
| Goals | Understand application integration |
| | Send clips from Final Cut Pro to Motion |
| | Animate graphics in 3D using behaviors |
| | Use and modify Library content |
| | Update Motion projects embedded in Final Cut Pro |
| | Understand which elements are retained when sending clips from Final Cut Pro to Motion |
| | Reconstruct Final Cut Pro effects in Motion |
| | Speed up workflow using multiple selections and keyboard shortcuts |

# Lesson 4
# Using Motion with Final Cut Pro

As the saying goes, no man (or woman) is an island. Well, that applies to software as well. If you are using Motion, there's a good chance you are using other applications in the Final Cut Studio suite. For example, if you are doing any kind of editing, you are probably using Final Cut Pro. In fact, you may be not only editing, but also creating motion graphics and effects directly in Final Cut Pro. Motion can seamlessly complement, extend, or replace the work you have been doing in Final Cut because the two applications work tightly together.

In this lesson, you'll explore the workflow between Final Cut Pro and Motion by sending two clips that are part of a short promotional sequence from Final Cut Pro to Motion. You'll then send clips from multiple tracks in a Final Cut Pro sequence that include some effects to see how those effects are handled in Motion.

## Final Cut Pro to Motion and Back: The Workflow

When you have completed a Motion project, you can import that project directly into Final Cut Pro without first exporting it as a movie. This process is called *embedding* a Motion project into a Final Cut Pro sequence.

Once you have a Motion project file embedded in a Final Cut Pro sequence, subsequent changes you make to that Motion project are automatically updated in Final Cut Pro, eliminating the need to repeatedly render out movies every time you need to make a change.

But the integration between Final Cut Pro and Motion goes deeper than the one-way process of opening Motion project files in Final Cut. You can *create* a Motion project using video clips in a Final Cut Pro sequence. You do so by *sending* a clip or clips from Final Cut Pro to Motion, optionally embedding the resulting Motion project file into the Final Cut Pro sequence. This process is called *round-tripping*.

Round-tripping between Final Cut Pro and Motion allows you to leverage the strength of each application. For example, you can capture or transfer your footage and do all your editing in Final Cut Pro—and perhaps create temporary, or *temp*, graphics which you can then replace with more polished versions in Motion.

To see the cross-application workflow in action, you will send two video clips from a Final Cut Pro sequence to Motion and composite an animated title on top of them.

**1**   Navigate to Motion4_Book_Files > Lessons > Lesson_04 and open Lesson_04_Start.

   This file is a Final Cut Pro project file, so it opens in Final Cut Pro.

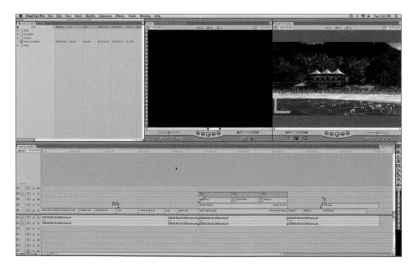

**2** Click in the Timeline window to make it active, and if necessary, press Shift-Z to fit all the clips to the window to get an overview of the entire project.

**3** Drag between the windows to make the Canvas wider and taller.

You'll be using only the first column of the Browser and not using the Viewer, so you can make the Canvas quite wide.

**4** Choose File > Save Project As and save the project to the Student_Saves folder in Lesson_04.

**NOTE ▶** A window other than the Viewer must be active for the Save Project As command to be available.

**5** Press Option-R to render the sequence, and then play the project.

The sequence is a 60-second promo for a surfing contest. It has been carefully edited to match the voice-over, or VO, and it has a few effects already incorporated. But it needs some titling at the beginning to reinforce the location and the surfer names, and the titling and effects in the middle could use some polish.

**NOTE ▶** Depending on your hardware, the project may play back without rendering. If you see red or orange render bars above the ruler area, you'll need to render to play the project at full quality.

**6** Press Home and play the first two clips again.

These two clips are establishing shots, giving viewers a wide view from both the ocean and the sky to show the event location. Adding some animated text will reinforce that location. You will create the text in Motion, but first you'll send the clips to Motion so that you can design that text in the context of the video.

**7**    Click the first clip to select it; then Shift-click the second clip to add it to the selection.

**8**    Control-click (or right-click) the selected clips, and choose Send To > Motion Project.

**NOTE ▸** The Send To command is also available from the File menu.

The Export Selection to Motion Project dialog appears. You are replacing the selected clips in the Timeline with a Motion project, and the dialog prompts you to choose a name and location for that Motion project.

**9**    Name the project *Pipeline Title* and then navigate to Motion4_Book_Files > Lessons > Lesson_04 > Student_Saves.

The checkbox options control what will happen when you click Save. When the Launch "Motion" checkbox is selected, Motion will open so that you can continue work on the project. When the Embed "Motion" Content checkbox is selected, the clips selected in the Final Cut Pro sequence are replaced by the Motion project.

**10** Leave both checkboxes selected and click Save. Motion opens, and the first frame of the first clip is displayed in the Canvas.

**11** Return to Final Cut Pro.

> **TIP** A quick way to move among open applications is to hold down the Command key while pressing the Tab key. A row of icons for each open application appears in the center of your screen with a box identifying the selected application.

Before you begin to work with Motion, let's look at what has happened in your Final Cut Pro sequence. Three things have changed:

▶ In the sequence, the clips that you sent to Motion have been replaced by a Motion project file, indicated by the extension in the clip name, *Pipeline Title.motn*.

▶ In the Browser, the same Pipeline Title.motn Motion project appears as a clip.

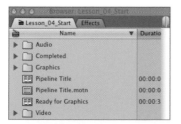

▶ A new sequence appears in the Browser with the same name, *Pipeline Title*.

The Motion project will update in both the Timeline and the Browser to reflect the changes you make in Motion. The new Pipeline Title sequence is a handy backup of the original clips.

**12** In the Browser, double-click the Pipeline Title sequence to open it in the Timeline.

This sequence contains the original clips you sent to Motion—so if you ever want to replace the Motion project with the original clips, you can copy them from here.

**NOTE** ▶ You may notice the "(81%)" in the name of the first clip. This number indicates that a speed change has been applied. The speed change is retained in Motion. You'll work with speed changes in a later lesson.

**13** Control-click the Pipeline Title sequence tab and choose Close Tab.

You won't need this sequence for the rest of this lesson.

**14** Return to Motion.

By keeping Final Cut Pro open, you'll be able to quickly switch back to it after you are done working on the clips in Motion.

## Building an Animated Lower Third

You could have created a new, empty Motion project to build the opening titles, but you will discover several advantages to sending the clips from Final Cut Pro:

▶ The project already has the codec, frame rate, and duration to match the Final Cut Pro sequence.

▶ The project contains the video clips you need.

▶ All the changes you make will automatically appear in Final Cut Pro.

Because you sent these clips from Final Cut, it's easy to get straight to work creating titles. You will use graphics for the titles, edit them into place, use behaviors to animate them, and finish by adding an animated background element, which you'll choose from Motion's Library.

### Adding Titles

In this exercise, you will add a line of text over each of the two video clips to identify the locations: "Pipeline Surf Break" for the first clip and "North Shore, Oahu" for the second clip. You will be using a font that isn't part of the standard font set, so you'll apply it as a graphic. But first, some housekeeping is in order to organize the project.

1   Press F5 to open the Project pane, and then open *Group 1*.

    The two video clips are contained in this group.

2   Rename *Group 1* to *video clips*.

3   Press Command-Shift-N to create a new group, name it *text graphics*, and select it.

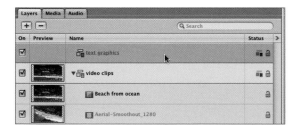

    You will place both of the text graphics in this group.

4   In the File Browser, navigate to Motion4_Book_Files > Media > Pipeline > Graphics.

5   Shift-click **north_shore.psd** and **surf_break.psd** to select them, and then click Import.

    The text graphics are placed inside the selected group and centered in the Canvas. You are going to reposition them and trim them to match the duration of each video clip.

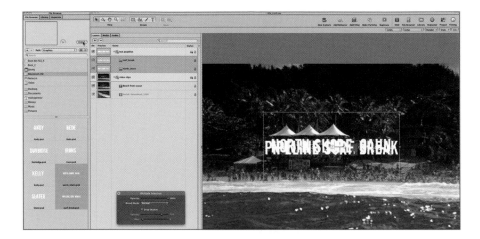

6   From the View and Overlay pop-up menu, choose Safe Zones to turn on the title safe and action safe guides.

> **TIP** The keyboard shortcut for safe zones is the ' (apostrophe) key.

7   In the Layers tab, select the *surf-break* layer; then, in the Canvas, drag it to the bottom left corner inside the title safe guides.

8   Move the *north_shore* layer to the bottom right.

The words overlap right now, but you will trim them so that they don't appear on the screen at the same time. Because you want to match the duration of each graphic with that of the corresponding video clip, you can trim them quickly using keyboard shortcuts.

**9**  In the Layers tab, select the **Beach from ocean** clip, and press Shift-O to move the play-head to the clip's Out point.

**10**  Select the *surf_break* layer, and press O to trim its Out point to the playhead.

**11**  Select the *Aerial-Smoothout_1280* layer, and press Shift-I to move the playhead to its In point.

**12**  Select the *north_shore* layer, and press I to trim its In point to the playhead.

**13**  Press F6 to open the Timing pane, and in the Timeline, verify that the duration of each graphic matches the duration of each video clip.

**14**  Press the Left and Right Arrow keys to view either side of the edit point, and confirm that the graphics change at the same time as the video.

These last two steps aren't strictly necessary, but it's a good habit to check your work.

It's difficult to read the second graphic because the white text is composited on top of the white surf. To improve legibility and keep the design consistent, lets add a drop shadow to the group containing the text layers.

**15**  In the Layers tab, select the *text_graphics* group.

**16**  Press F1 to go to the Properties tab of the Inspector, and select the Drop Shadow checkbox. Feel free to click the disclosure triangle for the drop shadow and adjust the parameters to suit yourself.

**NOTE ▶** You may notice the blue light that turned on next to the Drop Shadow check-box when you selected it. This light indicates that turning on the drop shadow forces the group to be *rasterized*, or *precomposed*. In the Layers tab, you'll see that the symbol next to the group name now has a box around it, which indicates the same thing. Rasterization means that the group is converted to a bitmap image. Therefore, any blend modes applied to layers in the group will not interact with layers outside the group. You won't be using blend modes here, so the rasterization will not have any impact. Rasterizing groups can also affect how they appear in 3D compositions, which we'll explore in later lessons.

**17**   Save your work, press F6 to close the Timing pane, and play the project.

With the text nicely matching the shots, you'll now give it a little more character by adding some animation.

## Creating a 3D Spin Effect

You are using a still image of text in this project rather than a Motion text object. So, instead of using a Text behavior to create animation, you will apply a Basic Motion behavior. The Spin behavior can make each line swing gently like a door—rotating around their y-axes in 3D space.

**1**   Start playback.

Because you are now animating, working while the project plays gives you instant feedback.

**2**   Click the *surf_break* and then Shift-click the *north_shore* layer.

> **TIP**▸ Shift-clicking makes a contiguous selection. If you need to select layers that are separated by effects, separated by other layers, or in different groups, Command-click each clip.

Because you want to apply the same behavior to both layers, you can do it in one step when they are both selected.

**3**   In the Toolbar, click the Add Behavior icon and choose Basic Motion > Spin.

The behavior is added to each of the selected layers.

**4** In the HUD (heads-up display; press F7 if it isn't visible), drag counterclockwise from the top outside edge of the circle for about half a revolution.

The text graphic now spins counterclockwise around its anchor point. It is rotating around its z-axis, which points directly into the screen. You want it to swing more like a door around its y-axis, which runs vertically through the anchor point.

The two rounded arrows in the center of the HUD indicate the rotation axis.

**5** Drag down on the upper rounded arrow.

The arrows rotate within a spherical mesh, but it can be difficult to line them up exactly horizontally so that they point around the y-axis.

**6** Press Command-Z to undo, and then Shift-drag straight down on the top arrow.

The rounded arrows now snap to the horizontal axis. The undo command also reset the spin amount, so you'll restore it.

**7**   Drag counterclockwise from the top of the circle to about halfway around.

As the project plays, the text graphic starts flat to the screen and begins to rotate. It would look more balanced if it started from a position that was already swung in the opposite direction.

**8**   Press F1 to go to the Properties tab of the Inspector.

**9**   Click the disclosure triangle for the Rotation parameter.

The separate parameters for rotation in each of the axes of 3D space—X (horizontal), Y (vertical), and Z (depth)—are displayed. As the project plays over the second graphic, the Spin behavior causes the Y property to change.

**10**   Stop playback and press Shift-I to move the playhead to the In point of the behavior.

It's easier to adjust the rotation while looking at the first frame of the animation.

**11**   In the Rotation Y value field, drag to set a value of about 10 degrees.

Before viewing the results, you'll adjust the Spin behavior on the first text graphic so that it travels in the opposite direction.

**12**   In the Layers tab, under the *surf_break* layer, select the Spin behavior.

**13** In the Properties tab of the Inspector, open the Rotation property and set the Y value to -10 degrees.

This value will start the first line of text rotated by the same amount, but in the opposite direction.

**14** In the HUD, drag counterclockwise from the top of the circle to about halfway around the circle.

It can be a little easier to change the axis in the Inspector than in the HUD.

**15** In the Inspector, click the Behaviors tab and set the Axis pop-up menu to Y.

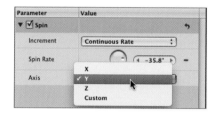

**16** Play back the project, tweak the rotation values as desired, and then save your work.

## Fading the Text

You will finish your text animation by making each line fade in and fade out.

**1** In the Layers tab, Command-click both of the *text graphic* layers. In the Toolbar, click the Add Behavior icon and choose Basic Motion > Fade In/Fade Out.

**NOTE ▶** If a Spin behavior is still chosen, Command-click to remove it before applying the behavior; otherwise, you'll end up with two Fade In/Fade Out behaviors applied to that layer.

**2** Play the project.

Each text graphic now fades in and out, but the default duration of 20 frames doesn't provide enough time for your viewers to read the text.

**3** In the Layers tab, Command-click each of the Fade In/Fade Out behaviors to select them both.

4    In the HUD, adjust both the Fade In and Fade Out durations to 5 frames.

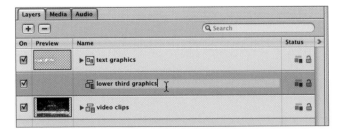

With the text animation completed, we'll finish this lower third by adding a background element to frame the text and separate it from the video clip.

### Using Library Content

Now you will dip back into Motion's extensive Library for an animated graphic, which you'll transform and filter to work with this project. But first, you'll create a new group to keep things organized.

1    In the Layers tab, close both groups and select the *video clips* group.

2    Click the Add button (+) to create a new group, and name it *lower third graphics*.

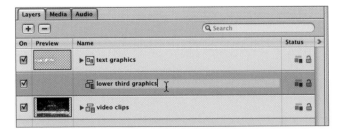

The group is created above the selected group, which will place the graphics over the video and underneath the text, just where you want them.

**3**   In the Library, choose Content > Drawings, locate Ornament 11, and watch the preview.

This growing vinelike drawing curls like a wave, and could work well to lead the viewer's eye across the text.

**4**   While the project is playing, drag the Ornament 11 image into the *lower third graphics* group.

A new group, *Ornament 11*, appears in the *lower third graphics* group, and the animation plays in the Canvas.

**5**   Open the *Ornament 11* group to see what's inside.

The group contains over a dozen paint stroke layers, each with a behavior applied to animate the strokes onto the screen. You'll work more with paint strokes in a later lesson.

6　Close the *Ornament 11* group, and in the Canvas, move the graphic to the lower left of the screen so that it appears to grow into the screen from the left side.

A blend mode and a change in color will help integrate the graphic into the scene.

7　In the HUD, change Blend Mode to Add.

You won't see any change because the Add blend mode adds the values of the pixels above to the pixels below. Because white is the highest value you can have, it just stays white.

8    In the Toolbar, click the Add Filter icon and choose Color Correction > Colorize.

9    Click the Remap White To color well and choose a medium-dark blue.

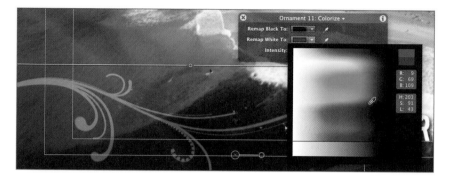

By first changing the blend mode, you can see its impact as you try out different colors.

10   Close all open groups and save your work.

You now have a nicely animated lower third that helps establish the location of the event. Let's see how your work looks back in Final Cut Pro.

## Completing the Round Trip: Returning to Final Cut Pro

When you've completed and saved your work in Motion, the Motion project embedded in your Final Cut Pro sequence updates automatically.

After viewing the Motion clip in the context of the rest of the Final Cut sequence, you may decide that you want to make a change. Luckily, it's easy to do so. You can use Final Cut's "Open in Editor" command to round-trip to Motion and back as many times as you like.

1    Press Command-Tab to return to Final Cut Pro.

You'll see a colored render bar over the Pipeline Title.motn project file. To play the Motion project at full frame rate and full quality, you'll need to render the project. However, you can get a feel for how the file looks without rendering.

> **TIP ▶** The color of your render bar will vary depending on your hardware configuration. For best playback performance of unrendered material, choose Unlimited RT in the RT pop-up menu at the top left of the sequence.

**2**    Press Home, and then press Option-P to play the Motion project.

> **NOTE ▶** Pressing Option-P renders each frame into RAM and plays the frames as fast as your hardware allows. You generally won't see real-time playback, and you won't hear any audio, but this is a useful technique for checking your work without rendering.

The Motion project plays in the Canvas. It should look identical to the project as it appeared in Motion.

> **NOTE ▶** Before you create your final render of the Motion project, you can adjust the way Final Cut Pro will handle the rendering. Choose Sequence > Settings and go to the Render Control tab. In the Master Templates and Motion Projects section, you can set the Quality level and force Best Quality when rendering.

Now that you see the lower-third animation in the context of the rest of the sequence, you may decide you want to stylize the footage in the first two shots.

The integration between Final Cut Pro and Motion lets you make changes to embedded Motion projects that are immediately reflected in Final Cut Pro.

**3**    Control-click the **Pipeline Title.motn** clip in the sequence and choose "Open in Editor."

The Motion application comes forward. If Motion was closed, it will open with this project.

**4**   In the Layers tab, select the *video clips* group.

**5**   Click the Add Filter icon and choose Color Correction > Desaturate. Both video clips are now grayscale.

**6**   Choose File > Save.

You must save your changes for them to appear in Final Cut Pro.

**7**   Press Command-Tab to return to Final Cut Pro.

**8**   Press Home; then press Option-P to play the Motion project without rendering.

The clips in Final Cut are also desaturated. It's interesting, but now that you can see it in context, the cut to the next clip in full color after the first two clips in black and white is jarring.

**9**   Press Command-Tab to return to Motion, and delete the Desaturate filter.

**10**  Press Command-S to save your changes; then press Command-W to close the project.

You are finished with the opening title, but you will be sending some other clips from Final Cut Pro to Motion, so you will leave Motion open.

**11**  Return to Final Cut Pro.

In the process of creating the lower-third title, you have learned the basics of moving between Final Cut Pro and Motion. In the next exercise, you will build on this foundation by sending a more complex set of modified clips, generators, and transitions.

## Sending Motion Graphics and Effects from Final Cut Pro to Motion

Many Final Cut Pro editors create motion graphics and effects directly in Final Cut Pro because it allows them to transform clips, add filters, create text, and animate properties like position, scale, or blur by setting keyframes. But by using Motion and Final Cut Pro together, you open up even more creative options.

At one end of the spectrum, you can use Final Cut just to import video from its source—such as tape, P2 cards, or SxS cards—and then send it from the Browser to Motion to apply all of your editing and effects.

Or you can perform your complete edit and insert animated titles, motion graphics, and effects in Final Cut Pro. Then you can send a few clips or the entire sequence to Motion to add a few effects that can't be created in Final Cut Pro or are easiest to do in Motion.

When editing, it's a common workflow to create *temp* effects—roughed-in titles, cross-dissolve transitions, a split frame, or a background element—that are meant to indicate a general style. These temp effects can be completed in Motion using its more complete tool set and real-time design engine built specifically for creating effects and animation.

When you send clips from Final Cut Pro to Motion, many of the transformations and effects you made in Final Cut will arrive intact. But a few effects do not "make the trip" to Motion. You can work most efficiently when you know which elements will arrive in Motion unaltered and which will need to be re-created.

In this exercise, you will send a section of a Final Cut Pro sequence to Motion that contains clips that have been transformed, still images, generators, transitions, and keyframed clips.

Once you are in Motion, you'll re-create any effects that didn't make the trip, and then you'll create animated titles to complete the sequence.

## Sending Clips with Effects

The promo you've been working on in this lesson contains a section near the middle that introduces three surfers in the competition.

Because these surfers are a big draw for the audience, you want to emphasize their importance by adding text and other elements. You've already created many of these elements inside Final Cut Pro. You now want to refine them in Motion.

First, let's examine what you'll be sending to Motion.

**1** Move the playhead to the beginning of the set of stacked clips and play through them.

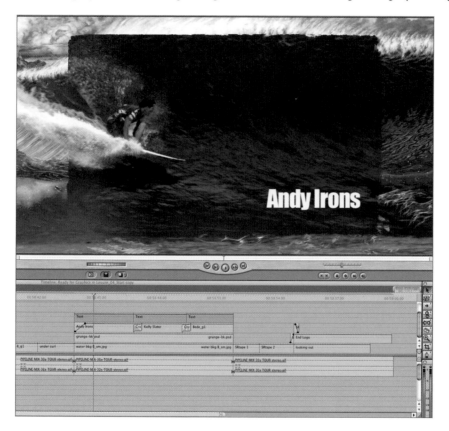

The audio track mixes a voiceover with the music that announces the name of each surfer. You will want to hear this VO in Motion in case you need to time any graphics to it.

**2** Select all the clips on tracks V2, V3, and V4; then Control-click and choose Clip Enable to hide these tracks.

Only the bottom V1 track is now visible, an illustration of a wave from underwater.

**3** Double-click **water bkg B_sm.jpg** to load it into the Viewer, and click the Filters tab. A Gamma filter is applied to make the clip darker.

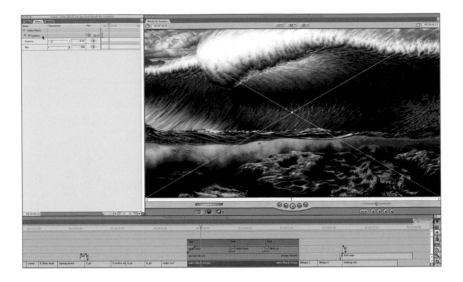

4    Control-click **grunge-bk.psd** on V2, and choose Clip Enable to turn it on.

5    Double-click the clip to load it into the Viewer, and click the Motion tab.

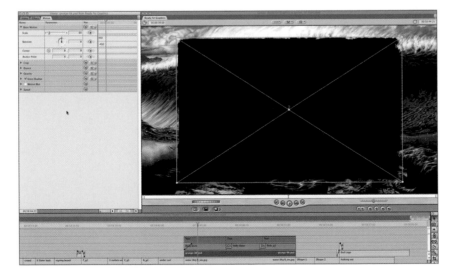

This clip is a black rectangular image with a rough edge and the Drop Shadow
selected. It is used as a matte for the surfer video clips.

6    Select all the clips on V3 and V4, and press Control-B to turn them back on.

**NOTE** ▶ Control-B is the keyboard shortcut for toggling Clip Enable.

The surfer clips each have a composite mode applied to combine them with the lower clips.

**NOTE** ▶ Composite modes in Final Cut Pro are the same as blend modes in Motion.

**7**  Press Command-Shift-A to deselect everything; then Control-click the first surfer clip, **Andy Irons**, and from the shortcut menu, choose Composite Mode.

The Lighten composite mode is applied to this video clip. Notice that only the bright part of the ocean spray appears over the wave illustration. Because everything in the video clip is lighter than the black rectangle, the entire video clip is displayed above it.

Notice also that this first video clip has its opacity keyframed, indicated by the sloping clip overlay line in the Timeline with diamonds placed at the keyframes. The clip starts at zero opacity and fades up to full opacity.

Cross-dissolve transitions have been placed between the surfer clips, which fade out the outgoing clip while the incoming clip fades in.

8   Examine the composite mode of the Kelly Slater clip.

It also is set to Lighten with the same result: The brighter parts of the ocean spray show up outside of the rough rectangle.

9   Move the playhead over the **Bede_g1** clip and examine its composite mode.

This clip has a different composite mode applied, Travel Matte – Alpha. The composite mode uses the transparency, or alpha channel, of the clip directly underneath the surfer clip to determine which parts of the surfer clip are made visible. So in this case, you only see the ocean spray from the surfer inside the rough rectangle.

**10** In track V4, double-click the last **Text** clip to open it in the Viewer. Click the Controls tab.

The text clips are generators—found in the Generator menu at the bottom right of the Viewer's Video tab or in the Effects tab of the Browser—and they each have been set to Impact, 36 points, and positioned at the lower right of the Canvas.

Before you send this content to Motion, let's review its details:

▶ The clips you are about to send to Motion include audio clips, still images, video clips, and generators.

▶ The wave image has a filter applied.

▶ The black grungy rectangle has a drop shadow applied from the Motion tab.

▶ The three video clips each have a composite mode applied.

▶ The first video clip has its opacity keyframed.

▶ There are cross-dissolve transitions applied between the video clips.

With this list in mind, let's send these clips to Motion and see what happens.

**11** Select the stack of clips, including the audio.

**12** Control-click the selected clips and choose Send To > Motion Project.

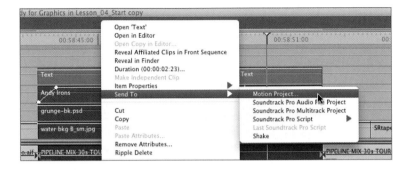

**13** Name the project *Top Surfers* and save it to Lesson_04 > Student_Saves.

**14** Verify that the Launch "Motion" and Embed "Motion" Content checkboxes are selected, and click Save.

Motion appears with the project opened.

**NOTE ▸** You can also send entire sequences from Final Cut Pro to Motion by selecting them in the Browser. All the clips from the sequence will appear in Motion, but no option is available to embed the Motion project into a Final Cut Pro sequence because sending a sequence is a one-way trip. This workflow is most useful for short projects, when you are finishing an entire project in Motion for export to the web or perhaps for use as a menu in DVD Studio Pro. If you do want to return to Final Cut Pro, you could import the Motion project.

## Cleaning Up a Motion Project

Let's see which elements made the trip.

**1** Press Shift-Z to fit the Canvas to the window, and then start playback.

Because you can hear the audio, you know it made the trip, as did the background wave illustration and the surfer clips, which you can see in the Canvas.

But the text is gone, and the third surfer fills the whole frame instead of being matted to the black rectangle. Let's investigate, starting from the bottom up, as you did in Final Cut Pro.

**2**   Stop playback after the VO says "Andy Irons," and press F5 to open the Project pane.

There are four groups in the Layers tab, and you can tell by the small icon in the Preview column that each group contains the clips from the corresponding tracks in Final Cut Pro. When you send clips on separate tracks from Final Cut Pro to Motion, Motion always separates those tracks into their own groups.

**3**   Open all the groups, and then Option-click the *water bkg B_sm.jpg* layer's activation checkbox to solo that layer.

> **NOTE ▶** You won't be able to open *Group 4* because it's empty. You know it's empty because it lacks a disclosure triangle.

The illustration is there, but the Gamma filter is missing. That's because filters do not make the trip from Final Cut Pro to Motion. However, Motion has its own filters that are usually similar or exactly the same, so you can apply them in Motion.

**NOTE ▶** Not every filter in Final Cut Pro has an exact match in Motion—some have different names, and some, like Final Cut Pro's Color Corrector 3-way, have no analogous Motion filter.

4   Select the *water bkg B_sm.jpg* layer; then, in the Toolbar, click the Add Filter icon and choose Color Correction > Gamma.

But how can you adjust the Gamma amount to exactly match the setting you used in Final Cut Pro?

5   Return to Final Cut Pro.

You'd like to open this clip in the Viewer to see the setting you used here, but the clip is gone, replaced by the Motion project! That's OK. Remember that when you send clips to Motion, Final Cut Pro creates a new sequence that contains those clips.

6   In the Browser, locate and open the Top Surfers sequence. Ah, there it is!

**7**   Double-click **water bkg B_sm.jpg** to open it in the Viewer, and in the Filters tab, note the Gamma setting of 0.52.

**8**   Close the Top Surfers sequence. Return to Motion, and in the Filters tab of the Inspector, set Gamma to 0.52.

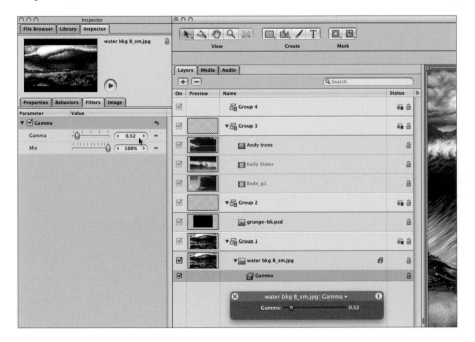

**TIP**   It can be easier to enter a precise value in the Inspector than to use the slider in the HUD.

**9**   Option-click the activation checkbox for the *water bkg B_sm.jpg* layer to unsolo it, and then select the *Andy Irons* layer.

In the HUD, notice that the Lighten composite mode from Final Cut Pro is maintained in Motion as a blend mode. Motion will recognize most, but not all, of Final Cut Pro's composite modes.

**10** Move the playhead forward until you see the third surfer, Bede Durbidge, in the Canvas; and then select the Bede_g1 layer.

The HUD tells you that the blend mode is Normal. This is the clip that had the Travel Matte – Alpha composite mode applied in Final Cut Pro. Final Cut handles travel mattes differently than Motion, so if you used either Travel Matte – Alpha or Travel Matte – Luma in Final Cut, you'll need to replace it in Motion.

One way to approach this task is to use an *image mask*. An image mask in Motion is an effect that you apply to a layer or a group. Rather than creating transparency based on a rectangle or circle, such as the shape masks you used in Lessons 1 and 2, an image mask uses the alpha channel or luminance of another layer or group to determine transparency.

You'll apply an image mask to all three video clips to create a consistent look for the clips.

**11** Shift-click the *Andy Irons* and *Kelly Slater* layers to select all three video clips, and in the HUD, change Blend Mode to Normal.

Because you'll be using an image mask, you won't need the Lighten blend mode.

**12** Select the *Group 3* group and choose Object > Add Image Mask.

The HUD contains a rectangle, called a *well*, to hold the source of the mask.

**13** Drag the *grunge-bk.psd* layer from the Layers tab to the well in the HUD.

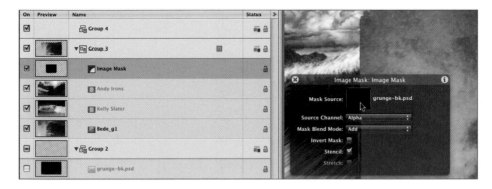

The *grunge-bk.psd* layer's activation checkbox is automatically deselected in the Layers tab, and all the video clips in the group are now matted to the grungy rectangle. But what has happened to the drop shadow?

**14** Select the *grunge-bk.psd* layer, and press F1 to go to the Properties tab of the Inspector.

Sure enough, the Drop Shadow checkbox is selected—but the drop shadow doesn't show in the Canvas because the layer was automatically turned off when it was used as an image mask. Turning it on won't help, however—the drop shadow will just be added to the mask. A better solution is to add a drop shadow to the group of video clips.

**15** Select the *Group 3* group and select the Drop Shadow checkbox in the Properties tab. All three video clips now have a consistent drop shadow.

**16** Save your work and play the project.

An obvious missing element is the text. It's missing because generators in Final Cut Pro—text, color mattes, color bars, shapes, slugs, and so on—don't make the trip to Motion.

A less obvious loss is that the cross dissolves are no longer present. As the project plays, the first surfer clip fades up, but then straight cuts occur between the next two clips.

So, opacity keyframes from Final Cut Pro make the trip, but transitions do not.

You could replace the cross dissolves with the Fade In/Fade Out behavior, after extending the duration of the clips to create enough overlap; but the straight cuts actually work well enough so that you'll leave them as they are.

To summarize, here's what happens to clips and effects sent to Motion from Final Cut Pro, including some additional information:

▶ Video clips and graphics make the trip to Motion with their In and Out points and handles intact. Markers added to clips in Final Cut Pro will also show up in Motion.

▶ All clip property changes in the Motion tab in Final Cut Pro make the trip to Motion—including scale, rotation, position, drop shadow, opacity, and even speed changes. Any keyframes applied to these parameters will also be retained in Motion.

The Motion tab from Final Cut Pro—if you modify any of these properties, except for Motion Blur, or if you add keyframes to change the properties over time, your changes will be retained in Motion.

▶ Filters, transitions, and generators applied to clips in Final Cut Pro do not make the trip to Motion. The one exception to this rule is Final Cut's SmoothCam filter, which is translated into Motion's Stabilize behavior.

▶ Freeze frames from Final Cut (created by choosing Modify > Make Freeze Frame) come into Motion as video clips with the Hold Frame behavior applied to create the freeze frame.

▶ Audio tracks sent from Final Cut Pro arrive intact in Motion, but the audio does not become part of the embedded Motion project file in Final Cut Pro. Instead, Final Cut leaves the original audio tracks in place.

Armed with this information, you can choose the motion graphics and effects work you want to start in Final Cut Pro and finish in Motion.

Because the text in Final Cut Pro was a placeholder element, you'll now add and animate the surfer names in Motion.

## Adding Title Graphics

You'll use graphics for the surfers' names just as you did with the lower-third intro titles. After adding the graphics and trimming them to match the clips, you'll animate the first and last names to move in opposite directions.

First, though, you'll label the groups.

1   Rename *Group 1* to *Background*, *Group 2* to *Matte*, *Group 3* to *Video*, and *Group 4* to *Titles*.

It's always a good idea to descriptively label your groups based on their contents.

2   Move the playhead to the start of the project.

3   Press Command-1 to go to the File Browser, select all six name graphics, and drag them to the *Titles* group.

> **TIP** Elements will be ordered in the Layers tab in the order in which you select them in the File Browser, from the bottom up.

With all the text graphics in the project, you can make quick work of matching them to each video clip using keyboard shortcuts.

4   Select the *Andy Irons* video layer, and press Shift-O to move the playhead to the layer's Out point.

5   Command-click to select both the *Andy* and *Irons* graphic layers, and press O to trim their Out points to the playhead.

6   Press the Right Arrow key once.

   This action places the playhead on the first frame of the *Kelly Slater* video layer because the video clips have no empty frames between them.

7   Select both the *Kelly* and *Slater* graphic layers, and press I to trim their In points to the playhead.

8   Select the *Kelly Slater* video layer, and press Shift-O to move to the Out point.

9   Select both the *Kelly* and *Slater* graphic layers, and press O to trim their Out points to the playhead.

10  Press the Right Arrow key once.

   This action moves the playhead to the first frame of the *Bede Durbidge* video layer.

11  Select the *Bede* and *Durbidge* graphic layers, and press I to trim their In points.

**12** Press F6 to open the Timing pane, and in the Timeline tab, verify that the duration of each of the name graphics matches the duration of each video clip.

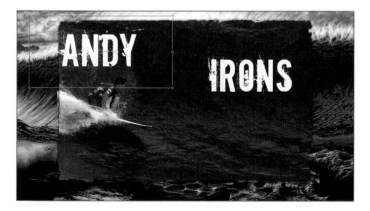

**NOTE ▶** You may need to open the *Titles* group in the Timeline to see each name graphic. Also, the order of your name graphics may be different from what's in the image above, depending on how you selected them. Feel free to reorder the name graphic layers to put first and last names next to each other.

**13** Press F6 to close the Timing pane.

**14** Select all of the name graphics, press F1 to go to the Properties tab, and in the Scale value field enter *90*.

This action scales down all the graphics by the same amount so that they don't crowd the surfers.

**15** Select each name graphic (move the playhead, if necessary, so that you can see the name in the Canvas), and reposition the names to read properly without blocking the surfers. Vertically offset them from each other.

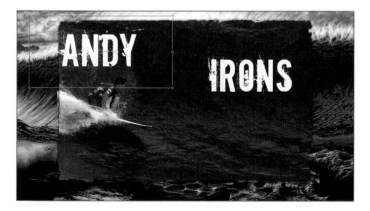

Scrub through each clip to make sure that the letters don't overlap the surfer's face as he moves.

With the names positioned, we'll use a behavior to add some subtle animation.

## Animating Title Graphics

In this exercise, you will use a Throw behavior to make each name graphic slowly drift across the screen, with the first and last names moving toward each other.

In the previous exercise, you selected multiple layer to add Spin behaviors to all the layers at once. Now, you'll add just one behavior, adjust it, and then copy it onto the other layers.

By first setting a play range around each video clip, you'll be able to quickly adjust the animation for that clip before moving to the next clip.

1   Select the "Andy" name graphic, and press Shift-O to move the playhead to the clip's Out point.

2   Press Command-Option-O to set a play range Out point at the playhead.

3   Start playback.

   **NOTE** ▸ You may want to mute the audio by clicking the Play/Mute audio button in the transport controls at the bottom of the Canvas.

   You are now playing just the first video clip, over which you will animate the *Andy* and *Irons* title layers.

4   Click the Add Behavior icon, and choose Basic Motion > Throw.

5   In the Behaviors tab of the Inspector, click the disclosure triangle for the Throw Velocity to reveal the X, Y, and Z parameters, and set the X value to 40.

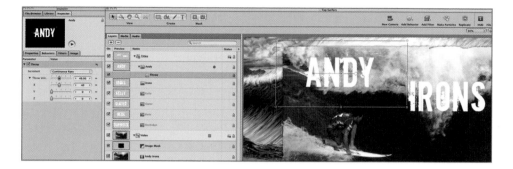

The red motion path in the Canvas indicates the distance that the graphic travels. While you could use the HUD to create this motion, using the Inspector allows you to enter a precise value, which will come in handy momentarily.

6   In the Layers tab, Option-drag the Throw behavior from the *Andy* layer to the *Irons* layer.

Using the Option modifier key copies the behavior rather than just moving it to the target layer.

7   Select the copied Throw behavior, and in the Behaviors tab, change the X value to -40.

The first and last names now drift toward each other.

**NOTE ▶** You may need to adjust the position of each of the name layers so that they don't overlap or block the surfers as they move. Just drag the layers as the project plays; or stop playback, go to the last frame of the animation, and reposition the layers.

If you had used the HUD for the first behavior, you would have ended up with a fractional value, such as 39.83, that would take more time to reenter as a negative value. It may not sound like much of a timesaver, but when you are working on a large project, every click or keystroke you don't have to perform really adds up.

Now you can copy each of these behaviors to the first and last name layers for the other surfers. First, though, let's rename the behaviors so that it's clear what they do.

8   Rename the Throw behavior to *Throw Right* and the Throw copy behavior to *Throw Left*.

9   Option-drag the Throw Right behavior onto the *Kelly* layer and then to the *Bede* layer.

10  Option-drag the Throw Left behavior onto the *Slater* layer and then to the *Durbidge* layer.

11  Stop playback, and press F6 to open the Timing pane.

In the Timeline, you can see what happened when you copied the behaviors to the other layers. The copied behaviors are automatically matched to the beginning of the layer to which they were copied; but the duration of the behavior is unchanged, and needs to be trimmed.

In the last exercise, when you simultaneously applied the Spin behavior to multiple layers, each behavior exactly matched the duration of each layer. So there are advantages and disadvantages to each approach.

12  In the Timeline under the *Kelly* and *Slater* layers, drag the Out points of the behaviors to trim them to match the duration of those layers. Shift-drag to snap to each layer's Out point.

You will see a thick black vertical line where the behavior Out point snaps to the In or Out point of another layer.

You can accomplish this same task using keyboard shortcuts. Let's try it.

**13** In the Timeline, select the *Bede* layer, and press Shift-O to move to its Out point. Select the Throw Right copy behavior underneath the layer, and press O to trim it to the playhead.

**14** Under the *Durbidge* layer, select the Throw Left copy behavior and press O to trim it.

Whether you drag or use keyboard shortcuts is really up to you. When using keyboard shortcuts, you don't need to open the Timeline, but if you already have the Timeline open, dragging may be faster.

**15** Set a play range around the second video clip, and adjust the positions of the name graphics as necessary; then repeat these steps for the third video clip.

**16**  Close the Timing pane, close all open groups in the Layers tab, and save your work.

Your work in Motion is done. All that's left is to check your results in Final Cut Pro.

**17**  Return to Final Cut Pro, move the playhead to the start of the **Top Surfers** clip, and press Option-P to play the project.

Fantastic! You now have a good grasp of how to move smoothly between Final Cut Pro and Motion, and you have also learned a few more Motion techniques. Plus, you've built some "muscle memory" by repeating useful and frequently used operations, such as setting play ranges and moving the playhead to the beginnings and ends of layers.

▶ **Motion, DVD Studio Pro, and Soundtrack Pro**

In addition to integrating with Final Cut Pro, Motion also integrates with other Final Cut Studio applications.

Motion is an ideal tool for creating alpha transitions and motion menus for DVD authoring in DVD Studio Pro. You can create button overlay files and set a menu loop point right in Motion. And, just as with Final Cut Pro, you can import a Motion project file directly into DVD Studio Pro, where you can apply it as a menu. If you want to change your menu, you can use the "Open in Editor" command that you explored in this lesson.

Motion even integrates with Soundtrack Pro. From the Audio tab in the Project pane, you can send any audio clip to Soundtrack Pro for repair or sweetening, and your changes will be automatically reflected in Motion.

For more information, see the Motion Help file under the Help menu.

## Lesson Review

1.  How do you send clips from Final Cut Pro to Motion?

2.  When sending clips from a Final Cut sequence to Motion, which two options are selected by default?

3.  If you choose to embed a Motion project file when sending clips from a Final Cut sequence to Motion, what happens to the original clips?

4.  In Motion, can you apply a behavior to more than one layer at a time?

5. Name three attributes of a Final Cut Pro video clip that are retained when you send the clip to Motion.

6. Which elements in Final Cut Pro are not retained when sending clips to Motion?

7. When does Motion create separate groups for clips sent from Final Cut Pro?

8. How do you edit a Motion project embedded in Final Cut Pro?

*Answers*

1. Select the clips; then Control-click them and choose Send To > Motion Project. Or, select the clips and choose File > Send To > Motion Project.

2. Launching Motion and embedding the Motion project file in Final Cut Pro.

3. The Motion project file replaces the clips in the sequence, but Final Cut creates a new sequence in the Browser with the name of the Motion project file that contains just the clips that were sent to Motion.

4. Yes, by first selecting the layers, and then choosing the behavior from the Add Behavior icon in the toolbar or dragging the behavior onto one of the selected layers from the Library.

5. All attributes in the Motion tab of the Viewer (except Motion Blur): Scale, Rotation, Center, Anchor Point, Crop, Distort, Opacity, Drop Shadow, and Speed.

6. Filters (with the exception of the SmoothCam filter), transitions, and generators.

7. Motion creates a group for every video track of clips in Final Cut Pro; even if the track contains only generators, which Motion won't import, it creates an empty group.

8. By using the Open in Editor command, accessed by Control-clicking the clip or by choosing Clip in Editor from the View menu.

## Keyboard Shortcuts

| | |
|---|---|
| **Shift-I** | Move the playhead to the selected layer's In point |
| **Command-Option-I** | Set the play range In point at the playhead |
| **Shift-O** | Move the playhead to the selected layer's Out point |
| **Command-Option-O** | Set the play range Out point at the playhead |
| **Right Arrow** | Move the playhead one frame later in time |
| **Left Arrow** | Move the playhead one frame earlier in time |

# 5

| | |
|---|---|
| **Lesson Files** | Motion4_Book_Files > Lessons > Lesson_05 |
| **Media** | Motion4_Book_Files > Media > Pipeline |
| **Time** | This lesson takes approximately 30 minutes to complete. |
| **Goals** | Export a project |
| | Create a custom export preset |
| | Share a project with specific devices |
| | Modify a Share output in Compressor |
| | Save effects, layers, and groups as favorites |
| | Apply saved favorites |
| | Share project components |

# Lesson 5
# Sharing Your Project

Your project is finally done. Well, let's face it—a project is never done. There's always something that can be improved: the timing of an animation, the color of a shot, or a new graphic to add. But eventually the client comes calling and you need to deliver your work. So how do you get it out of Motion?

If you plan to integrate your Motion project into a larger work in Final Cut Pro or DVD Studio Pro, you can import and embed the Motion project file into either of these Final Cut Studio applications.

But if you want to create a self-contained QuickTime movie of your project to output to tape, add to iTunes, watch on an Apple TV, share on your iPhone, or post to the web, you will need to export your project.

Motion offers two exporting methods that you'll explore in this lesson: Share and Export. Share makes exporting a movie incredibly simple, while Export lets you customize your exported movie in a variety of ways.

Sometimes you want to share just a part of your project. Perhaps you've created a logo animation that you want every motion graphics artist in your workgroup to use. Or you want to save a particular combinationof effects that you've applied to a clip. In this lesson, you'll also explore how you can easily save and reuse any combination of effects, layers, and groups, and share them with any Motion user.

## Sharing Projects

The Share command lets you export directly to specific formats with one-click simplicity. You can choose to export files for Apple TV, iPhone, iPod, MobileMe, and YouTube accounts; or you can export for several of these platforms by setting up a single batch process. You can even choose a post-Export action.

1   In the Finder, navigate to Motion4_Book_Files > Lessons > Lesson_05 and open **Top Surfers**. You worked on this project in Lesson 4. You now want to share it.

2   Choose File > Share or press Command-Shift-E to open the Share window, containing one output for Apple TV. The default destination is the Documents folder, which you will use for this exercise.

Let's export a version of this movie for the iPhone.

**3**  From the Output Type pop-up menu, choose iPhone. Notice that the menu also includes presets for Blu-ray Disc, DVD, iPod, MobileMe, YouTube, and other platforms and formats.

**NOTE** ▶ You can choose which presets appear in this menu by choosing Other, navigating to the desired presets, and selecting the In Menu checkbox. Any Compressor presets, including custom presets that you create, can be added to this menu.

By default, the file is named by combining the project name with the preset name. In this case, the default name is *Top Surfers-iPhone*.

**4**  Rename the file to *TopSurf_i*. The shorter name is more iPhone friendly.

**5**  Select the "Add to iTunes Library" checkbox. The next time you sync your iPhone, it will automatically upload the movie.

**6**  Click the Show Info button to the right of the filename. The balloon displays the output settings. You can't modify these settings from the Share window, but you do have some options.

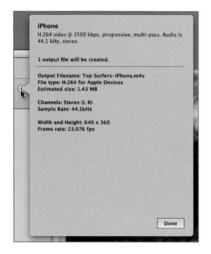

**7**  Click the Done button to close the Info balloon.

Perhaps, in addition to an iPhone version, you'd like to publish your movie on YouTube. The Share window lets you output the same project file in multiple formats.

**8**  To the right of the Show Info button, click the Add Output button. A new output appears underneath with the default Apple TV preset.

**9**  From the Output Type pop-up menu, choose YouTube; then select the "Publish to YouTube" checkbox that appears.

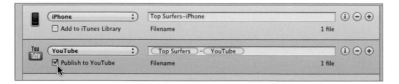

The Action drawer slides into view. Here, you can enter your YouTube account information and describe, tag, and categorize your movie.

**10** Click the Output button.

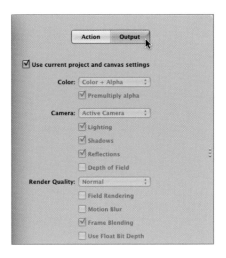

In the Output drawer, you can modify the current project and Canvas settings. For example, you can change Render Quality to High or turn on Motion Blur.

**11** Click Export to start the export process.

That's how to use the Share command. You can export to multiple formats and sites in one batch without the need to choose a codec or set a quality slider or a frame rate. If you want more control over your exports, you can use the Export command.

## Exporting Projects

When you want to export a single QuickTime file from Motion, and you want to control the way your project is exported, choose the Export command. You can choose to export a movie, a still image, or an image sequence; you can export the entire project or just the play range; you can modify the export settings; and you can decide what happens after the project is exported.

**1**  Using the same project, choose File > Export or press Command-E.

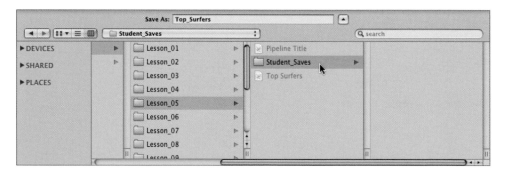

The Export dialog lets you choose a name and location for your file, what file type you want to export, what codec to use, what to include with the file, and what to do after exporting the file. By default, the exported file is named using the Motion project filename. Because this file is destined for the web, it's best if it doesn't have any blank spaces in its name.

**2**  In the Save As field, type *Top_Surfers*.

**3**  To the right of the Save As field, click the arrow button to open a navigation window, and navigate to Lesson_05 > Student_Saves.

The Export pop-up menu is set to QuickTime Movie, which is what you want to export in this exercise. You could also choose to export the current frame or an image sequence.

Exporting the current frame is useful for grabbing representative frames of a project for promotional purposes or for sharing with a client. Exporting image sequences can be useful when creating an intermediate file for use in another compositing or editing application. If a long render is interrupted for any reason, you won't lose the entire render as you would with a movie.

By default, Motion uses the current project and Canvas settings, and exports to a movie using the ProRes 4444 codec. These settings will create a high-quality, near-lossless file that includes any transparency information—a good choice if you want to use the file in another compositing or editing application. In this case, however, you want to create a compressed file to post on your website.

**4**  Click the Options button. This opens the Export Options dialog, where you choose a codec and adjust it to meet your needs. For the web, H.264 is a good choice.

**5**  From the Compressor pop-up menu, choose H.264.

**6**  Set the Quality slider to 75%, which will keep the quality high but will yield a smaller file size.

**NOTE ▶** The best settings will vary according to the type of material you are compressing and trade-offs among file size, resolution, and frame rate.

**7** Click the Advanced button. The Compression Settings dialog opens. In this dialog, you can adjust the settings for the selected codec. For example, for many projects, using a lower frame rate can reduce the exported file's size while maintaining good image quality.

**8** From the "Frames per second" pop-up menu, choose 12.

**9** Click OK to return to the Export Options dialog; in the Audio section, click the Advanced button. In the Sound Settings dialog that opens, you can choose a different codec and a lower sample rate to reduce the exported file size without significantly impacting audio quality.

**10** Set Format to AAC and Rate to 24 kHz.

**11** Click OK to return to the Export Options dialog, and then click the Output tab.

In the Output tab, you can override the project and Canvas settings. In this exercise, you want the web version of your project to be half the size of the HD project.

**12** Deselect the "Use current project and canvas settings" checkbox; then, from the Resolution pop-up menu, choose Half.

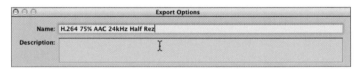

**TIP** In your project, you may have never enabled certain properties—such as motion blur or field rendering—or you may have turned them off to improve playback performance while you work. In the Output tab, you can turn on these and other properties just for the currently exporting file. It's a good idea to look through the settings in this tab each time you export to confirm which settings are on and off.

Now that you've created a customized export setting, you can save it as a preset.

**13** In the Name field, type a descriptive name, such as *H.264 75% AAC 24kHz Half Rez*. You can also enter a description if you wish.

**14** At the bottom of the dialog, click the Save As button. The preset is saved, the Export Options dialog closes, and you are returned to the original Export dialog. Your new preset appears in the Use pop-up menu.

**TIP** This new custom preset will also appear in Motion Preferences, in the Presets section, where you can edit it. (Choose Export Presets from the Show pop-up menu.)

Because you want to include both the video and audio in the exported file, you'll leave the Include pop-up menu set to "Video and Audio."

The After Export pop-up menu includes several options. By using the default value, "Open in viewer window," you can see your file immediately after exporting it.

**TIP** The "Import into project" option in the After Export pop-up menu can be useful for rendering a part of your project, such as an animated background that contains lots of elements, and then using the rendered file in place of the original layers to improve playback performance. To export a selected group or groups, choose File > Export Selection, and then choose "Import into project" to automatically add the rendered file to the project. Turn off the original group(s), but don't delete them, in case you want to change them later.

Finally, you can choose to export just a play range that you set. In this exercise, you want to export the entire project.

**15** Click the Export button. A dialog opens to show the export progress. When it's complete, your movie opens in a viewer.

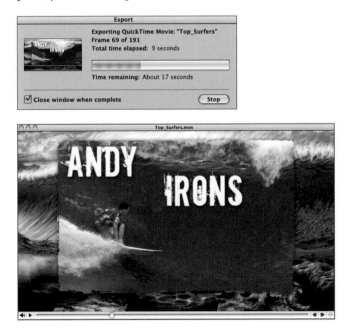

**16** Play the movie, and then close the viewer window.

That's it! You've exported your project to a web-friendly format and created a preset that will make the export process faster next time around.

## Saving and Sharing Project Components

You've applied an effect to your project—a filter, behavior, or mask—and you've tweaked it to make it look just the way you want. Perhaps you are colorizing a video or animating a line of text.

You'd like to save the settings you used so that you can apply the same color or animation to a different project, or perhaps you want to share the setting with someone in your workgroup across the hall or with a colleague halfway around the world.

Motion lets you save these project components—effects, layers with effects applied, even entire groups of layers and effects—and reuse them in other Motion projects. And you can send these saved files to anyone else using Motion.

In this exercise, you'll look at the options for saving and sharing project components, including saving to the Library and saving to the File Browser.

### Saving Favorites

To save project components for later use, you save them to the Favorites folder or Favorites Menu folder in the Library.

1   Press F5 to open the Project pane of the Top Surfers project. Open the *Background* group, and then display and select the Gamma filter applied to the *water bkg B_sm.jpg* layer.

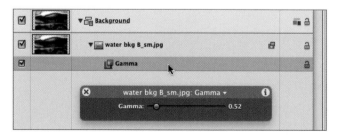

You used this Gamma filter to darken the midtones of the background image. You want to darken other background images by the same amount. Rather than writing down or memorizing the setting, you can save a copy of the filter with this setting applied.

2   Press Command-2 to go to the Library, and then select the Favorites folder. The folder is one location used for saving customized effects (filters, behaviors, and masks), any type of layer, and even groups of layers.

**3**  Drag the Gamma filter from the Layers tab into the Favorites folder. The customized filter appears in the stack. The small silhouette icon indicates that it is a user-created file. You can give it a more descriptive name.

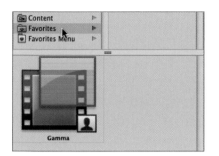

**4**  Control-click (or right-click) the Gamma filter in the Library, choose Rename, and name the file *Gamma 0.52*.

You may have many dozens of files in the Favorites folder, so detailed names can help remind you of what they are for. Next, you'll save a behavior.

**5**  Open the *Titles* group. Open the *Andy* and *Irons* layers, Command-click the Throw Right and Throw Left behaviors to select them, and drag both of the behaviors to the stack area of the Library, but don't release the mouse button.

These are the behaviors that cause the surfers' first and last names to drift toward each other. You want to make sure you use the same speed and duration settings for a similar project.

Motion offers two options in the drop menu that appears for adding these files to Favorites: "Multiple files" and "All in one file." You'll want to apply these behaviors to separate layers.

**6**  Drop the files onto the "Multiple files" well of the drop menu. Each behavior appears in Favorites. Because you already renamed these behaviors in the Layers tab in an earlier lesson, you don't need to do so here.

**TIP** ▶ Drag the slider at the bottom of the Library to change the size of the icons; or, if you prefer, view them as a list by clicking the List View button near the top of the Library.

You can also save components to the Favorites Menu folder. You will try that next, using two layers.

**NOTE** ▶ You can also save Motion Library items directly to the folder from which they originated. For example, you can save a customized filter to the Filters category or a customized behavior to the Behaviors category. The same process applies to Library elements such as Generators, Shapes, Particle Emitters, and Replicators.

**7**  In the *Titles* group, Command-click the *Kelly* and *Slater* layers to select them. Drag them to the Favorites Menu folder (not the Favorites folder), wait a moment, and then drop them onto the "All in one file" well in the drop menu.

**8**  Open the Favorites Menu folder so that you can see its contents.

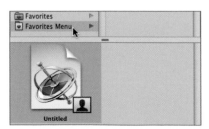

A single file with a Motion icon and a user preset icon appears. It has this icon and is named *Untitled*, because it consists of more than one object.

**9**   Rename the file to *Name Animation*.

Finally, you'll save an entire group.

**10**   Drag the *Background* group from the Layers tab to the stack of the Library.

Groups are always saved as a single file—no matter how many you select.

**11**   Rename the Background file to *Water bg with gamma*. That's more accurate than *Background*.

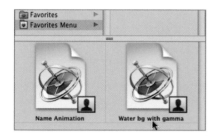

Once you have saved favorites to either the Favorites folder or the Favorites Menu folder, they are available for you to use in any project on your system.

## Using Favorites
Now you'll apply the favorites to a new project.

**1**   Choose File > New, and choose the HDV 720p24 preset.

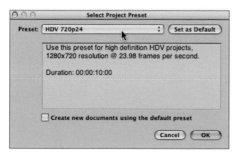

This is the same preset used for the Top Surfers project. By matching project settings, you ensure that your favorites will appear at the same locations in the Canvas and play for the same duration.

2   Click OK, and in the File Browser, navigate to Motion4_Book_Files > Media > Pipeline > Graphics, import **water bkg B_sm.jpg**, and scale it up to fill the Canvas.

> **NOTE ▸** When you have multiple Motion projects open at the same time, you see only the active project. To select a project that is not active, use the Window menu, or hold down the Command key and press the ` (grave accent) key until the project you want appears. Note that pressing Command-` toggles between the utility window and the Canvas before toggling to other open projects, so it may require more keystrokes than you expect.

3   Navigate to the Library, select the Favorites folder, and drag the Gamma 0.52 filter onto the graphic in the Canvas.

The image darkens, and the HUD (heads-up display) tells you that the correct setting has been applied.

4   In the Toolbar, choose the Text tool. In the Canvas, type *ANDY,* and use the HUD to format the text in any way you wish.

5   Position the text layer near the upper left of the Canvas, and then Option-drag a copy of it to the right and place it lower than the original text layer. Change the copied text to "IRONS."

You will apply the saved behaviors to these two text layers.

**6**  From the Favorites folder in the Library, drag the Throw Right behavior onto the *Andy* layer and the Throw Left behavior onto the *Irons* layer, and then play the project.

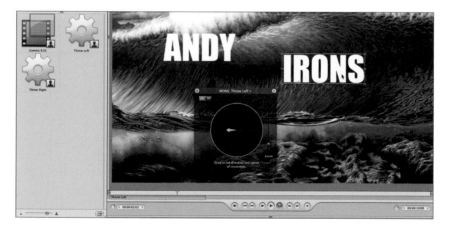

The behaviors retain the speed and direction settings you made in the original project, and in the mini-Timeline you can see that their durations also remain the same.

Now apply the saved layers and groups, this time from the Favorites menu.

**7**  Stop playback. To start from scratch, move the playhead to the start of the project, press Command-A to select all, and press Delete.

**8** From the Favorites menu, choose "Water bg with gamma." The entire *Background* group, with the water graphic and the Gamma filter, appears in the Canvas.

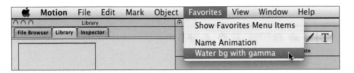

**9** Press Command-Shift-N to create a new group above the *Background* group. This group is for the surfer name layers you previously saved as a favorite.

**10** From the Favorites menu, choose Name Animation, and then play the project.

The *Kelly* and *Slater* name layers, with the attached behaviors, appear in the group and on the Canvas, and the behaviors animate the text.

Note that the positions of the layers in the Canvas are the same as in the original, and the durations of the layers, visible in the mini-Timeline, are also the same.

**NOTE** ▶ Both of these favorites refer to image files stored on your computer. If you move these images, you may get an offline warning when you apply the graphic and a prompt to locate the files to reconnect the media to the project. If you save favorites that include your own media files, be sure to keep those media files in the same relative path.

That's how easy it is to save effects, layers, and groups as favorites and use them again in other projects. As you work, keep in mind that anything you create can be saved and reused. And if you want to share your project components with other Final Cut Studio users, you can do that as well.

## Saving to the File Browser

Saved favorites can be shared with anyone else using Final Cut Studio. To copy your favorites to another computer, you need to know where they are located, and then copy them to the same location on the target machine.

**1**   Press Command-Tab as many times as necessary to switch to the Finder.

**2**   Press Command-N to open a new Finder window.

**3**   Press Command-3 to switch to column view.

**4**   Navigate to [*home folder*]/Library/Application Support/Final Cut Studio/Motion/ Library/Favorites. Your favorites are stored here and in the Favorites Menu folder, in the .molo file format.

If you copy the .molo files to the same path on the destination computer, the favorites will appear in that user's Motion Library. However, you don't have to save favorites to the Library to use them or share them. You can save them directly to any folder on any connected drive, and apply them directly from the File Browser.

**5**   Press Command-Tab to return to Motion.

**6**   Press Command-1 to go to the File Browser, and then, in the sidebar, select the Desktop folder.

**7**   Drag the *Background* group from the Layers tab to the stack, at the bottom of the File Browser.

The Background project appears on the desktop. From here, you can import it into any Motion project, or copy it to any other Final Cut Studio workstation.

If you want to quickly send a component of your Motion project to a coworker so that she can apply the same animation or style to her project, save the file to a convenient location, email it to her, and tell her to apply it directly from the File Browser.

**NOTE ▶** If the .molo project references media files, you will need to include those files on the target computer, and you will need to reconnect the media files when prompted to do so.

Using Motion's ability to save any component of a project, you can quickly build a library of favorite effects and styles, or a collection of standardized reusable components that you can apply over and over, such as for an opening title sequence for an episodic show. Motion's many export and sharing options allow you to share your final project in just about any format, on just about any device.

## Lesson Review

1. You are in the Export dialog and you realize that you forgot to enable Motion Blur. How can you enable it without canceling the export?

2. Which command lets you export multiple outputs: Export or Share?

3. How can you automatically publish your project to YouTube with the Share command?

4. Name two folders in the Library where you can save effects, layers, and groups.

5. True or false: You can save project components only to the Library.

6. What options do you have when dragging multiple effects and/or layers to the Library?

7. If you save a group as a favorite that contains a graphic that is not part of Motion's Library, what precautions do you need to take and why?

### Answers

1. Select the Output tab, deselect the "Use current project and canvas settings" checkbox, and select the Motion Blur checkbox.

2. Share allows you to create multiple outputs in the Share window.

3. Select the YouTube output type, select the "Publish to YouTube" checkbox, and then fill in the account information in the Action drawer.

4. The Favorites folder and the Favorites Menu folder.

5. False. You can save project components to any connected drive in the File Browser.

6. You can add them as multiple files or all in one file.

7. You need to keep the source file in the same location with the same name to avoid an offline media warning. If you share the favorite with another computer, you also need to provide a copy of the media file.

### Keyboard Shortcuts

| | |
|---|---|
| **Command-E** | Export the project |
| **Command-Shift-E** | Share the project |
| **Command-Option-E** | Export the selection |

# Animation

# 6

| | |
|---|---|
| Lesson Files | Motion4_Book_Files > Lessons > Lesson_06 |
| Media | Motion4_Book_Files > Media > Rockumentary-behaviors |
| | Motion4_Book_Files > Media > Stage |
| Time | This lesson takes approximately 60 minutes to complete. |
| Goals | Create animation with Basic Motion behaviors |
| | Adjust, copy, and trim behaviors |
| | Use Simulation behaviors |
| | Apply Parameter behaviors |
| | Clone animated groups |
| | Compare animating with behaviors and keyframes |

# Creating Animation with Behaviors

Motion has a unique approach for putting the "motion" in motion graphics, by using *behaviors*. So what are behaviors? They are an *effect*, like a filter or a mask, so you can apply them to a layer or group of layers. They allow you to create animation *procedurally*—that is, they contain a set of instructions that describe how to make an element move, or spin, or fade, so you don't have to animate the layer manually.

Motion includes a huge variety of behaviors that you can use to animate layers, shapes, particle systems, and text; stabilize footage; track objects; simulate gravity; and even animate cameras to fly around in 3D space.

In this lesson, you will use Basic Motion and Simulation behaviors to create the animation in the first half of a DVD motion menu for the Rockumentary project you started in Lesson 2. After that, you will explore Parameter behaviors in a new project.

## Adding Basic Motion Behaviors

If you want to float a layer across the screen, rotate it, or have it fade into view, then reach for the Basic Motion behaviors. They create animation using simple drag-and-drop techniques, and they even work in 3D. In the upcoming exercises, you'll use several Basic Motion behaviors to make graphics appear to tumble down through space like raindrops from a cloud's point of view.

First, view the final Rockumentary animation to see what you'll create in this lesson; then we'll examine the partially completed project, set things up, and add your first behavior.

**1**   In the Finder, navigate to Motion4_Book_Files > Lessons > Lesson_06, open **Rockumentary_Menu.mov**, and play the movie.

You want to illustrate the years that the rock group Pale Divine was on tour by creating a cascade of dates and images. In the first 15 seconds of the menu, you can animate dates and photos to fade in, drop back in space as they spin, and fade out.

**2**   Return to the Finder, navigate to Motion4_Book_Files > Lessons > Lesson_06, open Rockumentary_behaviors_start, and save it to the Student_Saves folder inside the Lesson_06 folder. You can leave the QuickTime movie open for reference if you like.

**3**   Press F5 to open the Project pane, and then open all groups and layers.

**TIP** You can drag up between any two layers or groups to resize all the layers and see more of them without scrolling.

There are two top-level groups: The *Background gradients* group contains two still-image layers with filters applied to create an aged, vignetted background look; and the *Opening animation* group contains a group of dates, a group of photos, and a group with a brayer image. All of the layers in the *Opening animation* group are dimmed because they don't exist at the current playhead location.

4   Press F6 to open the Timing pane, and in the Timeline, open the *dates* and *photos* groups. Use the Zoom slider if necessary to fit the full project duration into the window.

**TIP** You can increase the size of the Timing pane by dragging up on the double dashes in the center of the separator bar (located between the Timing pane and the transport controls). You can also resize the layers and groups by dragging between any two of them, but they won't get as small as they will in the Layers tab.

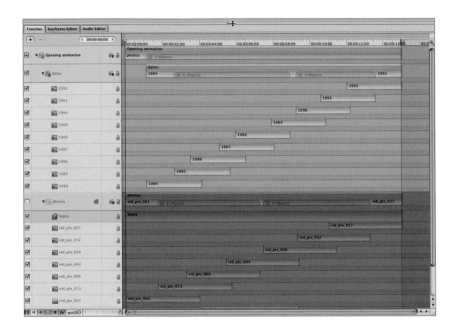

The *dates* and *photos* layers are staggered in a staircase-like pattern to introduce one after the other. The layer bars in the *photos* group are dimmed because the group's visibility is turned off, enabling you to focus on the dates.

5   Press F6 to close the Timing pane, and close the *Background gradients*, *photos*, and *far_brayer* groups. Press the Spacebar to play the project, and then click each of the layers in the *dates* group.

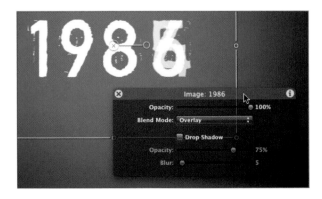

The HUD (heads-up display) shows that each of the layers has the Overlay blend mode applied.

NOTE ▶ If the HUD isn't visible, press F7 or choose it in the Toolbar.

Now that you have a feel for the project's structure, you can animate the dates. First, set a play range around one layer.

6    Stop playback, select the bottom *1984* layer, and press Shift-I to move the playhead to the layer's In point.

7    Choose Mark > Mark Play Range In or press Command-Option-I.

8    Press Shift-O to move the playhead to the layer's Out point, press Command-Option-O to set a play range Out point, and then press the Spacebar to play the play range.

NOTE ▶ In the transport controls at the bottom of the Canvas, make sure that Loop playback is turned on and that the audio is muted.

The next two layers, *1985* and *1986*, overlap the *1984* layer, which makes them pop on in a distracting way.

9    Turn off the visibility of the *1985* and *1986* layers. You are now set up to animate this layer by adding several Basic Motion behaviors.

10   Press Command-2 to open the Library. Choose Behaviors, and then choose the Basic Motion folder. The folder contains eight behaviors.

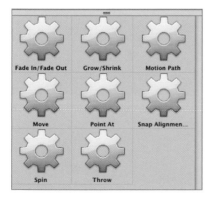

**11** Select the Grow/Shrink behavior. The Preview area shows an animation of what the behavior does, along with a written description. You can use this behavior to create the illusion that the layer is falling "back" in space.

**12** Drag the Grow/Shrink behavior onto the *1984* layer in the Layers tab or in the Canvas.

Because the behavior is an effect, it appears under the layer it is applied to, just like a filter or a mask. In the mini-Timeline, a purple bar representing that behavior matches the duration of the layer between the play range In and Out points. In the HUD, a graphical interface allows you to manipulate the behavior. In the Canvas, although the project is playing, nothing appears to be happening. Many behaviors must be adjusted to create animation.

**13** In the HUD, drag inward on a corner of the square. The layer shrinks over the duration of the behavior, appearing to fall back in space.

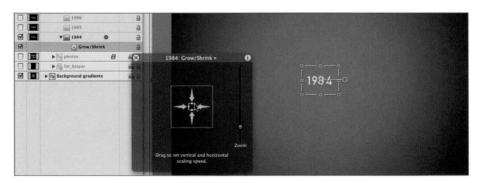

**TIP** Be sure to drag from a corner. If you drag from an edge, the layer will scale nonproportionally.

**14** Save your work.

It's a good start, but the animation could use more pizzazz. Luckily, it's easy to add multiple behaviors to the same layer.

## Stacking Behaviors

You can add many behaviors to a layer, and Motion will combine their effects. In this exercise, you use a behavior to make the layer fade into view and then disappear, and a second behavior to make the layer tumble as it appears to fall away.

**1**  From the Library, drag the Fade In/Fade Out behavior onto the *1984* layer.

**2**  Drag in the HUD to increase the Fade In duration to 30 frames.

To make the layer tumble, use the Spin behavior. When you are more familiar with using behaviors, it can be faster to select them from the Toolbar.

**3**  In the Toolbar, click the Add Behavior icon and choose Basic Motion > Spin. The Spin behavior appears underneath the *1984* layer, stacked on top of the other behaviors.

**4**  In the HUD, drag clockwise 360 degrees around the edge of the circle. An arrow indicates the direction and amount of spin; the "x1" at the lower right of the HUD indicates the number of revolutions.

The layer now spins around its anchor point, but it is only rotating parallel to the screen. It would be more interesting if the layer tilted (like a laptop screen) and swung (like a door).

5   In the HUD, drag the 3D arrows inside the circle. The layer now rotates on all three axes and tumbles as it shrinks.

Now that you have three behaviors applied to this layer, you can adjust each of them in the context of the completed animation while playing the project. You can quickly switch between the behaviors in the HUD, or use the Inspector to apply more precise adjustments.

6   Press the D key to select the next behavior, the Fade In/Fade Out behavior, and adjust it as desired in the HUD.

Pressing D repeatedly cycles through all the behaviors and filters applied to a layer and the layer itself, making it easy to quickly make changes in the HUD, even if the Layers tab is closed.

7   Press F2 to open the second tab of the Inspector: the Behaviors tab. Here, you can precisely adjust all of a behavior's parameters, some of which are not available in the HUD.

**8**   In the Spin behavior section, from the Axis pop-up menu, choose Y. The layer now swings around only its vertical y-axis.

**9**   Reset the Axis pop-up menu to Custom, and adjust the Latitude and Longitude parameters to your liking.

**10**   Stop playback and save your work.

Your first animation with behaviors is complete. We'll animate the other dates by copying some of these behaviors and applying new ones.

## Using Basic Motion Behaviors in 3D

In later lessons, we'll work with all the 3D features in Motion, but let's get a feel for them now. In 3D space, you can change a layer's rotation and position along all three axes: the horizontal, or x-axis; the vertical, or y-axis; and the depth, or z-axis (the one pointing straight out of the screen).

Every layer in a Motion project can be rotated and positioned along the x, y, and z axes, even without turning on 3D features—such as 3D groups, 3D tools, views, or cameras—that you will use in later lessons.

You already animated the *1984* layer in 3D by rotating it on all three axes. But it's not really moving "back" in space, it's just shrinking in size. Instead of using the Grow/Shrink behavior to simulate this 3D movement, you can make the layer move back in z-space using the Throw or Motion Path behavior. Let's try each to see what it can do.

**1**   Turn on the *1985* layer, select it, and set a play range around it by dragging the play range In and Out points in the mini-Timeline, or by using the keyboard shortcuts you used earlier.

> **TIP**   If you Shift-drag the play range In and Out points, they will snap to the layer's In and Out points.

**2**   Turn off the *1984* and *1987* layers so that they won't distract you, and start playback.

**3**   In the Toolbar, click the Add Behavior icon and choose Basic Motion > Throw.

4   In the HUD, drag the Zoom slider to about a third of the way from the bottom, and then, starting from the crosshair in the center of the circle, drag out in any direction.

**TIP** ▶ To move a layer only vertically or horizontally, Shift-drag from the HUD crosshair.

The layer moves in the Canvas, with a red line indicating the direction and length of travel. The Zoom slider in the HUD determines how far you can move. By default, the behavior moves the layer only horizontally and/or vertically along the x and/or y axes. But what about the z-axis?

5   In the HUD, click the 3D button and set the Speed slider near the top of the range. Drag in the circle to move the 3D arrow until it points away from you.

After you've enabled 3D for the behavior, you can throw a layer in any direction in 3D space. To make it fly directly away from you, it's easiest to use the Inspector.

**6**    If the Behaviors tab isn't already selected, press F2. Click the Throw Velocity disclosure triangle, and set X, to 0, Y to 0, and Z to -1000.

To make the layer spin and fade, you can copy those two behaviors from the *1985* layer. You'll need to modify the copied Spin behavior so that the animation doesn't look exactly the same in each layer.

**7**    In the Layers tab, under the *1984* layer, Shift-click the Spin and Fade In/Fade Out behaviors to select them. Then release the Shift key and Option-drag them onto the *1985* layer.

The behaviors are copied to the *1985* layer and exactly fill the play range in the mini-Timeline, so that they match the location and duration of the layer.

**NOTE ▶** When you copy a behavior from one layer to another, the behavior automatically starts at the beginning of the target layer. However, the behavior's duration is not changed, so it may need to be trimmed to match the Out point of the target layer. In this case, all the layers have the same duration, so no trimming is necessary.

The HUD indicates that multiple objects are selected.

**8**  Click the Spin copy behavior, and in the HUD, adjust it to vary the tumbling animation from the *1984* layer.

The Throw behavior is great for animating a layer in a specific direction at a specific speed, but if you want a layer to change direction or point in the direction in which it's moving, then the Motion Path behavior is a better option. You can experiment with this behavior on the next layer.

**9**  Turn on and select the *1986* layer, set a play range around it, and turn off the *1985*, *1987*, and *1988* layers.

**10**  Click the Add Behavior icon, choose Basic Motion > Motion Path, and start playback. The 1986 layer slides off the screen along a red motion path line.

**11**  Hold down Command-Spacebar and drag left to change the zoom level on the Canvas so that you can see both ends of the motion path line.

> **TIP** ▶ After changing the zoom level with Command-Spacebar, you can move the Canvas around to re-center it by holding down the Spacebar until the pointer changes to a hand tool, and then dragging.

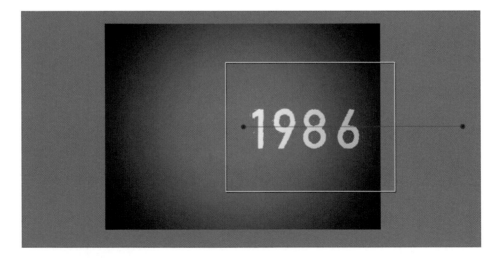

> **NOTE** ▶ If Spotlight opens when you press Command-Spacebar, choose Apple > System Preferences, click the Spotlight icon, and turn off the menu keyboard shortcut or change it to a different key combination.

The red dots at each end of the motion path line are control points. You can reposition them and add more points to create a customized, curving path.

**12** Move the left-hand control point off the left side of the Canvas; then double-click the motion path line to add more control points, moving them and adjusting the Bezier handles to create a curving, looping path.

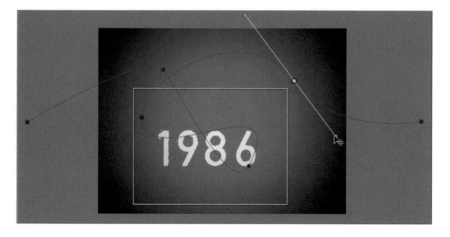

The layer moves along the path at a constant speed, no matter how many twists and turns it contains, but it doesn't rotate. To make it point in its direction of travel, let's use another behavior.

**13** Click the Add Behavior icon and choose Basic Motion > Snap Alignment to Motion. The layer now rotates as it follows the path.

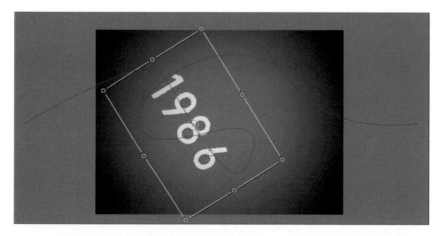

The Motion Path behavior is very flexible. For this project, you don't need many twists and turns. All you really need are the two original control points. And you don't need to align the movement to the motion path, because that would conflict with the Spin behavior that will be added shortly.

**14** Delete the Snap Alignment to Motion behavior, select the Motion Path behavior, and in the Behaviors tab, click the hooked arrow to reset the behavior to its default values.

You can set specific values for each control point in X, Y, and Z in the Inspector.

**15** Stop playback. Then in the Behaviors tab of the Inspector, click the Control Points disclosure triangle, and enter *0, 0, 0* for Point 1 and *0, 0, -5000* for Point 2. The layer now flies straight back in z-space along the motion path. To make it spin and fade, copy behaviors from the first layer.

**TIP** ▷ Press Shift-Z to return the Canvas to Fit in Window, or press Option-Z to zoom it to exactly 100 percent size.

**16** From the *1984* layer, Option-drag the Spin and Fade In/Fade Out behaviors to the *1986* layer. Then adjust the Spin behavior so that it isn't the same as the other two animations.

You've used three different methods to animate three layers to fade, spin, and fall back in 3D space. To animate the date graphics, let's copy these behaviors to the other layers.

**17** Option-drag the three behaviors from any of the layers you've worked with to each of the layers that haven't yet been animated. Then modify the Spin behavior of each.

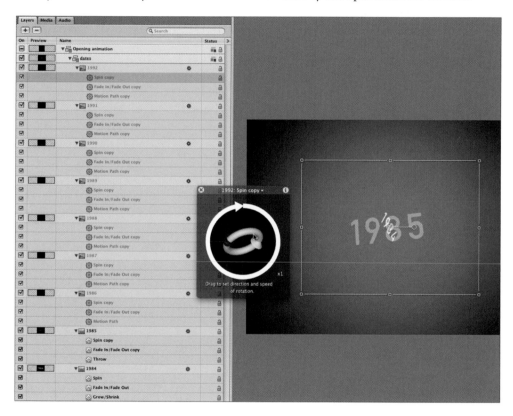

**18** Turn on all layers in the *dates* group, press Option-X to reset the play range, play the animation, and adjust as desired.

**19** Stop playback, press Home, close the *dates* group, and save your work.

Great job! You've used several of the Basic Motion behaviors to animate the dates falling in space. Now turn your attention to animating the photos using a different behavior-based technique.

## Using Simulation Behaviors

Motion graphics animators often try to mimic real-world movements, such as an object accelerating as it starts to move or slowing to a stop. Simulation behaviors are great for mimicking movement that results from inertia, gravity, and other natural forces.

To animate the photos falling back into z-space, we will apply an Attractor behavior to an invisible layer. The layer will act like a hidden planet that attracts passing meteors.

1    Turn off the *dates* group, and then turn on, select, and open the *photos* group. The photos are much larger than the Canvas, so they will look as if they are falling into the scene very close to your view.

   To make a behavior work in 3D in this group, first make the group itself a 3D group.

2    Choose Object > 3D Group.

   Rather than applying a behavior to each layer to move it back in z-space, place a shape layer where you want the photos to move, and apply one behavior to animate them all toward that shape layer.

3    In the Toolbar, choose the Rectangle tool.

4    Drag in the Canvas to create a rectangle of any size or shape. You won't be seeing the rectangle in the final animation, so the shape doesn't matter. However, you do want to place it in the center of the Canvas and 5000 pixels back on the z-axis, much like the end of the motion path in the previous exercise.

5    Press Esc to return to the Select/Transform tool; then press F1 to open the Properties tab of the Inspector. Set the Position values to 0, 0, -5000.

   The rectangle should get much smaller as it jumps back in z-space. Now you can apply the behavior to attract the photos.

6    Turn off the rectangle's visibility. Press Command-2 to open the Library, and choose the Simulation folder of behaviors. Click each of the behaviors to preview it.

7   Drag the Attractor behavior onto the *Rectangle* layer and start playback. The pictures change from one to the next, but they don't move. By default, the Attractor does not work in z-space.

8   In the Include section of the HUD, click the Z button. There is still no change because the rectangle is 5,000 pixels away from the photos, but the Influence parameter is set to 1,000 pixels by default.

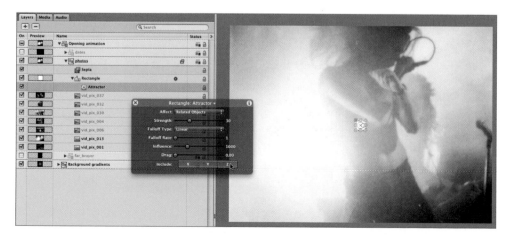

**9**   Drag the Influence slider all the way to the right. It goes only to an insufficient 4,000 pixels. When the HUD won't let you enter the value you want, try the Inspector.

**10**   Press F2 to open the Behaviors tab of the Inspector, and set the Influence value to 6,000 for good measure.

Finally, the pictures move back in z-space, but not very quickly.

**11**   Select the Attractor behavior again, and in the Behaviors tab of the Inspector, increase the Strength value to about 200.

The animation is starting to look better, but it would be more interesting if each photo started from a different position. To change this, open up some working room around the Canvas, and then enable a feature that lets you see layers outside the Canvas.

**12**   Stop playback, press Home, and then press and hold down Command-Spacebar and drag left to create a lot of extra space around the Canvas—enough to easily see the bounding box of the first photo. By default, everything outside the Canvas is gray, and you can see only the bounding box of a selected object.

**13**   Choose View > Show Full View Area or press Shift-V so that layers outside the Canvas will appear at lower opacity.

**14**   Drag each layer off-center in a different direction. If you Shift-select all the layers in the Layers tab when you are done, you should see all of their bounding boxes and red motion paths.

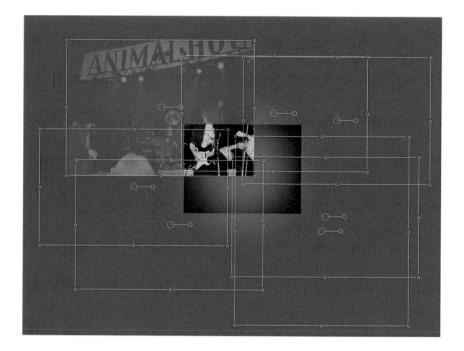

**NOTE** ▶ You will see an image outside the Canvas only for layers at the current playhead location.

**15** Play the project to check the animation, and save your work.

By applying a Simulation behavior to a "dummy" or "null" shape layer, you made one behavior do the work of many. Now you can make the layers fade and spin by copying the behaviors from the *dates* group. But the photos have a different duration, so some trimming will be in order.

### Trimming and Applying Behaviors to Multiple Layers

In this exercise, let's use the Timeline to check the durations of copied behaviors and trim them.

**1** Click in an empty part of the Canvas to deselect everything. Press Shift-Z to fit the Canvas to the window, stop playback, and press Home.

**2**    Open the *dates* group. Below the *1984* layer, Shift-select the Spin and Fade In/Fade Out behaviors, and Option-drag them onto the *vid_pix_001* layer.

**3**    Press F6 to open the Timing pane, and in the Timeline, close the *dates* group. Scroll down, then select and open the *vid_pix_001* layer. The behaviors start at the right frame, but they aren't long enough.

**4**    Press Shift-O to move the playhead to the layer's Out point.

**5**    Shift-click both behaviors, and press O to trim their Out points to the playhead.

All the photo layers have the same duration, so you could now copy these two behaviors to all of them with no further trimming. However, that's not always the case, so we will use a different method that will automatically match every behavior to the layer's length.

**6**    In the Layers tab, Shift-click all the remaining photo layers that do not have the fade and spin behaviors applied.

**7**    Click the Add Behavior icon and choose Basic Motion > Fade In/Fade Out. The behavior is applied to all the selected layers and matches the length of each. It would do so even if the layers had different durations. Since this is a new behavior, you need to modify it to match the others.

**8**    In the Layers tab, Command-click each of the six new Fade In/Fade Out behaviors.

> **TIP** You could also select the behaviors in the Timeline. Command-clicking allows you to make a noncontiguous selection of the behaviors by skipping the layers themselves.

**9**  In the HUD, increase the Fade In time to 30 frames. The HUD title, "Multiple Selection," tells you that this adjustment will affect all the selected behaviors at once. Now add the Spin behavior.

**10**  Command-click the photo layers to select them without selecting the behaviors. Then click the Add Behavior icon and choose Basic Motion > Spin.

**11**  Select each Spin behavior one at a time, and in the HUD, give each a unique Spin Rate, Latitude angle, and Longitude angle.

As a final step, animate the brayer graphic in the *far_brayer* group.

**12**  In the Timeline, close the *photos* group, open the *dates* group, and open the *1984* layer. Shift-click just the Fade In/Fade Out and Grow/Shrink behaviors, and Option-drag them to the *ko_brayer.03e_blk* layer. This layer doesn't need to spin, but you may want to change its starting position and rotation a little.

**13**  With both layers still selected, Shift-drag the Out points to the right until they snap to the end of the layer.

14 Turn on the *far_brayer* and *dates* layers, press F6 to close the Timing pane, and close all the groups in the Layers tab. Press Shift-V to turn off the full view area, and play the project.

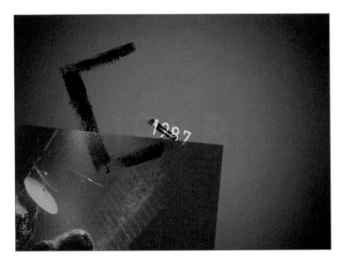

You should now have a nice animation of falling dates and photos, with one brayer graphic that will set us up for additional graphic elements in the next lesson.

15 Make any final adjustments you choose, and save your work.

You've used a variety of Basic Motion and Simulation behaviors to create animations, and learned several ways to add, adjust, copy, and trim those behaviors. To conclude this lesson, we'll use a different project to explore another type of behavior—the Parameter behavior.

## Applying Parameter Behaviors

Parameter behaviors are powerful little critters that work differently from the other behaviors you've worked with so far. You use them to create animation by applying them to a specific parameter you want to animate.

In this exercise, you will use several Parameter behaviors to animate a set of gears that appear to open the curtains of a stage. You'll learn a couple of methods for applying and adjusting Parameter behaviors, clone groups of animated layers, and combine Parameter behaviors.

You can choose the parameter you want to animate with a Parameter behavior either before or after you apply the behavior. Let's try both methods.

1   Close any open projects. In the File Browser or the Finder, navigate to Motion4_ Book_Files > Lesson_06, open Parameter_behaviors_start, and save it to the Student_ Saves folder. Press F5 to open the Project pane, and then open both groups.

The project contains two groups: the top-level *Stage* group, which contains several layers, as well as a group titled *Gears,* which contains the four cogs you see in the Canvas. There is also a Light layer, which is disabled. Currently, nothing in the scene is animated.

Your first task is to rotate the left-hand gear. Your first inclination might be to apply a Spin behavior from the Basic Motion category to rotate the cog, and that would certainly work. But a Parameter behavior is another option.

2   Press Command-2 to open the Library, choose Behaviors, and then choose the Parameter folder.

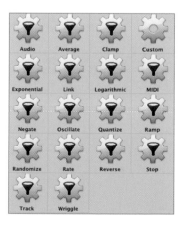

The 18 behaviors in this folder are unique because you apply them to a specific parameter of a selected layer, effect, or group. One way to apply a Parameter behavior is to add it to an object, and then choose which parameter to animate.

3   Start playback, and then drag the Rate Parameter behavior from the Library to the *Cog1* layer in the Layers tab. Nothing happens, because you need to tell the behavior which parameter you want to animate.

4   In the HUD, from the Go pop-up menu, choose Properties > Transform > Rotation > Z.

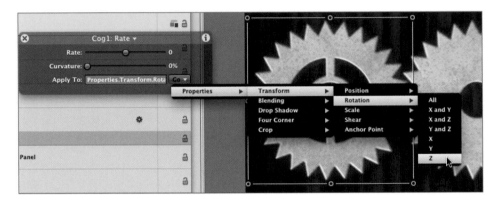

5   Drag the Rate slider to about -50. The cog now rotates at a constant rate of speed.

   **NOTE** ▸ In Motion, negative rotation is clockwise.

Another way to apply a Parameter behavior is to decide first which parameter to animate, and then choose the appropriate behavior. Let's use this approach to animate the second large gear layer, *Cog2*.

6   Select the *Cog2* layer and press F1 to open the Properties tab of the Inspector. You want the *Cog2* layer to rotate as well, so Control-click (or right-click) the word "Rotation." The shortcut menu contains the Parameter behaviors you saw in the Library.

   **NOTE** ▸ The list does not include the Track and Custom Parameter behaviors, which are used in more specialized circumstances.

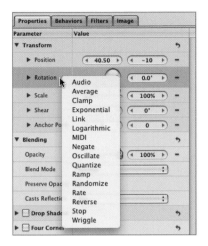

**7**  Choose Link. You could choose Rate again and try to manually match the speed of the first cog in the opposite direction. However, by applying the Link Parameter behavior, you can connect the animation of one layer to the animation of another.

The HUD indicates that the parameter is applied to the rotation of the layer, but you still need to tell it what source object to use.

**8**  Drag the *Cog1* layer into the Source Object well in the HUD.

**NOTE ▶** Be sure to hold down the mouse button as you drag the layer to the well. If you click the *Cog1* layer and release the mouse button, you can select the layer, and the Link behavior will no longer appear in the HUD. If that happens, reselect the Link behavior and try again.

**TIP** ▶ You can also drag a source object directly onto the Link behavior in the Layers tab.

The *Cog2* layer now rotates, exactly matching the rate of the *Cog1* layer, but this isn't quite right. The cog should spin in the opposite direction. The Scale slider in the HUD goes down only to 0, but we can change this value in the Inspector.

**9** In the Behaviors tab of the Inspector, in the Scale value field, type *-1.* (minus one period) and press Enter. The *Cog2* layer now rotates in the opposite direction, and its teeth mesh perfectly with *Cog1*.

The same Link behavior can be used to animate the two smaller cogs.

**10** In the Layers tab, Option-drag the Link behavior from the *Cog2* layer to the *cog3* layer.

**11** Select the Link copy behavior, and in the Behaviors tab, set the Scale value to 2.25. This cog needs to rotate in the same direction as the first one, and because it's smaller, it needs to rotate more quickly.

**12** Option-drag the Link copy behavior from the *cog3* layer to the *cog4* layer; select the copy; and in the Behaviors tab, change the Scale value to -2.25. All the cogs now animate nicely together.

**13** Turn off the Rate behavior applied to the *Cog1* layer by deselecting its activation checkbox. All the cogs stop turning because they are linked to the *Cog1* layer.

**14** Turn the Rate behavior on, stop playback, press Home, and save your work.

With the base animation complete, you will fill the area above the curtains with gears by using clones.

## Cloning a Group

To create more animated gears, you will copy the *Gears* group. You could duplicate the group, but by creating clones instead, certain changes to the original will pass through to the clones that will come in handy a little later. First, however, you should scale and reposition the cogs to fit into the gold bar at the top of the curtains.

1   Close and select the *Gears* group. Then, in the Canvas, scale down the group to about 28% to fit in the gold bar, and move it to the left.

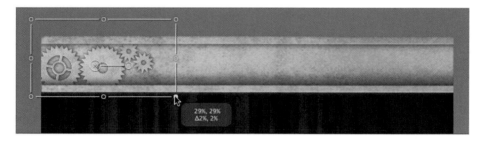

**TIP** ▶ Shift-drag a bounding box handle to scale the box proportionately. If the dynamic guides make it difficult to precisely scale and/or position the group, press N to turn off snapping.

Now, let's clone this group to place more gears along the top.

2   Choose Object > Make Clone Layer or press K.

**NOTE** ▶ Make sure the playhead is placed at the start of the project or is moving when you create the clone; otherwise, the clone layer will start at the playhead location.

3   In the Canvas, drag the clone layer to the right of the original, and line up the layers so that the teeth of the cogs appear to mesh with each other.

**TIP** It can be helpful to change the zoom level of the Canvas to get a closer look at the gears as you position the clone layer. Do so by pressing Command-Spacebar and dragging right on the location you want to see more closely. Press Shift-Z when you are finished, to fit the Canvas back into the window.

4   Press K to make a clone of *Clone Layer*, and position *Clone Layer 1* to the right of the other cogs.

**TIP** You may want to turn off the visibility of the layer's bounding box in the Canvas so that you can see the cog teeth more clearly. From the View and Overlay pop-up menu, choose Show Overlays, or press Command-/ (slash). Remember to turn on the overlays again when you are done.

5   Press K to clone *Clone Layer 1*, and position *Clone Layer 2* at the far right. It's OK if it goes off the screen. You now have a fully assembled gearbox.

6   Press the Spacebar to start playback. All the cogs rotate and mesh together nicely.

7   Open the *Gears* group. Open the *Cog1* layer and turn off the Rate behavior. All the gears stop.

If you had duplicated the *Gears* group rather than cloning it, each duplicate would have its own Rate behavior, and you'd need to turn off each of them to stop the animation. With clones, changes you make to the source of the clones pass through to all of them.

8   Turn on the Rate behavior and save your work.

Now we can make it look as if the cogs are opening the curtains.

## Combining Behaviors and Adding a Light

To animate the curtains opening, you will first link them to each other, and then link their positions to the rotation of the very first *Cog1* layer—the source of all the animation so far. And since you want the curtains to open and come to a stop, let's add a Stop Parameter behavior to the *Cog1* layer to stop the rotation at a specific point in time.

1. Select the *red right* layer; press F1 to go to the Properties tab of the Inspector; and, if necessary, click the disclosure triangle for Position to reveal the individual X, Y, and Z position parameters.

   You want to link the right curtain's horizontal or X position to the same parameter of the left curtain but have it move in the opposite direction.

2. Control-click the X, and choose Link.

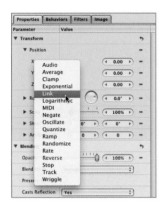

3. Drag the *red left* layer from the Layers tab to the Source Object well in the Behaviors tab, and then set the Scale value to -1.

4. Select the *red left* layer, and in the Canvas, drag the layer around; then undo.

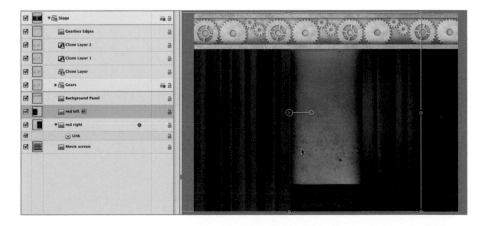

As the left curtain moves left, the right curtain moves right and vice versa; but moving the left curtain up or down has no effect on the right curtain because only the horizontal position is linked.

To make the left curtain move, you will link its position to the rotation of the *Cog1* layer.

5   With the *red left* layer still selected, go to the Properties tab. Control-click the X under Position, and choose Link.

6   Drag the *Cog1* layer from the Layers tab to the Source Object well in the HUD.

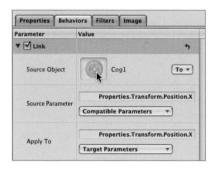

Note that Motion assumes that you want to link the position of the left curtain to the *position* of the *Cog1* layer as it says in the Source Parameter box. But you want the *rotation* of the cog to drive the position of the curtain.

7   From the Compatible Parameters pop-up menu, choose Properties > Transform > Rotation > Z. The curtains now open as the project plays, but too quickly.

**8**   In the Behaviors tab, Option-drag left in the Scale value field to about 0.4 as you watch the animation in the Canvas.

> **TIP ▶** Option-dragging in a value field "gears down" the rate of change to one-hundredth the normal speed; Shift-dragging makes the value change ten times faster.

It's not bad, but the animation would work better if the gears and curtains came to a stop before the curtains moved all the way out of view. We'll use another Parameter behavior to make them stop.

**9**   Stop playback and move the playhead to 5:00. At this point, the curtains are open but still visible.

**10**   Select the *Cog1* layer; in the Properties tab of the Inspector, Control-click the word *Rotation,* and from the shortcut menu, choose Stop. The new Parameter behavior appears in the mini-Timeline, with its In point at the playhead.

**11**   Resume playback. The curtains open and suddenly come to a stop at 5:00.

The stop is a bit abrupt, but let's leave it for now. In the next lesson, we'll learn how to use keyframes to create different kinds of movement. For example, you could make the gears and curtains slow down before they come to a stop.

As a final touch to this project, add a light for mood and make the screen flicker, like an old-fashioned movie projector.

**12**   Select the activation checkbox for the Light layer. Nothing happens because lights only affect 3D groups.

> **NOTE ▶** If you accidentally select the Light layer when you turn it on, the default Select/Transform tool changes to the Adjust 3D Transform tool and new red, green, and blue arrows appear in the Canvas. We'll work with this tool and these controls in other lessons; for now, press Shift-S to return to the default selection tool.

**13**   Select the Stage group and choose Object > 3D group. The light now affects the scene. You'll explore several types of lights and how to manipulate them in a later lesson.

Let's finish by making the screen flicker with a final Parameter behavior. If the parameter you want to animate is available in the HUD, you can apply it from there.

**14** Select the *Movie screen* layer, and in the HUD, Control-click the word "Opacity" and choose Wriggle.

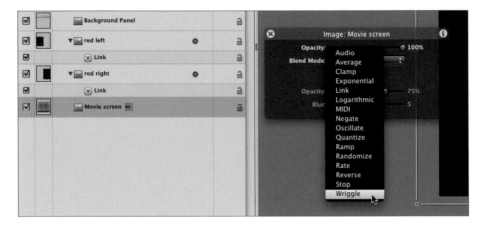

**15** In the Behaviors tab, set Amount to 50% and then Apply Mode to Subtract, and adjust the Frequency and Noisiness sliders to suit yourself. Save your work.

You have now worked with many types of behaviors in two different projects, and have even done a little 3D and keyframing.

For extra credit, you could add some content to the movie screen you just made by dragging the Rockumentary_behaviors_finished Motion project from the File Browser to just above the *Movie screen* layer in the Layers tab, and setting the blend mode for both groups to Overlay.

## Lesson Review

1.  Name three of the Basic Motion behaviors.
2.  You've applied a Motion Path behavior and added control points to create a curved path. How can you make the layer turn as it moves along the path?
3.  If you copy a behavior from one layer to another, will it always match the duration of the target layer?
4.  What type of behaviors mimic physical phenomena such as gravity, inertia, and random movement?

5.  Describe two ways to apply a Parameter behavior.

6.  What's one difference between duplicating a layer and cloning a layer?

*Answers*

1.  Fade In/Fade Out, Throw, Spin, Motion Path, Snap Alignment to Motion.

2.  Add the "Snap Alignment to Motion" behavior from the Basic Motion category.

3.  No, the copied behavior will match the In point of the target layer but its duration won't change, so if the target layer is longer or shorter than the source layer, the Out point of the behavior must be trimmed to match it.

4.  Simulation behaviors.

5.  Drag a Parameter behavior from the Library to a layer (or select it using the Add Behavior icon), and then select the parameter to apply it to in the HUD or Behaviors tab. Alternatively, choose the parameter to apply it to first by Control-clicking the name of the parameter in the HUD or Inspector and selecting the Parameter behavior from the shortcut menu.

6.  A duplicated layer is independent of the original, while a clone will change when you change certain aspects of the original—for example, changing the animation of the original.

## Keyboard Shortcuts

| | |
|---|---|
| **A** | Turn keyframe recording on and off |
| **Shift-V** | Turn the full view area on and off |

# 7

**Lesson Files**   Motion4_Book_Files > Lessons > Lesson_07

**Media**   Motion4_Book_Files > Media > Stage

Motion4_Book_Files > Media > Rockumentary

**Time**   This lesson takes approximately 60 minutes to complete.

**Goals**   Record keyframes

Set keyframes manually

Use the Keyframe Editor

Change keyframe interpolation and adjust keyframe curves

Add, move, and change the values of keyframes on a curve

Set keyframes for multiple layers simultaneously

Change keyframe timing in the Timeline

Choose keyframe curves for editing in the Keyframe Editor

## Lesson 7
# Animating with Keyframes

In the previous lesson, behaviors allowed you to create animation *procedurally*—you applied a behavior that contained a set of instructions for making the layer move. Setting keyframes is a way of *articulating* an animation: manually identifying exactly what, when, and how you want to animate.

The term *keyframes*, or *key frames*, originates from traditional hand-animation techniques in which a senior artist would draw "key" poses of a character and turn over those images to a junior artist, who would draw the in-between frames to create smooth character animation from one keyframe to the next.

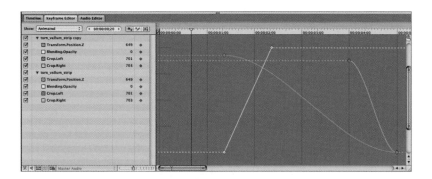

In Motion, keyframes work much the same way: You are the senior artist, creating your composition and identifying the frames you want to establish as keyframes; and the computer acts as the junior artist, creating in-between frames of animation through a process called *interpolation*.

Whether you use keyframes or behaviors to animate is not always a clear-cut decision, but as a rule of thumb, if you want repeated, continuous motion—such as a graphic drifting across the screen, a pendulum swinging, or a neon sign blinking—use behaviors. If you want animation that starts, stops, and changes direction at specific points in time, use keyframes.

In this lesson, we'll open the stage project from the previous lesson and animate the curtains with keyframes to compare their use with behaviors, experimenting with interpolation types and adjusting keyframe Bezier handles. We'll then return to the Rockumentary project to set and adjust keyframes to animate multiple layers to form a composition.

## Recording Keyframes

The easiest way to set keyframes is to turn on recording. When recording is turned on, every change you make to any keyframeable parameter will be recorded as a keyframe at the playhead location, locking in the new value at that point in time. This exercise uses recording to set a keyframe for the rotation value of the first cog, which will cause the curtains to part.

1    Navigate to Motion4_Book_Files > Lessons > Lesson_07, open the Keyframes_start project, save it to the Student_Saves folder, and then press F5 to open the Project pane.

This is the stage project that you worked with in the previous lesson. The position of the curtains is linked to the *Cog1* layer with the Link behavior, as is the rotation of all the other Cog layers, but the *Cog1* layer is not currently animated. You can test the animation by rotating the *Cog1* layer.

2    Select the *Cog1* layer, and in the Canvas, drag the rotation handle.

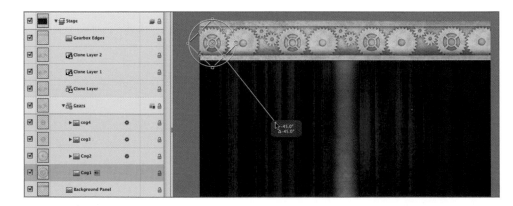

Rotating the *Cog1* layer clockwise turns the other cogs and opens the curtains. In the previous lesson, you animated the rotation of this layer using a Rate behavior and stopped the rotation with a Stop behavior. The result was a rather abrupt ending. Here, you'll animate the rotation by recording keyframes.

**3**    Press Command-Z to undo the rotation, and then at the bottom of the Canvas, click the Record button. The button pulses red to let you know that recording is enabled.

**4**    Press F1 to open the Properties tab of the Inspector.

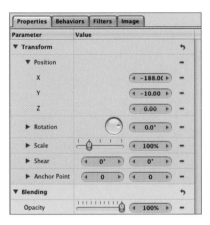

The value fields for all parameters are now red, another warning sign that recording is enabled. If you change any red parameter, it won't change for the whole project; it will change only at the playhead position. Let's see how this works.

**5**    Type 5. (period) in the Current Time value field at the bottom left of the Canvas, and then press Return or Enter to move the playhead to 5 seconds. This is the frame where you want the curtains to stop opening.

> **TIP** ▸ You don't have to first click in the Current Time field to enter a number—as long as the Timing pane is closed when you start typing, Motion assumes that you want to move the playhead and enters the number in the Current Time field.

**6**  In the Properties tab, drag left in the Rotation value field to about -300 degrees as you watch the curtains open in the Canvas.

A solid diamond appears to the right of the value field, where the dash used to be. This diamond indicates that a keyframe for this parameter is now placed at the current playhead location. The dash and the diamond are part of a menu called the *Animation menu*, which we'll explore later in this lesson.

**7**  Play the project. The curtains animate open until 5:00, and then stop.

**8**  Stop playback on any frame other than 5:00 or 0:00. The solid diamond for Rotation is now hollow. A hollow diamond indicates that at least one keyframe for this parameter exists somewhere, but not at the current playhead location.

**9**  Press Home to move the playhead to the start of the project. The diamond turns solid again, indicating that a keyframe exists at the playhead. But wait a minute. You only set a keyframe at 5:00, not at 0:00. Why is there one here?

A single keyframe will not create any animation: It locks in the value of the keyframed parameter at a point in time, but the parameter will have that same value at all other points in time. *To animate with keyframes, you need at least two keyframes with different values.*

When you use recording to set keyframes, Motion assumes you want the value to change over time, so it automatically sets a keyframe with the original value at the beginning of the layer that you are animating. It's important to remember that recording will always do this because sometimes it's not what you want.

By default, when recording is enabled, any other changes you make to the *Cog1* layer, such as adjusting its position or scale, set a keyframe for that parameter as well. Sometimes you want to make an overall adjustment to a parameter without setting a keyframe, but you'd still like to be able to add keyframes to a parameter that you've already animated.

**10**  Double-click the Record button. The Recording Options dialog opens. One of the options in this dialog is to record keyframes on animated parameters only.

**11**  Select the "Record keyframes on animated parameters only" checkbox, and click OK. Press A to toggle on recording, and scrub the playhead a few frames to update the interface.

> **NOTE ▶** Opening and closing the Recording Options dialog turns off recording if it's turned on, so you may need to turn it on again.

Now only the Rotation value field is red, indicating that keyframes will be applied only to changes to this parameter.

**12**  Change the Position Y value for the *Cog1* layer and play back the project. The *Cog1* layer and its clones are all in new locations, but their positions don't change over time as they would with keyframes.

**13**  Press Command-Z to undo the position change, double-click the Record button, deselect the "Record keyframes on animated parameters only" checkbox, and click OK. You are returned to the default setting, and recording should be turned off.

You've now animated the *Cog1* layer and the curtains linked to it, using keyframes. But the resulting animation is very similar to the one in the last lesson: The curtain movement comes to an abrupt stop at 5:00. You can make the curtains slow to a smoother stop by changing the keyframe interpolation.

## Changing Keyframe Interpolation

When you recorded a keyframe for a cog rotation value of -300 degrees at 5:00, Motion automatically set a keyframe at the start of the layer with the original value, 0 degrees.

Therefore, the layer needs to change from 0 degrees at 0:00 to -300 degrees at 5:00. To get from 0 to -300 over the course of 5 seconds, Motion changes, or interpolates, the value from frame to frame. You can change the type of interpolation in several ways in the Keyframe Editor.

1   Press F6 to open the Timing pane, and select the Keyframe Editor tab.

> **TIP** ▶ Pressing F6 opens the Timing pane but doesn't select a particular tab. You can press Command-8 to go directly to the Keyframe Editor tab.

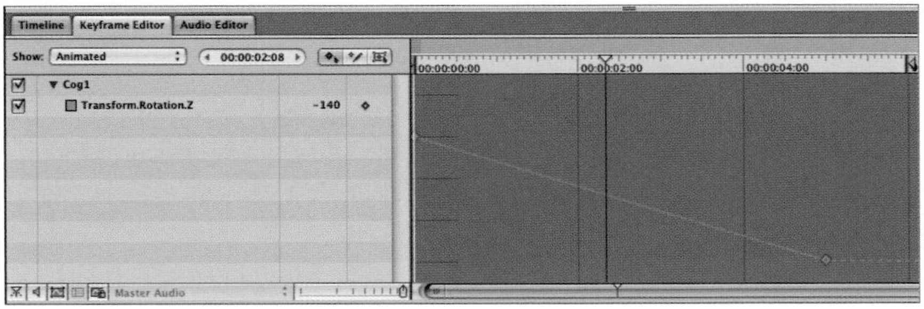

The sole animated parameter for the *Cog1* layer, Transform.Rotation.Z, appears on the left side of the window. Next to it is the value of the parameter at the current frame (-140) and a hollow diamond, indicating that keyframes exist for this parameter, but not at the playhead.

> **NOTE** ▶ By default, the Keyframe Editor displays all animated parameters for the selected layer(s) or group(s), as indicated by the Show pop-up menu.

On the right side of the window, a pink line connects two diamonds. The diamonds are the keyframes, and the line is the keyframe curve. The curve is straight because the default interpolation for rotation is linear, meaning that the rotation value changes at a constant rate. You can change the interpolation using the Animation menu, which is tucked under the black hollow diamond.

> **NOTE** ▶ The Animation menu in the Keyframe Editor is similar to the Animation menu in the Inspector, but contains more options.

2   Start playback, click the Animation menu, and choose Interpolation. There are six different interpolation options.

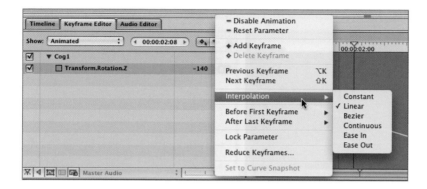

3   Choose Bezier.

Bezier interpolation creates smoother, more real-world animation by imitating the effect of inertia: Objects with mass take some time to get up to speed and to slow to a stop. Instead of a constant rate of change, the rate of change starts out low, increases over time, and then decreases again.

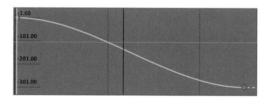

The curve starts out flat, gets steeper in the middle, and then flattens out at the end. The curtains now start opening slowly, speed up, and then slow down to a smooth stop, a more realistic animation.

4   Experiment with the other interpolation options:

▶   Constant holds the keyframe value all the way until the next keyframe, when the value changes instantaneously.

▶ Continuous is similar to Bezier. It's easier to create smooth motion with Continuous interpolation; however, the curve cannot be adjusted as with Bezier interpolation.

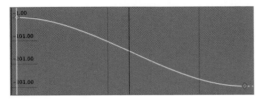

▶ Ease In, when applied to a curve, creates a smooth start followed by a linear, abrupt finish.

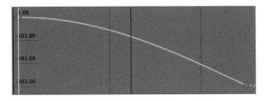

▶ Ease Out, when applied to a curve, creates a smooth ending after an abrupt linear start.

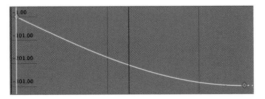

**TIP** ▶ You can also change the interpolation of individual keyframes along a curve by Control-clicking (or right-clicking) a keyframe and selecting an interpolation type.

5 Return the interpolation type to Bezier. Bezier interpolation gives you the most creative flexibility to fine-tune your animation. Using it, you can make the curtains come to an even slower stop, and then speed up the time it takes them to open at the beginning.

6 Click the keyframe at 5:00 to select it, and then drag out the Bezier handle to the left to make it longer and flatten out the curve coming into the keyframe.

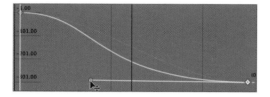

**TIP** ▶ Be careful not to pull the Bezier handle down, or the curve may dip below the keyframe value and the curtains will start to close again before fully opening.

**7**  Click the keyframe at 0:00, and adjust the Bezier handle to create a steeper curve and, therefore, faster initial movement.

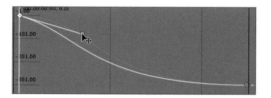

Currently, the animation starts at 0:00 because keyframe recording automatically added a keyframe at the start of the layer. But what if you want the curtains to stay closed for the first second to build a little suspense? Setting keyframes manually gives you the most creative control.

## Setting Keyframes Manually

In addition to recording keyframes, you can set keyframes manually, whether or not recording is enabled. Manually setting keyframes is a great solution when you don't want to change a value but just want to lock it in at the current frame.

Here, you'd like the curtains to stay closed for the first second. In other words, you want the rotation of the *Cog1* layer to remain at 0 degrees from 0:00 to 1:00, and *then* start to change. So, let's delete the current keyframe at 0:00 and create a new one at 1:00.

**NOTE** ▶ It's not strictly necessary to delete the first keyframe, but it's useful to know how to do it.

**1**  If it's not still selected, in the Keyframe Editor, select the keyframe at 0:00 and press Delete.

Only the keyframe at 5:00 remains, and the flat dotted line indicates that there is no animation, because you need at least two keyframes with different values to create animation. The Rotation value at the keyframe of -300 is the same for the entire layer, and the curtains remain open. You want them to be closed at 1:00.

2    Type *1.* (period) and press Return or Enter to move the playhead to 1:00.

3    In the Keyframe Editor, click the Animation menu and choose Add Keyframe. When adding keyframes manually, you must *first* add the keyframe, and *then* change the value. If you change the value first, you change the value of the parameter for the full duration of the layer, not just at the playhead.

**TIP** Once you've set a keyframe and moved the playhead, you can press Control-K to set a keyframe for that same parameter, or choose Object > Add Keyframe. In this case, it would read Object > Add Rotation Keyframe.

4    Double-click the value field for Transform.Rotation.Z, type *0*, and press Enter. Depending on your screen resolution, the top of the curve may disappear from the window.

**5** At the bottom left of the Keyframe Editor, click the "Fit visible curves in window" icon. You can now see the full curve.

**6** Play the project. The curtains stay closed for the first second, then animate open from 1:00 to 5:00.

**7** Adjust the Bezier handles on each keyframe to suit yourself. You can also add and adjust keyframes directly on a curve.

**8** Double-click anywhere along the curve to add a keyframe.

**9** Drag the keyframe up or down to change its value. Shift-drag up and down to avoid dragging left or right and changing the timing of the keyframe. As you drag, the numbers that appear in parentheses indicate the timecode of the keyframe location and the value of the keyframe, in that order.

**NOTE ▶** If you switch from timecode to frames by clicking the watch icon next to the current frame field or project duration field, frames will be visible in the Keyframe Editor.

**10** Double-click the keyframe to enter a specific value.

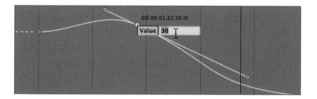

By adding keyframes, you can radically alter the animation. For this project, two keyframes will suffice.

**11** Delete any extra keyframes, save your work, and close the project.

**TIP ▶** You can delete multiple keyframes by first dragging a marquee to select them.

You've now explored the basics of creating keyframes by recording them or setting them manually for one single parameter on one single layer. Next, we'll explore some techniques for applying and adjusting keyframes of multiple parameters on multiple layers.

## Using Keyframes on Multiple Parameters and Layers

Because keyframes are so targetable and flexible, they are often used to animate several layers to move, spin, or blur, all at a specific point in time. In this exercise, we'll return to the Rockumentary project, this time animating all of the DVD menu elements to fall into place to form the final menu composition. Motion lets you set keyframes for parameters on multiple layers quickly, and lets you choose which keyframes appear in the Keyframe Editor for editing.

### Keyframing Multiple Layers

The first step is to add keyframes to lock in place all the layers that are to be animated.

1   Navigate to Motion4_Book_Files > Lessons > Lesson_07, open Rockumentary_ keyframes_start, save it to the Student_Saves folder, and open the Project pane.

In a previous lesson, you created the second half of this project, the composite image of the DVD menu with the series of photos. You also animated the initial photos and dates "falling" through space. Now we'll concentrate on the middle part of the project: animating the DVD menu elements into position. Unlike the photos and dates that fell away with continuous movement, these layers need to fall and then stop in a specific arrangement, a great task for keyframes.

**NOTE ▶** This project does not include the opening sequence of falling dates and pictures, but will start with the DVD menu elements that you will animate into position.

As with many motion graphics projects, it will be easiest to approach this task backward: first setting keyframes that "lock" every layer into its final position, and then setting keyframes at the start of the project to spread out the layers in z-space, completely offscreen.

Let's first look at the layers to animate.

**2**   Open the *Graphics Over* and *Graphics Under* groups, adjusting the layer heights as needed to fit everything into the view. These are the layers that will start offscreen and then animate by "falling" into place.

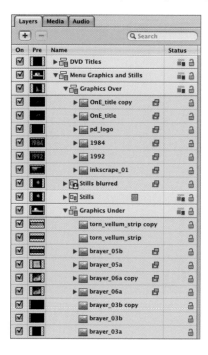

**3**   Move the playhead to 5:00.

At 5:00, you want all the layers to have landed in position, so set a keyframe here to lock them in place on this frame. Rather than setting a position keyframe for each layer individually, you can set it for all layers in a group at the same time.

**4** Shift-click the first and last layers in the *Graphics Over* group, and then press F1 to open the Properties tab of the Inspector.

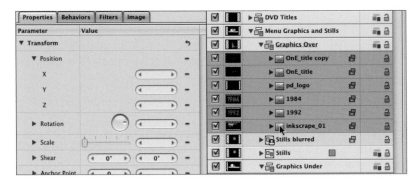

The value fields for Position are blank because you have multiple layers selected, each with a different position value. But you can still set a keyframe for all of them at the same time.

The small dash to the right of each parameter is the Animation menu, much like the Animation menu you worked with in the Keyframe Editor in the previous exercise.

**5** From the Animation menu for the Position Z parameter, choose Add Keyframe. A solid diamond appears in the Animation menu, indicating that there is a keyframe at the playhead.

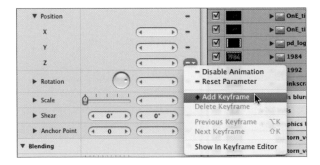

**6** In the Layers tab, click each layer in the *Graphics Over* group to select just that layer, and examine the Position values.

Each layer has a different position value, but all have a keyframe for Position Z. Now let's create the same keyframes for the layers in the *Graphics Under* group, this time using a shortcut.

**7** Select all the layers in the *Graphics Under* group; then, in the Properties tab, Option-click the Animation menu for Position Z to add a keyframe for all the selected layers.

With the layers safely locked in place in their assembled positions, you can now start at the beginning of the project and move them away in z-space. Since you are setting keyframes manually, the key here is to *first* set the keyframe, and *then* change the value for each layer.

**8** Move the playhead to the start of the project.

**9** With all the layers in the *Graphics Under* group still selected, Command-click each of the layers in the *Graphics Over* group to add them to the selection.

**10** In the Properties tab, Option-click the Position Z Animation menu to add a keyframe to all the selected layers.

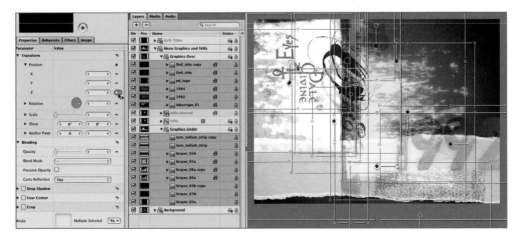

Now that a keyframe is set at 0:00, when you change the Z-position of each layer at this frame, it will change only *at this frame*, and it will animate back to its original position by the next keyframe at 5:00.

Each layer now has two keyframes, but if you play the project, nothing is animating because both keyframes for each layer have the same value. With the beginning and ending keyframes in place, you can start animating.

## Animating Layers and Groups with Keyframes

To animate the layer positions, you can give each layer a new Position Z value on the first frame, and then animate the rotation of the group containing both of the layers to add a nice spin to the overall animation as the layers "assemble" themselves.

1   With the playhead at Home, select the lowest layer in the *Graphics Under* group, and in the Inspector, drag right in the Position Z value field to set it to about 500 pixels, enough to make the layer disappear off the edge of the Canvas.

2   Continue up the group, select the next *brayer* layers, and set a Position Z value for each one at around 500 to 900 pixels, until each one is offscreen. Give each layer a different Position Z value to spread them out.

3   When you get to the two *vellum* layers, Shift-click each to select it, and then change both their values at the same time.

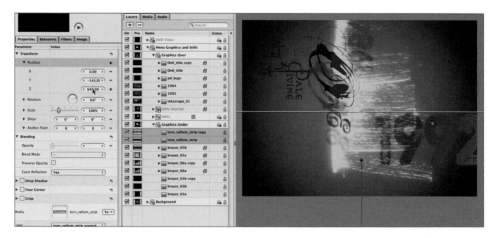

4   Continue to the layers in the *Graphics Over* group, selecting each layer in the group and changing its initial Position Z value to move it off the screen. When you are done, there should be nothing but the background image in the Canvas.

5   Play the project. The layers all move into position and come to a soft landing. Why don't they stop abruptly, like the curtains in the last exercise?

6   Select all the animated layers in the two groups, and press Command-8 to open the Keyframe Editor.

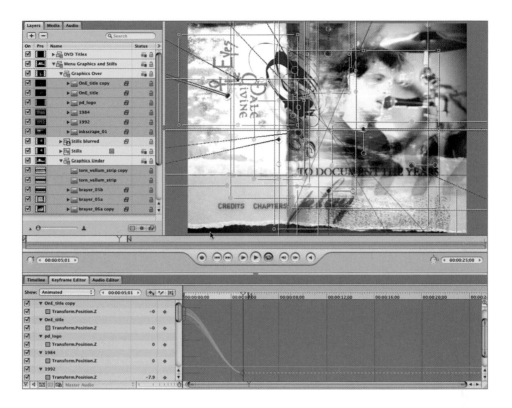

The red motion paths in the Canvas are straight lines that indicate the path of travel. The keyframe curves in the Keyframe Editor are curved, indicating that the speed of each layer changes over time. This is because the default interpolation for the Position parameters is Bezier (as opposed to the Rotation parameter, which has a default interpolation of Linear).

It's nice that the layers already come to smooth landings, but the animation needs more work. First, we will animate the opacity of all the layers to make them fade in. Then, we'll animate the rotation of the group.

**7** Press Home to return to the first frame, and with all the layers still selected, Option-click the Opacity parameter in the Properties tab, and set the Opacity value to 0.

> **NOTE ▶** Another option for changing the opacity of a layer or group of layers over time is to use the Fade In/Fade Out behavior.

**8**   Move the playhead to 1:00, set a keyframe for Opacity, and set the value to 100%. Remember, set the keyframe first, and *then* change the value. Because Opacity is now animated, its curve for every selected layer appears in the Keyframe Editor. Now all the layers fade up as they start moving.

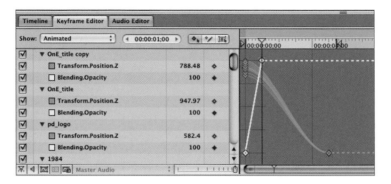

To rotate the group containing all the layers, let's work backward from its final position. You want to move the playhead to the same frame as the other keyframes at 5:00. Rather than entering the time value, you can jump the playhead directly to a keyframe.

**9**   In the Properties tab, click the Animation menu for Position Z and choose Next Keyframe, or press Shift-K.

> **NOTE ▶** The keyboard shortcuts for jumping to keyframes—Shift-K for the next keyframe and Option-K for the previous keyframe—are the same as in Final Cut Pro.

**10**   Select the *Menu Graphics and Stills* group, and set a keyframe for the rotation of the group by Option-clicking the Animation menu for Rotation in the Properties tab.

**11**   Move the playhead to the start of the project, set an initial keyframe for the rotation of the group, and then set the Rotation value to -90 degrees.

**12**   Play the project.

All the layers now rotate as they fall into position. However, they all come in at pretty much the same time, and they land without much punch. You'll now work in both the Keyframe Editor and the Timing pane to liven things up.

## Working with Multiple Keyframe Curves

You'd like all the layers to suddenly snap into final position. Rather than adding keyframes to each layer's Position Z property, you can achieve the effect using just one keyframe on the group. Then, in the Timing pane, you can adjust the timing of keyframes on individual layers to create more of a cascading effect as the layers fall into place.

1    Stop playback, and press Shift-K to move the playhead to the ending keyframe for the *Menu Graphics and Stills* group.

2    In the Keyframe Editor, frame the curve by clicking the "Fit visible curves in window" button.

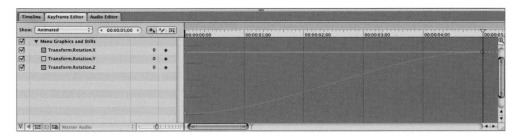

Currently, only rotation is animated for the group. We will now animate the scale over the last ten frames of the project.

3    In the Properties tab, Option-click the Animation menu for Scale to add a keyframe.

4    Type *-10* and press Enter to move the playhead back 10 frames.

5    Add a keyframe for scale, and set the value to 70%. The scale now changes from 70% to 100% over the last ten frames, but it's 70% for the entire project before the last ten frames.

6    Go to the first frame, set a keyframe, and set the Scale value to 100%. Now the layers all scale down slowly from 100% to 70%, then quickly scale up to 100% at the end, but do so too smoothly.

7    In the Keyframe Editor, drag a marquee to select all the middle Scale keyframes so that you can see their Bezier handles.

**NOTE ▶** If you just click the keyframe to select it, only Transform.Scale.X is selected and not Y and Z, which are directly underneath it.

8    Drag out the right Bezier handle to make a steeper curve up into the final keyframe. The layers now scale down, then pop back up and appear to snap onto the screen.

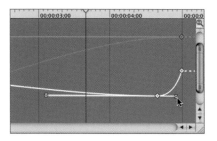

Your final step is to stagger the keyframes on the layers so that they don't all appear at once. When you want to change the timing of keyframes, it's frequently easiest to use the Timeline rather than the Keyframe Editor.

9    Click the Timeline tab, drag up on the middle of the separator bar to make the window bigger, open the *Graphics Over* and *Graphics Under* groups, and drag between any two layers in the Timeline to shrink the layer height.

10   If it's not already active, click the Show/Hide Keyframes button to display the keyframes under each layer bar.

There are three reasons why it can be easier to change just the timing of keyframes in the Timeline rather than the Keyframe Editor:

▶    You can see the relationships of keyframes applied to multiple layers.

▶    Each keyframe at a given frame is actually a "bundle," representing all keyframes at that point in time, so it's easy to select and move all of them.

▶    You can't accidentally drag a keyframe up or down, which would change its value.

Here, you want to stagger the introduction of each layer in time by moving the first two keyframes a different amount for each layer while keeping the distance between them constant.

**11** Select the second to last layer in the *Graphics Under* group, *brayer_03b*.

You don't have to select a layer in order to select its keyframes, but it makes it easier to see which keyframes are related to that layer.

**12** Shift-click the first and second keyframes, and then drag them to the right a small amount.

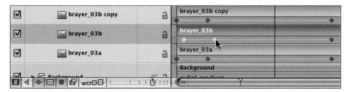

The first keyframe "bundle" includes the Position Z keyframe and the Opacity keyframe. The second is the Opacity keyframe alone. By moving them together, you ensure that opacity still animates over the same 1-second duration.

**13** Select the first two keyframes on the *brayer_03b copy* layer, and move them to the right a little bit more than in the *brayer_03b* layer.

**14** Repeat for all the layers in the *Graphics Under* group. When you reach the upper *vellum* layer, Shift-drag to snap it to the lower *vellum* layer. As you drag, thin vertical lines appear on the layer bar, representing all possible snapping points.

**15** Repeat the process for the layers in the *Graphics Over* group, staggering the first two keyframes. Then play the project and adjust the keyframe locations to suit yourself. The layers now fade in and drop into the scene at different times, but they all end up in their final positions at the same 5:00 frame.

For a final touch, you can animate the strips of vellum to spread out just before they land.

## Animating Crop with Keyframes

To make the strip of vellum appear to open up, let's animate its Crop parameter. Because the graphic is composed of two layers, we will animate them in tandem.

**1** Stop playback, press F6 to close the Timing pane, and move the playhead to the start of the project.

Start by working in the Layers tab.

**2** In the Layers tab, Shift-select the *torn_vellum_strip* and *torn_vellum_strip copy* layers, and press Shift-K three times to move the playhead to the third keyframe at 5:00. In the Properties tab, a solid diamond appears in the Position Z Animation menu, confirming that you are parked on a keyframe.

**3** Select the Crop checkbox, and click the disclosure triangle to display the Crop parameters. Option-click the Animation menu for the Left and Right parameters to set keyframes.

Once again, you are working backward, locking the final crop values. Now back up in time and crop the layers.

**4** Drag the playhead back to a point where the layers are still rotated, at about 4:00.

**5** Set keyframes for the Crop Left and Crop Right parameters, and then increase their values so that the crop lines cross in the middle of the layer, making the layers disappear, at just over 700 pixels each.

**6**  Play the project. It looks good, but let's say you'd like to modify the keyframe interpolation.

**7**  Press Command-8 to open the Keyframe Editor.

By default, the Keyframe Editor shows the curves for all animated properties—in this case, Z-position, opacity, and the left and right crop. Sometimes you want to focus on just one or two curves.

**8**  In the Properties tab, from the Animation menu next to the Crop Left parameter, choose Show in Keyframe Editor.

**9**  Do the same for the Crop Right parameter. Now only those two keyframe curves appear in the Keyframe Editor. However, only the keyframes for one of the selected layers appear.

**TIP** You can select keyframed parameters from different layers or groups, and they will each be added to the Keyframe Editor—a great way to match up the timing of multiple elements without cluttering the window with other curves.

Because you want to see the keyframes for both layers to adjust them together, you will use a different method to display them.

**10** In the Keyframe Editor, from the Show pop-up menu, choose Animated.

**11** Deselect the Transform.Position.Z and Blending.Opacity activation checkboxes to turn off the visibility of those curves, leaving just the Crop.Right and Crop.Left curves for the two layers showing.

**12** Click the "Fit visible curves in window" button, drag a marquee to select both keyframes at each frame, and then adjust the Bezier handles to taste.

**13** Save your work.

Great job. You now have a good foundation for recording keyframes and setting them manually, changing interpolation and adjusting Bezier curves, and adding and adjusting multiple keyframes at the same time.

## Lesson Review

1. How does Motion let you know that recording is enabled?

2. What parameters of a layer or group will be keyframed when recording is turned on?

3. How many keyframes do you need to create animation?

4. The position of a video is keyframed at 1:00 and 5:00, but it does not move. Why?

5. You want to set a keyframe at 3:15 for the scale of three layers that are each in different groups. How can you set it for all of them at once?

6. When you set a keyframe with recording enabled at a frame that is not at the beginning of a layer, what does Motion do automatically?

7. When setting keyframes manually, which do you do first—set the keyframe or change the value—and why?

8. What parameters can be keyframed?

### Answers

1. The Record button turns red and glows, and all keyframeable value fields in the Inspector turn red.

2. All keyframeable parameters will be keyframed by default. You can change the recording options by double-clicking the Record button and selecting the checkbox to record keyframes on animated parameters only.

3. At least two.

4. Because the keyframes have the same value.

5. Command-click each of the layers to select them; then click the Animation menu in the Properties tab of the Inspector for Scale and select Add Keyframe, or Option-click the menu.

6. Motion automatically sets a keyframe at the beginning of a layer if recording is enabled when you change the value of a parameter at any other point in time.

7. Always set the keyframe first and then change the value when setting keyframes manually; otherwise, the value will change for the entire duration of the layer, not just at the keyframe.

8. Any parameter of any layer, group, or effect that has an Animation menu in the Inspector.

## Keyboard Shortcuts

| | |
|---|---|
| **A** | Toggle recording on and off |
| **Control-K** | Add a keyframe for the last animated property |
| **Command-8** | Open the Keyframe Editor |

**When the Keyframe Editor is open, for the selected layer(s):**

| | |
|---|---|
| **A** | Show keyframe curves for all anchor point parameters |
| **H** | Show keyframe curves for all shear parameters |
| **O** | Show keyframe curves for opacity |
| **P** | Show keyframe curves for all position parameters |
| **R** | Show keyframe curves for all rotation parameters |
| **S** | Show keyframe curves for all scale parameters |
| **U** | Show keyframe curves for all animated parameters |
| **Y** | Show keyframe curves for all modified parameters |

# Motion Graphics Design

# 8

| | |
|---|---|
| Lesson Files | Motion4_Book_Files > Lessons > Lesson_08 |
| Media | Motion4_Book_Files > Media > Secret Agent |
| Time | This lesson takes approximately 90 minutes to complete. |
| Goals | Inspect project properties |
| | Extend video layers with hold frames |
| | Understand rasterization |
| | Align layers and keyframes to markers |
| | Apply, adjust, filter, and animate generators |
| | Use shapes |
| | Work with paint strokes |

# Lesson 8

# Creating Content with Generators, Shapes, and Paint Strokes

Some motion graphics projects are "assemble and animate" operations. You already have graphics and video that you created, purchased, or received, and you focus on compositing and animating these existing elements.

But often you have little to no content in hand, so you need to create almost everything from scratch. This is where Motion shines. In addition to the massive amount of material in the Content folder of the Library, Motion includes elements—generators, shapes, and paint strokes—that you can use to create an amazing variety of animated designs.

*Generators* are objects that create patterns—some very simple, some quite intricate. *Shapes* are open or closed splines that you create with several different tools and then animate with their own special behaviors. And *paint strokes* are a type of shape to which you can apply a dizzying array of shape styles to create beautiful effects.

The creative possibilities expand exponentially when you start to *combine* these objects with effects—filters, behavior, and masks—and then animate the objects or the effects with keyframes and behaviors.

This lesson starts with a partially completed project containing just two video clips with a few masks, filters, and keyframes, and some markers that indicate proposed timing. It's up to you to bring the project to life with dynamic background elements that support the look and feel of those existing elements.

## Working with Video

You are completing a web spot for a financial services company.

The client provided two video clips, a logo, and the key messages—that's it. A colleague started working on the project before suddenly leaving for an extended vacation, so it's up to you to create animated graphics to complete the spot.

You'll begin by inspecting the project and slipping a clip to change its content. Then you'll create hold frames, turn on filters and masks, and learn about rasterization.

1   Navigate to Lessons > Lesson_08; open Lesson_08 Start and save it to the Student_ Saves folder.

    If you inherit a project from someone else or start working on a project you haven't seen for a while, it's a good idea to check the properties of the project so that you know exactly what you are working with.

2   Choose Edit > Project Properties or press Command-J. The General tab of the Project Properties window provides important information about the project, much of which can be modified if necessary.

    This is a 12-second project that uses the DVCPRO HD 720p24 preset because it matches the video used in the project. The DVCPRO HD codec uses a nonsquare pixel aspect ratio to display a 960 x 720 image in a full 1280 x 720 HD frame. You can use this information to verify that the Canvas is properly displaying the image.

**Project Properties**

General | Render Settings

Project Description:

Preset: DVCPRO HD 720p24

Width: 960

Height: 720

Bit Depth: 8 Bit          ☐ Dither

Pixel Aspect Ratio: HD (960x720, 1440x1080)    1.33

Field Order: None

Frame Rate: 23.98    fps

Duration: 00:00:12:00    Timecode

Start Timecode: 00:00:00:00

Background Color: ⬛ ▾

Background: Transparent

The background color is visible in the
canvas, but does not render as part of the
composition.

Cancel    OK

**3** Click Cancel to close the Project Properties window.

**4** At the top right of the Canvas, click the View and Overlay pop-up menu and confirm
that Correct for Aspect Ratio is selected. If no checkmark is visible next to the option,
click it to add one so that your project is displayed correctly in the Canvas.

| Render ▾ | View ▾ | ▢ ⬍ |
| --- | --- | --- |
| ✓ Show Overlays | ⌘ / |
| Rulers | ⇧⌘R |
| Grid | ⌘' |
| ✓ Guides | ⌘; |
| ✓ Dynamic Guides | ⇧⌘; |
| Safe Zones | ' |
| Film Zone | ⇧' |
| ✓ Handles |
| ✓ Lines |
| ✓ Animation Path |
| ✓ Show 3D Overlays | ⌥⌘/ |
| ✓ 3D View Tools |
| ✓ Compass |
| ✓ Inset View |
| ✓ 3D Grid | ⇧⌘' |
| ✓ 3D Scene Icons |
| ✓ Correct for Aspect Ratio |
| Show Full View Area | ⇧V |
| ✓ Use Drop Zones |
| Save View Defaults |

**5** Press F6 to open the Timing pane, select the Timeline if necessary, open the *Video*
group, and play the project.

**NOTE ▶** If you can't see the full project in the Timeline, drag the Zoom slider, or Control-click (or right-click) in the ruler and choose "Zoom to Project."

In the Canvas, two video clips play—a man jumping from an airplane and the same man floating down with a parachute. The video layers are not centered in the Canvas, and there is a period of empty frames between the clips. The second video scales up quickly over its first few frames, and then shifts to the right side of the screen.

In the Timeline, you can see bars for the video layers—*Bond_air* and *Bond_chute*—and the gap between them. Keyframes are present on the *Video* group, the *Bond_air* layer, and the Circle Mask, which is currently disabled.

**NOTE ▶** If you don't see the keyframes, click the Show/Hide Keyframes button at the bottom left of the Timeline.

Above the ruler area is a series of colored *project markers* with marker names next to each one. The green markers indicate where the text layers should be placed. (You will place that text in the next lesson.) The orange markers indicate the start of each transition in the project: the points in time at which one text message leaves the screen and the next one arrives.

A red *object marker* appears on the *Bond_air* layer. The name of a layer marker isn't displayed in the Timeline, but you can see it by opening the Edit Marker dialog.

**6**   Double-click the red marker.

The name *opening shot* indicates that this frame of the video (where the man emerges from the plane) should be located at the beginning of the project. It's currently located at 1:03, so you need to move the video so that this frame is located at 0:00. While you could drag the entire clip to the left and then drag the Out point to trim it, a more efficient method is to *slip* the clip. Slipping a clip changes the *content* but not the location of the In and Out points of a layer. In Motion, you slip a clip using a modifier key.

7   Click Cancel to close the Edit Marker dialog; then Option-drag the *Bond_air* layer bar to the left until the marker is at the start of the project.

The pointer changes to a slip pointer, and the *handles*—the extra media beyond the clip's In and Out points—appear. The information window displays the new In and Out points and the change in time.

**NOTE ▶** Make sure to drag the clip, but not the marker. If you drag the marker, you'll move the marker without slipping the clip. Also note that you must have handles available beyond a clip's In and/or Out points to slip a clip.

8   Press Home to move the playhead to the start of the project. The video clip now starts at the marker where the man emerges from the plane.

The next step is to fill the gaps in the project. The video clips don't play long enough to do so, so let's change the end condition of each video clip in order to extend it.

9   With the *Bond_air* layer still selected, press F1 to open the Properties tab of the Inspector. Near the bottom of the Inspector, from the End Condition pop-up menu, choose Hold. This setting freezes the Out point of a video layer for as many frames as you need.

10  In the Timeline, click the Out point of the *Bond_air* layer and Shift-drag it to the right until it snaps to the In point of the *Bond_chute* layer.

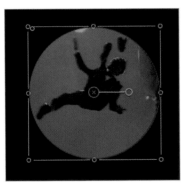

11 Select the *Bond_chute* layer, change its End Condition to Hold, and Shift-drag the layer's Out point to snap it to the end of the project (indicated by the play range Out point in the ruler). Now play the project.

Each clip freezes at its previous Out point, indicated in the Timeline by a small indent on the layer bar. The first video scales down quickly just before the second video scales up. It's not yet clear why they do so, or why they are off-center.

12 In the Timeline, select the Circle Mask checkbox. The mask frames the man in both video clips: as he jumps from the plane and freezes in mid-air, and as he floats from his parachute. The group containing both video clips scales down just before the edit point between the clips and scales up after the edit point to create a transition.

You will create an animated background to complement the video clips and support the text and logo. But first, there are a few more clues that will help you in the design process.

13 Stop playback, move the playhead to about 2:15 to see the freeze frame of the first video clip, and then click the disclosure triangle for the *Bond_air* layer to view the effects applied to it. The layer has three filters applied to its full duration, all currently inactive.

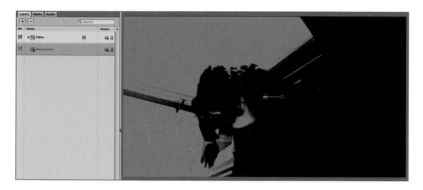

**14** Activate each filter by selecting its activation checkbox, starting from the bottom and working up, to see how they affect the video.

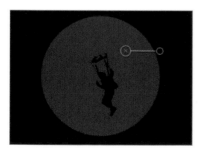

The Threshold filter converts the video to black and white and increases the contrast. The Levels filter increases the contrast more smoothly than could be achieved with only the Threshold filter. The Colorize filter gives the white areas an orange tint.

**15** Move the playhead so that you can see the *Bond_chute* layer, open the layer, and activate the filters. This clip has the same three filters applied to it, but with different settings and a blue tint.

You will incorporate these style choices to create a bold, graphic look based on circles and an orange and blue color palette.

**16** Save your work.

## Creating a Background with a Generator

Motion's generators are great for creating something out of nothing. Some generators are animated by default, while you can animate others using keyframes or behaviors. And when you add a filter to a generator and animate the filter, the creative possibilities become endless.

In this exercise, you will import a generator, customize it, and then add and animate a filter to create a dynamic background that matches the color and shape of the masked videos in the project.

1   Move the playhead to the start of the project, press F6 to close the Timing pane, and press F5 to open the Layers tab. Because the background will last for the full project, timing isn't important, and you can work most efficiently in the Layers tab.

2   Close the *Video* group, click beneath it to deselect everything, and click the Add (+) button to add a new group. Choose Object > Send Backward or press Command-[ (left bracket) to move the new group below the *Video* group, and then rename the group to *Background*.

> **TIP** ▶ If a layer or effect in the *Video* group is selected when you create a new group, the group is created above the selected layer *inside* the *Video* group. If this happens, drag the group down and to the left to move it out of the group; or press Command-Z to undo, and try again.

3   Press Command-2 to open the Library, and choose the Generators category. The Library contains 25 generators, 4 of which are text generators.

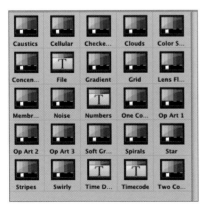

4   Select a few generators and inspect them in the Preview area. Then select the Grid
    generator, and click the Apply button at the top of the Library, which will place it in
    the *Background* group and center it in the Canvas.

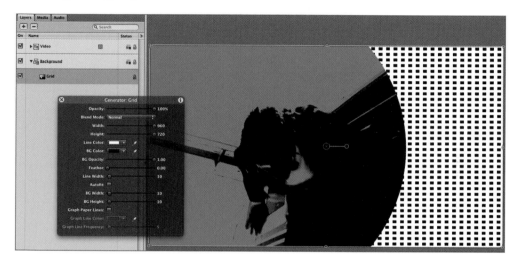

Right now, it's a little difficult to see how this design is going to work with the video.
That's where combining generators and filters comes in. First, let's find a good frame
on which to start working.

The markers you saw in the Timeline appear as faint vertical lines in the mini-
Timeline and on the Grid layer bar. There's one at the beginning of the freeze frame
at 2:02, which is a good place to start designing because it's the point at which the
first line of text will be animating onto the screen. Even with the Timing pane closed,
you can still snap to markers by pressing the Shift key.

5   Shift-drag the playhead to 2:02.

6   With the Grid layer still selected, click the Add Filter icon in the Toolbar and choose
    Distortion > Target. The filter transforms the appearance of the generator quite
    dramatically, the pointer now has no shaft, and some new controls are available in
    the Canvas.

**7** In the Canvas, drag the center of the concentric circles to the left to center them behind the video, and then drag the handle to change the Angle parameter in the HUD (heads-up display).

You want to position the filter precisely behind the video, so let's use the Inspector.

**8** Click F3 to open the Filters tab of the Inspector. In the Angle field, enter *166*, and then Option-drag in the two Center fields while observing the Canvas to fine-tune the filter location.

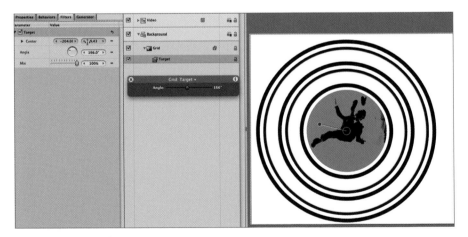

You can now adjust the Grid generator and see the results of your changes with the filter applied.

**9** Select the *Grid* layer, and in the HUD, change Line Width to 6, BG Width to 47, and BG Height to 95, and select the Graph Paper Lines checkbox.

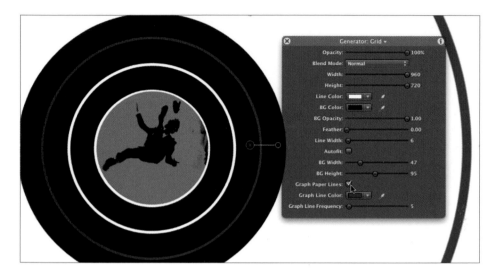

This combination of settings creates a nice open space to the right of the video that is framed by a thin blue ring. The colors still need some work to match the blue and orange tints of the video clips.

**10** Press F4 to open the Generator tab of the Inspector. Open the Line Color parameter, and set Red to 0.18, Green to 0.33, and Blue to 0.53.

> **NOTE** ▶ These specific settings were chosen to match the Lesson_08 Finished project. However, feel free to experiment with your own colors and settings for both the generator and the filter.

**11** Open the BG Color parameter, and set Red to 0.76, Green to 0.50, and Blue to 0.15.

**12** Open the Graph Line Color parameter, and set Red to 0.86, Green to 0.86, and Blue to 0.88. The background now contains colors that match and complement the video tint. The orange isn't an exact match, but we'll change that later.

Before you animate the generator, something very subtle but important happened when you first turned on the *Video* group's circle mask. It's easier to see and understand what occurred now that you have placed a background underneath the video.

Look at the icons to the left of the names of the *Video* and *Background* groups, and notice how they differ.

**13** Select the *Video* group, open it, and deselect the activation checkbox for the Circle Mask.

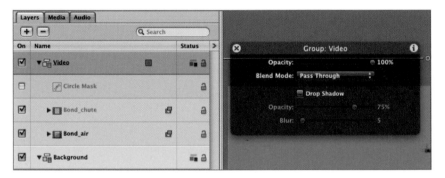

Now the icons look the same. The HUD indicates that the blend mode for the group is Pass Through, which means that any blend modes applied to layers within this group will pass through to the groups beneath them.

**NOTE ▶** You may need to deselect then reselect the Video group to update the HUD's blend mode.

**14** Select the *Bond_air* layer, and in the HUD, change Blend Mode to Overlay.

Because the blend mode for the group containing this layer is set to Pass Through, the Overlay blend mode on the *Bond_air* layer passes through to the *Grid* layer in the *Background* group beneath it. This is the default state for groups and blend modes. However, certain operations applied to a group will cause that group to

become *rasterized*—converted into a bitmap image—before it is composited
with other groups.

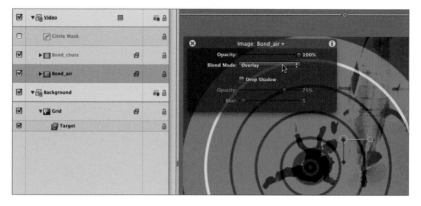

When a 2D group is rasterized, any blend modes applied to layers within it will
no longer pass through to the groups below.

**15** Select the *Video* group and select the activation checkbox for the Circle Mask.

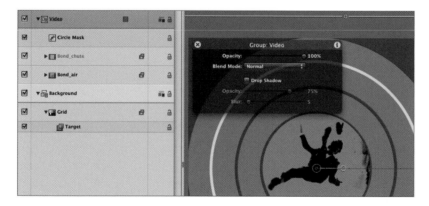

A box now surrounds the *Video* group icon to indicate that the group is rasterized.
The group's Blend Mode setting has been changed to Normal, and if you click the
Blend Mode pop-up menu in the HUD, you see that Pass Through is dimmed and no
longer can be selected. In the Canvas, the Overlay blend mode applied to the *Bond_air*
clip no longer affects the group underneath.

The point is that certain operations applied to a group will trigger rasterization and
stop blend modes on layers in that group from passing through to layers in the groups
below.

There's often another way to accomplish the same result. In this example, you could change the blend mode of the entire *Video* group rather than alter the individual layers within the group. However, for this project, no blend mode is needed.

16 Select the *Bond_air* layer, use the HUD to change Blend Mode back to Normal, close the group, and save your work.

> **NOTE ▶** Operations on a group that trigger rasterization include adding a mask; applying a filter; and selecting the Drop Shadow, Four Corner, or Crop checkbox. The operations that trigger rasterization for a 3D group are different, and the impact of a rasterized 3D group is also different. We'll work with 3D groups in later lessons.

## Animating a Background

The Grid generator and Target filter combination makes for an interesting background graphic, but it's currently static.

When faced with an animation task in Motion, you can choose to use keyframes, behaviors, or a combination of both. For this project, the animation should stop each time that text appears on the screen to focus the viewer's attention, and should stop with a specific design that frames that text. Because you want animation that starts and stops on precise frames and requires precise values, using keyframes may be the best approach.

Many of the parameters of both the generator and the filter will create interesting animation when keyframed. The Angle parameter of the Target filter works particularly well.

> **TIP ▶** A great way to figure out what to animate is to scrub in the value fields of all the parameters of a generator or filter and see what happens. If the results are interesting, try animating that parameter with keyframes or parameter behaviors.

1 Press F5 to close the Project pane, and press F6 to open the Timing pane. Close the *Video* group, open the *Background* group, if necessary, and select the Target filter.

You've just spent some time perfecting the look of the background at the frame where the video freezes, so let's lock it in place by setting a keyframe.

2 With the playhead placed at the first marker at 2;02, press F3 to open the Filters tab of the Inspector. Then Option-click the Angle parameter's Animation menu to set a keyframe.

With the design fixed in place at this marker, you can set a new starting value.

3   Move the playhead to the start of the project. Press A to turn on recording, and change the Angle value to 77 degrees.

The Angle parameter now animates from 77 degrees at 0:00 to 166 degrees at 2:02. From there, you want the animation to freeze from the first marker, *Are You Prepared?*, to the second marker, *Begin trans_1*, so that the text can animate onto the screen without distraction.

4   Choose Mark > Go To > Next Marker twice, or press Command–Option–Right Arrow twice, to move the playhead to the first orange marker at 3:23.

5   In the Filters tab, Option-click the Angle parameter to set a keyframe with the same value of 166 degrees.

Recording sets a keyframe only if you change a value, and you want the value to stay the same between these markers, so you need to set the keyframe manually.

From the *Begin trans_1* marker to the next marker, the background should animate again, and then freeze between the following two markers.

**6** Press Command–Option–Right Arrow to move the playhead to the *At ACB Financial* marker at 5:00, and in the Inspector or the HUD, change Angle to 90 degrees.

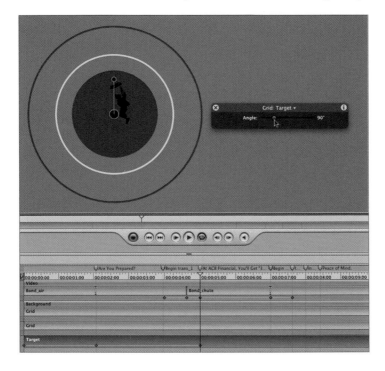

**7** Move the playhead to the *Begin trans_2* marker at 7:00, and manually set a keyframe for the same Angle value of 90 degrees.

You'll set one more keyframe to create animation during this second transition. Before you do, however, you must animate the center of the Target filter, because the masked video moves across the screen during the transition, and you want the center of the filter to follow it.

**8** Ensure that the playhead is still at the orange *Begin trans_2* marker at 7:00. In the Filters tab, locate the Target filter, and Option-click the Center parameter's Animation menu to set a keyframe. Setting a keyframe here locks this value in place so that the center won't move before this frame.

**9** Move the playhead to the *Investments* marker at 7:15, and then change the Center X value to 202.54 and the Center Y value to 9.24 to precisely center the filter behind the masked video.

**NOTE ▶** If these values don't align the video to the grid circles, go to the Filters tab of the Inspector and Option-drag in the Center value fields until it is aligned.

**10** Change the Angle value to 14 degrees.

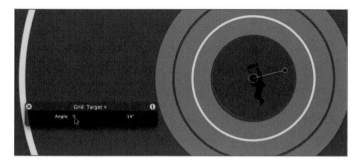

This Angle value creates a nice thin circle to the left to frame the text, similar to the circle you created at the first marker.

**11** Press A to turn off recording, and play the project.

Most of the animation works well, but when the masked video slides to the right, the center of the animated circles shifts out of sync, although it does start and stop moving at the same times as the video. This behavior indicates that the keyframe interpolation doesn't match.

**12** Click the Keyframe Editor tab; then, from the Center.X parameter Animation menu, choose Interpolation.

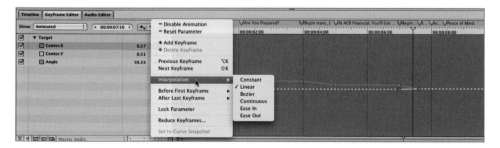

The Center keyframe interpolation is set to Linear. On the other hand, the masked video's Position parameter, which was keyframed to make the video slide across the screen, uses Bezier interpolation by default to create a realistic movement with acceleration and deceleration.

**13** Choose Bezier or Continuous. The grid circles now move across the screen in lockstep with the video.

> **NOTE** ▶ Another way to match the movement of one object to another is to use the Match Move behavior, which is one of the behaviors in the Tracking category. We'll work with tracking behaviors in a later lesson.

**14** Stop playback and save your work.

You've created an animated background that supports the shapes and colors of the existing project elements by keyframing a filter applied to a generator. Your next step is to add the "hero shot," the company logo.

## Understanding Fixed Resolution

A client may provide artwork created in a vector-based application such as Adobe Illustrator and saved in a format such as .ai (Illustrator) or .pdf (Portable Document Format). The vector nature of the artwork means that you can scale it as large as you like without losing resolution. To get started, let's create a new group for the logo.

**1** Press F6 to close the Timing pane, and press F5 to open the Project pane. Close any open groups, click in an empty area of the Layers tab to deselect everything, click the Add (+) button to create a new group above the two existing groups, and rename it to *Logo*.

**2** Move the playhead to the marker at 7:15 in the mini-Timeline. The logo will cover the man with the parachute at this frame, where the final three lines of text will begin to animate onto the screen.

**3** Press Command-1 to open the File Browser. Navigate to Motion4_Book_Files > Media > Secret Agent and select **ACB_logo.ai**.

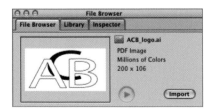

**4**   Click Import to place the file into the *Logo* group at the playhead location, and then use the dynamic guides to center it over the masked video.

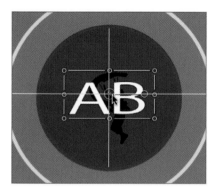

At 100% size, the logo is a little too small. To clearly see the impact of the next few steps, let's dramatically increase the size of the layer.

**5**   Shift-Option-drag a control handle on the layer's bounding box to increase the scale to about 500% while maintaining its proportions and keeping its anchor point stationary.

The letter outlines appear blurry, as if this layer were a bitmap rather than vector image. This is because, by default, the layer is set to *fixed resolution* to maximize performance. You can change this setting by selecting the underlying media for the layer instead of the layer itself.

**6**   In the Project pane, click the Media tab. This tab contains a list of all the graphics, image sequences, and QuickTime movies you have imported into your project.

**7**   Select the **ACB_logo.ai** file; then press F4 to open the context-sensitive Object tab of
the Inspector, which now is also named Media. The Media tab of the Inspector contains settings for the source media file.

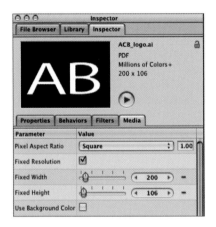

**8**   Deselect the Fixed Resolution checkbox. The logo layer now looks crisp and clear,
even at this very large scale.

> **TIP**  If you are not scaling the layer over 100%, there is no need to deselect the
> Fixed Resolution checkbox. Leaving it selected will optimize playback performance
> and render speed.

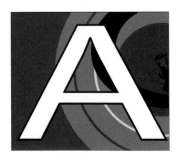

**9**   Press Command-4 to open the Layers tab; select the *ACB_logo* layer; and in the Canvas, Shift-Option-drag a control handle to scale down the layer to about 155%, so that it fits inside the blue circle.

## Using Shapes

Motion's shapes are incredibly diverse and versatile objects, and you have a choice of tools for creating shapes: anything from rectangles, circles, and lines to free-form shapes and paint strokes. Motion's Library also contains preset shapes and dozens of shape styles; and there is a set of specialized behaviors just for animating shapes.

The ACB company's logo has a transparent background, so you'll position a circle shape filled with a gradient behind it and use another circle shape for a frame, and then use a rectangle shape to create a vignette look for the whole project.

**1**   In the Toolbar, click and hold the Rectangle tool. Two other tools appear: the Circle and Line tools.

**2**   Choose the Circle tool, and then, from the center of the logo, Shift-Option-drag outward to create a circle just large enough to cover the video. Don't worry if it's not perfectly centered or scaled.

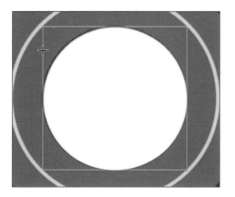

Holding down the Shift key constrains the circle so that it remains perfectly round, and holding down the Option key keeps the center of the circle at the point where you started dragging.

Notice that the pointer has changed to a crosshair, which indicates that the Circle tool is still selected. To manipulate the circle, you need to return to the default Select/Transform tool.

3   Press the Esc (Escape) key to exit the Circle tool.

Before adjusting the circle's position and scale, it can be helpful to get a closer look.

4   Command-Spacebar-drag the center of the circle to the right to zoom in on the Canvas. Then Spacebar-drag to pan the circle to the center of the Canvas.

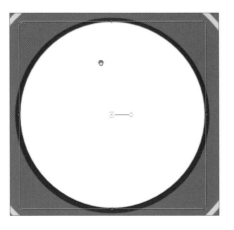

Dragging on a location in the Canvas while holding down the Command and Spacebar keys is a great way to zoom into a specific area quickly. Holding down just the Spacebar while dragging turns the pointer into a hand icon and lets you pan around on the Canvas.

**NOTE** ▶ If Spotlight turns on when you press Command-Spacebar, you need to change its default keyboard shortcut in System Preferences. found under the Apple menu.

5   Scale and reposition the circle as necessary to fit it just inside the thin blue circle around the video.

**TIP** ▶ Rather than dragging a layer to move it a small amount, you can nudge the layer by holding down the Command key and pressing the arrow keys repeatedly.

The default white fill is a little bland, so let's fill this shape with a gradient.

6    Press F4 to open the Shape tab of the Inspector. Change the Fill Mode to Gradient, and click the disclosure triangle next to the Gradient parameter.

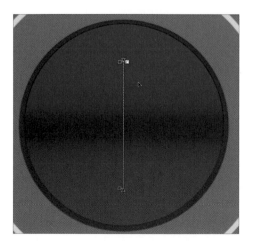

This action opens the gradient editor. The small red square and blue square boxes at the far left and right of the colored bar are *color tags*. In the gradient editor, you can change the color of each color tag; add, move, and delete color tags; and adjust the opacity of the gradient. Most of these tasks can be done directly in the Canvas as well.

7    Control-click in the Canvas and choose Edit Gradient. A vertical line appears to indicate the gradient's direction. The color tags on the left side of the line indicate the gradient colors, and the single white box on the right indicates its opacity.

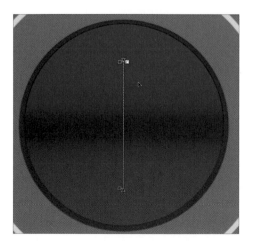

**8** Control-click the red color tag box, and choose a light blue color.

**9** Drag up on the top triangle and drag down on the bottom triangle to increase the spread of the gradient and smooth out the transition.

**10** Make the bottom color tag a darker blue that is closer to the color of the thin blue circle.

> **TIP** If you want to enter specific RGB values for gradient color tags, use the Inspector.

Let's see how the gradient looks with the logo placed on top.

**11** Press Command-[ (left bracket) to move the *Circle* layer below the *ACB_Logo* layer.

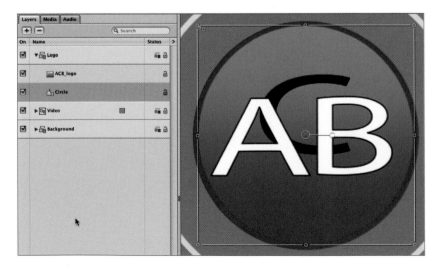

**12** If necessary, press the arrow keys to nudge the logo to center it in the circle, and then save your work.

Next, we'll use another shape to frame the logo, animate that frame, and give it some depth by applying a filter.

## Using Shape Behaviors

Shapes can be animated with any of the keyframing techniques or behaviors you've already used, but there is also a special category of behaviors just for animating shapes.

**1** Rename the *Circle* layer to *logo background*, press Command-D to duplicate it, and rename the copy to *logo frame*. Because you duplicated the existing shape, the copy is already perfectly centered.

**2** In the HUD, deselect the Fill checkbox, select the Outline checkbox, and increase Width to 19.

**3** In the Canvas, Option-Shift-drag a control handle to scale up the shape so that it covers the blue edge and is not touching the logo.

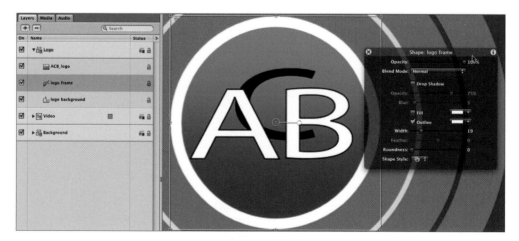

**4** Press Command-2 to open the Library. Choose Behaviors, and then choose the Shape folder.

These nine behaviors animate shapes in different ways. Some of them work only on paint strokes, which are shapes that have an outline and no fill. Some of them are designed to work with a pen and tablet input device rather than with a mouse.

5   Drag the Write On behavior from the Library to the *logo frame* layer in the Layers tab.

> **NOTE ▸** The icon for the *logo frame* layer is different from the one for the *logo background* layer because it has an outline and no fill. In other words, it is a paint stroke. You'll work more with paint strokes in the next exercise.

6   Move the playhead to 9:00, and press O to trim the behavior to the playhead. Now the shape will animate onto the screen from 7:15 to 9:00, or for 1.5 seconds. Let's set a play range around the behavior.

7   Press Command-Option-O to set a play range Out point at the playhead, press Shift-I to move the playhead to the behavior's In point, and then press Command-Option-I to set a play range In point at the playhead.

8   Start playback. The outline shape now appears to draw itself on the screen in a clockwise direction.

Let's reverse the behavior's direction and change the shape's color to better match the project.

9   In the HUD, from the Direction pop-up menu, choose Reverse.

10  Press the D key to select the *logo frame* layer, and then in the HUD, click the triangle next to the Outline color well and choose an orange color. The exact shade you

choose doesn't matter too much because next we'll add a filter to create some depth, which will alter the color.

**TIP** ▶ Pressing D selects the next element of a layer, rotating through the layer itself and each of the effects applied to it.

**11** In the Toolbar, click the Add Filter icon and choose Stylize > Indent.

**12** In the HUD, increase Softness and Brightness as far as possible, set Light Rotation to 360, set Depth to 4, and adjust the other parameters as you prefer.

As a final touch, you can animate the Light Rotation parameter so that a glint appears to move across the frame after it draws on. A Parameter behavior will do the job nicely.

**13**  In the HUD, Control-click the Light Rotation parameter and choose Rate.

**14**  In the HUD, set Rate to -60 degrees. Then drag the play range Out point to the end of the project so that you can see the animation.

**15**  Adjust the *logo frame* layer's color to a shade that you like. Press Shift-Z to fit the Canvas to the window, press Option-X to reset the play range, and play the full project. Stop playback, press Home, and save your work.

The project is coming along nicely. Next, another shape is used to create a vignette effect, darkening the frame's edges to add depth.

## Creating a Vignette Effect

Motion usually offers more than one way to accomplish a task, and creating a vignette effect is no exception. You could use the Vignette filter (in the Stylize category), but you'd first need to put all your groups into one "master" group and apply a filter to that group to affect the entire project. You could add a light, but that would require that all groups be converted to 3D groups. Instead, in this exercise, we'll apply a gradient to a shape and add a blend mode, a method that is simple and extremely flexible.

**1**  Close all open groups, and press Command-Shift-A to deselect everything. Press Command-Shift-N to create a new group, and rename it to *Vignette*.

You are going to draw a rectangle that completely covers the Canvas. First, it can be helpful to create some room around the Canvas.

**2**  Command-Spacebar-drag left to zoom out on the Canvas until some gray area appears around all sides.

**NOTE ▶** If you are working on a large monitor, you may already have space around the Canvas.

**3**  In the Toolbar, click and hold the Circle tool and choose the Rectangle tool, or press R. Make sure the playhead is at the start of the project.

**4**   In the Canvas, starting in the gray area at the top left, drag down and to the right to draw a rectangle that is larger than the visible area of the Canvas.

**5**   Press Esc to exit the Rectangle tool.

**6**   Press F4 to open the Shape tab. Change Fill Mode to Gradient. Open the gradient editor, and then change the gradient Type to Radial.

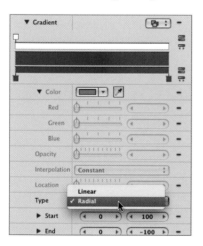

**7**   Control-click in the Canvas, and choose Edit Gradient.

**8**   Change the red color tag to white, and change the blue color tag to black. Then reposition the triangles to create a large soft white area in the center of the Canvas with dark corners.

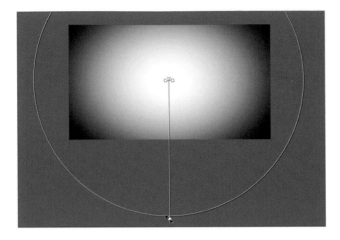

**NOTE ▶** You may need to zoom out and pan up on the Canvas to make enough room to reposition the gradient.

To turn this gradient into a vignette effect, we'll use a blend mode and moderate its impact by adjusting the layer opacity.

**9** In the HUD, change Blend Mode to Overlay and then decrease Opacity to about 70%. The blend mode makes the gradient darken the corners of the screen, and the orange color of the video now blends in better with the surrounding orange color.

**10** Press Shift-S to return to the Select/Transform tool. Press Shift-Z to fit the Canvas to the window. Play the project to see how it looks; then stop playback and save your work.

As a final step to prepare the project for text, we'll use animated paint strokes to bridge the transition from one scene to the next, drawing the viewer's eye along for the ride.

## Working with Paint Strokes

Any shape that has an outline but no fill—such as the frame you added to the logo—is a *paint stroke*. However, there is much, much more to paint strokes, including a paint stroke tool and a huge variety of presets, called *shape styles*, with which you can paint.

Your project includes two transitions. In the first, the video cuts from the man jumping from the plane to the same man hanging from a parachute. In the second, the video slides to the right and is replaced by the logo.

In this exercise, a shape style will create a streak of light that foreshadows the start of each transition and interacts with the text (which you'll add in the next lesson). A final streak of light around the logo will complete the effect.

1   Close all open groups. Select the *Logo* group, press Command-Shift-N to create a new group, and name it *Light Streaks*.

Because the *Logo* group was selected first, the new group is created just above it and below the *Vignette* group, so that the vignette will affect the light streaks as well as everything else in the project.

2   Move the playhead to 3:15, and press Command-Option-I to set a play range In point. The light streak will start drawing a little before the first transition, which begins at the marker at 3:23.

3   Move the playhead to 5:15. Press Command-Option-O to set a play range Out point, and then press Shift-Home to return the playhead to the play range In point.

> **TIP** ▶ Pressing Shift-Home and Shift-End moves the playhead to the play range In and Out points, respectively. On a portable computer, you also need to hold down the fn key.

The Out point at 5:15 is a little beyond the end of the first transition. The light streak should be gone by then.

Although you will not use the Paint Stroke tool to create your light streaks, it's a powerful tool, and understanding how it works will be useful to you.

4   In the Toolbar, choose the Paint Stroke tool.

The Paint Stroke tool works much like a brush, pen, or pencil. You use it to draw in a free-form manner with a mouse or a pen-and-tablet input device. Before you use the tool, you can choose what media you will paint, much as you would choose a color from a palette. But instead of choosing a color, you choose an image or even a movie with which to paint.

5   In the HUD, click the Shape Styles pop-up menu and browse through the categories.

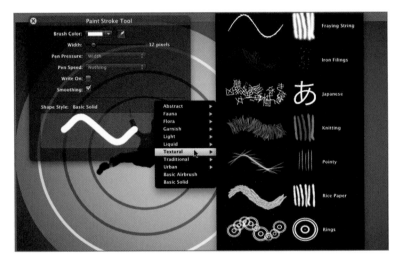

Each shape style is an image or a short movie, and when you paint, you create a trail of these images or movies, called *dabs*. When the dabs are sufficiently close together, they form a continuous stroke. In this exercise, you will use a shape style from the Light category.

6   Choose Light > Light Streak 01. In the HUD, drag in the large horizontal rectangle at the bottom; then click the Play button to see a preview of the stroke. The default width is a little narrow for this project.

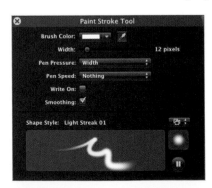

**7**   Increase Width to about 30 and draw a new stroke to preview in the HUD.

Now, you want to draw a straight line extending from the falling man to the right edge of the screen. This line will look as if it's pushing off the text, which you will create and animate in the next lesson.

**8**   In the Canvas, drag a horizontal line from the center of the video to the right edge of the Canvas, and then play the project.

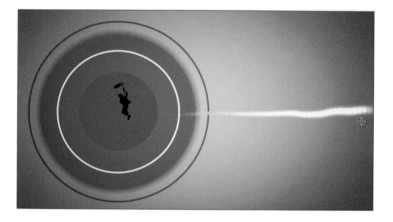

The light stroke animates on, but it's not very straight. While the Paint Stroke tool is great for an organic, hand-drawn look, in this case you'd like to draw a perfectly straight line. Luckily, a shape tool is available for that task.

**9**   Press Command-Z to undo. Stop playback, and press Shift-Home to return the playhead to the play range In point. In the Toolbar, click and hold the Rectangle tool, and choose the tool at the bottom of the pop-up list, the Line tool.

**10**  In the Canvas, Shift-drag from the center of the video to the right edge of the screen.

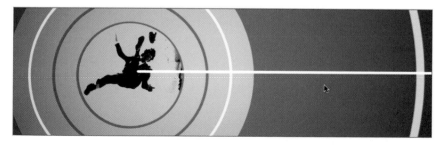

**TIP** ▶ Holding down Shift while drawing with the Line tool constrains the line either horizontally or vertically.

You now have a straight line, but it's too thin and doesn't animate. In the previous steps, you chose a shape style *before* you started to draw a stroke, but you can also choose a shape style and modify it *after* you draw.

**11** Press Command-2 to open the Library. Choose Shape Styles > Light > Light Streak 01, and drag it onto the *Line* layer in the Layers tab. Start playback.

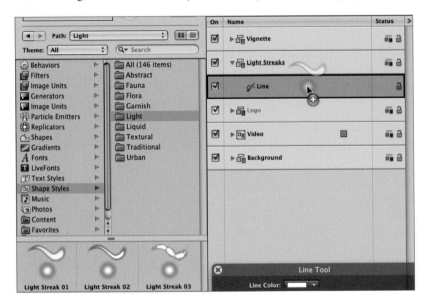

The style is applied, and it's automatically animated. The Line tool is still selected, so you need to return to the Select/Transform tool before you can adjust the line you just drew.

**12** Press Shift-S to choose the Select/Transform tool, and in the HUD, increase Width to about 42.

The light streak needs a little more work. Paint strokes have an incredible number of parameters that you can adjust. Let's try a few.

**13** Press F4 to open the Shape tab of the Inspector, and in the Style pane, set Spacing to 18%. This adjustment brings the dabs closer together and makes the stroke look more uniform.

**14** In the Shape tab, select the Stroke pane, and make sure the project continues to play.

In the gradient editor for the Color Over Stroke parameter, the opacity tags are animated, which is why the light streak appears to "write on" even though no Write On behavior is applied to it. The problem is that it takes too long to move off the screen. We'll adjust the keyframes to speed up the animation.

**15** Click the Color Over Stroke parameter's Animation menu (the hollow diamond) and choose "Show in Keyframe Editor."

**16** In the Keyframe Editor, choose the Box tool. This tool lets you proportionally scale a set of keyframes.

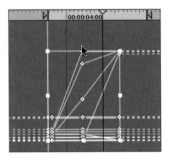

**17** Drag to create a box around the keyframes, Scale the box down by dragging on the right edge until the entire box is well inside the play range Out point.

The light streak now moves offscreen more quickly.

**18** Stop playback and save your work.

You will use a different tool for each of the next two paint strokes.

## Using the Bezier Tool

Unlike the Paint Stroke tool, which creates a stream of control points automatically as you draw, the Bezier tool lets you position each control point yourself. You use it to create precise shapes and lines, and it's perfect for creating a looping light streak.

**1** Set a play range Out point at the marker at 7:15, and set a play range In point between the third and fourth markers, at 5:22. In the Toolbar, choose the Bezier tool.

**NOTE ▶** The B-spline tool, located underneath the Bezier tool, is another option for creating smooth paths.

**2**   In the Canvas, click to create a looping path. If you drag as you click, the path will curve through the control point rather than making a sharp turn. Make a path that starts at the edge of the video, loops, and then exits to the right. We'll place this loop around some text in the next lesson. At the moment, you are just roughing it in to establish the timing.

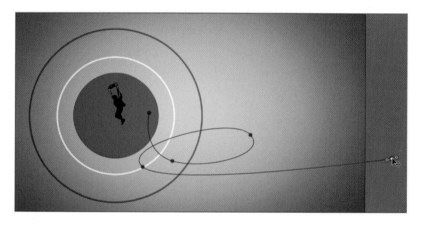

**3**   After setting the last control point, press Return to create the shape as an open path. In the HUD, select the Outline checkbox and increase Width to about 40.

Rather than dragging a shape style from the Library, you can apply it from the HUD.

**4**   In the HUD, from the Shape Style pop-up menu, choose Light > Light Streak 01.

**5**   In the Shape tab, in the Style pane, decrease Spacing to 18%. Play the play range.

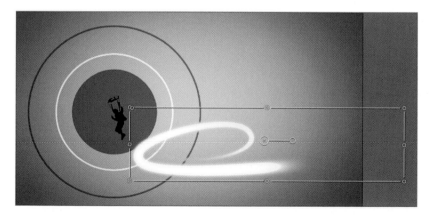

**6**    In the Stroke pane, from the Color Over Stroke Animation menu, choose "Show in Keyframe Editor." In the Keyframe Editor, use the Box tool to scale down the keyframes to fit within the play range.

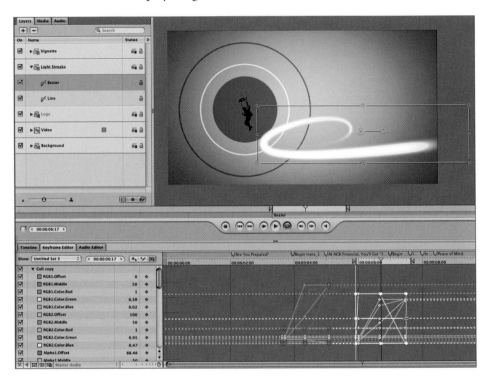

That's great for now. You will adjust the stroke once more when the text is in place. For the last paint stroke, you will use a copy of the logo frame.

**7**    Press F6 to close the Timing pane. Press Option-X to reset the play range, open the *Logo* group, select the *logo frame* layer, press Shift-I to move the playhead to the layer's In point, and press Command-Option-I to set a play range In point. Your goal is to create a paint stroke layer that seems to paint on the frame.

**8**    Press Command-D to duplicate the *logo frame* layer, rename it to *logo frame light streak*, and open it. Delete the Indent filter, and then drag the *logo frame light streak* layer into the *Light Streaks* group to keep things organized. Start playback.

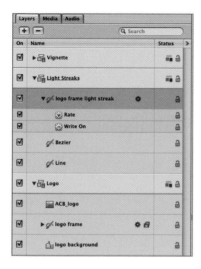

An unattractive brown circle animates on top of the frame. A few adjustments will make it look better.

9   In the Style pane of the Shape tab, under Outline, change Brush Type to Airbrush, Brush Color to an orange shade, Width to 75, and Spacing to 18%, and select the Additive Blend checkbox. The shape is now a bright streak, but it covers the entire frame layer and just sits there after it animates on.

10  In the Layers tab, underneath the *logo frame light streak* layer, select the Write On behavior; and in the HUD, set Shape Outline to "Draw and Erase." The light streak now erases after drawing on, revealing the frame underneath.

**11** Press Option-X to reset the play range. Review the project, tweak as necessary, and save your work.

You've covered a large amount of ground in this lesson, learning how to combine generators with filters to create and then animate a background with keyframes. You've also worked with shapes and paint strokes, and adjusted multiple keyframes in the Keyframe Editor. You are now ready to add text to your project and animate it.

## Lesson Review

1. How can you view the resolution and frame rate of a Motion project?

2. How can you view the name of a layer marker?

3. True or false: All generators are animated by default.

4. You've keyframed the positions of two layers at the same points in time to move them across the screen together. They start and end at the same time, but during the animation, they drift apart. Why?

5. How can you quickly select each of the filters and behaviors applied to a selected layer without opening the Project pane or the Timing pane?

6. How does the Paint Stroke tool differ from the Bezier tool?

7. Describe two ways to apply a shape style preset to a paint stroke.

8. What behavior can you use to animate the appearance and/or disappearance of a paint stroke from the first control point to the last?

*Answers*

1. Choose Edit > Project Properties or press Command-J.

2. Double-click the marker to open the Edit Marker dialog.

3. False. Some generators are animated, and some require that you apply keyframes or behaviors to their parameters to create animation.

4. The keyframe interpolations of the layers do not match.

5. Press the D key repeatedly to select each of the effects applied to a layer, or the layer itself.

6. The Paint Stroke tool creates a stream of control points as you draw to produce a hand-drawn look. The Bezier tool lets you set each control point directly as you draw each time you click in the Canvas.

7. Choose a shape style from the HUD pop-up menu, or drag it from the Shape Style category in the Library onto the paint stroke layer.

8. The Write-On behavior.

## Keyboard Shortcuts

| | |
|---|---|
| **B** | Select the Bezier tool |
| **C** | Select the Circle tool |
| **L** | Select the Line tool |
| **P** | Select the Paint Stroke tool |
| **R** | Select the Rectangle tool |
| **Shift-S** | Select the Select/Transform tool |
| **Esc** | Exit the Rectangle, Circle, or Line tool |
| **Shift-Home** | Move the playhead to the play range In point |
| **Shift-End** | Move the playhead to the play range Out point |

# 9

| | |
|---|---|
| Lesson Files | Motion4_Book_Files > Lessons > Lesson_09 |
| Media | Motion4_Book_Files > Media > Secret Agent |
| Time | This lesson takes approximately 45 minutes to complete. |
| Goals | Create, format, and style text layers |
| | Format glyphs |
| | Save and apply text style presets |
| | Animate text with text behaviors |
| | Customize the Sequence Text behavior |
| | Animate glyphs |
| | Save text animation favorites |
| | Work with motion blur |

Lesson **9**

# Creating Text Effects

Text and motion graphics were made for each other. When you combine video, motion graphics, audio, and animated text into a cohesive, integrated presentation, you have a powerful vehicle for informing, entertaining, educating, and persuading your audience.

The text engine in Motion is powerful and flexible. Using the text formating, styling, and animation tools, and text behaviors, you can create dynamic, engaging, and unique text treatments to complement your motion graphics.

In this lesson, you will edit, style, and animate text for the key messages of your financial services project. After creating the text layers, you'll animate each line onto the screen using behaviors, and animate individual characters, called *glyphs*, using keyframes.

## Creating, Formatting, and Styling Text Layers

The first step is to create your text at the appropriate time using project markers, and in the appropriate space relative to the background. After entering text with the Text tool, you will adjust the text's format and style in the HUD and the Inspector.

1    You can work with the project you finished in Lesson 8, or you can open Lessons > Lesson_09 > Lesson_09_Start and save it to the Student_Saves folder.

2    Press F6 to open the Timing pane, and select the Timeline, if necessary. If the playhead is not already at the start of the project, press Home, and then press Command-Option-Right Arrow to move the playhead to the first marker, *Are You Prepared?*, at 2:02.

Let's place the first teaser line of text at this marker, where the video and background have frozen.

3    In the Timeline, select the *Logo* group, click the New Group (+) button to create a new group, and rename the group to *Text*.

You placed the *Text* group below the *Light Streaks* group so that the light streaks will appear on top of the text. To create a text layer, you use the Text tool.

**4**   In the Toolbar, select the Text tool, or press T. Make sure the *Text* group is still
selected so that the text layer will be created inside it.

**5**   Press Option-Z to view the Canvas at 100% scale, and, if necessary, pan it so that
you're seeing the right half of the screen (You'll need to exit the Text tool before
panning with the Spacebar.). Then, click to the right of the orange circle, and type
*Are You Prepared?* In the HUD, drag the Size slider to 48 points, and, from the Font
pop-up menu, choose Optima.

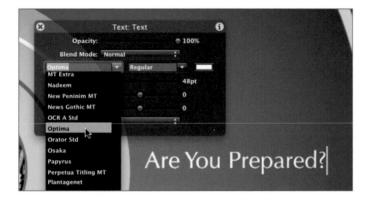

> **TIP** ▶ If you drag on the list of fonts, the text in the Canvas will update the font in
> real time, so that you can see exactly how each font looks.

**6**   Press Esc (Escape) to exit the Text tool and return to the Select Transform tool; then
drag the text in the Canvas, using the dynamic guides to position it in the horizontal
center, midway between the circles. You can continue to modify the text after return-
ing to the default Select/Transform tool. To access more parameters, let's use the
Inspector.

**7**  Press F4 to open the fourth tab of the Inspector, which is now the Text tab.

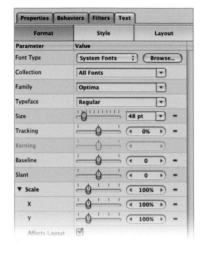

The Text tab contains a large number of parameters in three panes: Format, Style, and Layout. The Format pane contains many of the parameters also found in the HUD, such as the font Family, Typeface, Size, and Tracking.

**8**  Experiment by changing some of the other parameters in the Format pane, pressing Command-Z to undo after each change. Then click the Style button.

The Style pane lets you customize four attributes of a text layer: Face, Outline, Glow, and Drop Shadow. Each attribute has a similar group of parameters to adjust. The text color is pure white by default, so it doesn't quite match the off-white of the large ring.

**9**  Click the color well (not the triangle next to the color well) to open the Colors window, and then click the magnifying glass icon. Click the off-white ring to the right of the text to apply that color to the text layer.

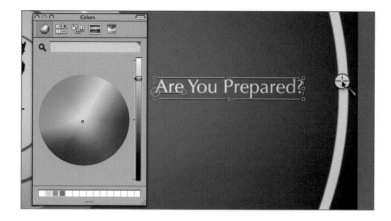

**TIP** ▶ You can also change the color of the text face by using the color well in the HUD.

An outline can help separate the text from the background.

**10** Close the Colors window, select the Outline checkbox, click the triangle next to the color well, and select a black color.

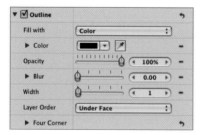

A soft, subtle drop shadow will add some depth.

**11** Select the Drop Shadow checkbox. Change Opacity to 50% and Blur to 4.

So far, you've applied format and style changes to the entire text layer. You can also apply these changes (and more) to individual text characters, or glyphs, using the Adjust Glyph tool.

**12** In the Canvas, Control-click (or right-click) the text, and from the shortcut menu, choose Transform Glyph.

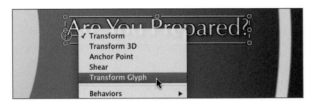

**TIP** ▶ You can also choose this tool by clicking and holding down the first button in the View tools in the Toolbar and choosing it from the pop-up list.

A bounding box surrounds the first glyph of the text layer, which you can use to change its scale. You use the red, green, and blue arrows to change the position of the glyph along the x-axis (horizontally), the y-axis (vertically), or the z-axis (toward or away from the viewer). You use the hollow white circle to rotate the glyph around each of the x, y, and z axes.

**13** Experiment with the various controls, undoing after each change. Then Shift-Option-drag a bounding box control handle to increase the glyph's size to about 200%, and drag the red arrow to move it closer to the next glyph, the letter "r."

**NOTE** ▶ An arrow turns yellow when you move the pointer over it or click it.

Notice that the glyph baseline (rather than the center) stays fixed when you change the scale while holding down the Option key. This is because the default location of a text layer's anchor point is along its baseline.

**14** Click the question mark glyph to select it, and in the Format pane of the Text Inspector, change Scale to 200%.

Changes that you make to the glyph in the Canvas using the Adjust Glyph tool are stored in the Scale, Offset, and Rotation parameters in the Format pane (not in the Scale, Position, or Rotation parameters in the Properties tab, which apply to the text layer as a whole).

**NOTE ▸** You may want to adjust the Drop Shadow Distance, Opacity, and Blur parameters for the "A" and the "?" to more closely match the other characters.

You can often improve the appearance and readability of text by adjusting the distance between individual characters, a process called *kerning*. And although you could kern each letter using the Adjust Glyph tool, there's a more efficient technique.

**15** Press the Tab key to return to the Select Transform tool. Double-click the text in the Canvas to select it, and then click once to place an insertion bar between the "a" and "r" of the word "Prepared."

   **TIP ▸** The Tab key cycles through all possible tools for the selected element.

These letters look a little too far apart relative to the others.

**16** Press Control–Left Arrow a few times to reduce the space between the letters.

**17** Press the Left and Right Arrow keys to move the pointer between the other characters, and adjust the kerning as you see fit. Press Esc to exit the Text tool, reposition the text layer as necessary, and save your work.

## Saving and Applying Text Style Presets

You have several other text layers to create for this project. Rather than starting from scratch each time, you can save your modified text as a preset, and then apply that preset to another text layer.

**1** With the text layer still selected, open the Style pane of the Text Inspector and click the Style Preset pop-up menu at the top of the pane.

In this menu, you can select one of the preset text styles from Motion's Library or save your own preset. When saving a preset, you have the option to save only the Format parameters—including Font, Size, and Tracking—or only the Style parameters—including Face, Outline, Glow, and Drop Shadow; or you can save all parameters from both the Format and Style panes.

2   Choose Save All, and in the Save Preset To Library dialog that appears, type *Optima Off-White Outline Drop Shadow*. Click Save.

The new custom preset now appears in the Style Preset pop-up menu and in the Text Styles section of the Library. Let's prepare for the next text layer and see how to apply the style.

3   In the Timeline, move the playhead to the third marker, *At ACB Financial*, at 5:00. This frame is where the first transition ends and the next line of text should appear. The text layer you just created should be gone by now, so let's trim it to end just before this frame.

4   Press the Left Arrow key to move the playhead back one frame, press O to trim the text layer's Out point to the playhead, and then press the Right Arrow key to return the playhead to the marker.

5   Press T to choose the Text tool. Click near the middle of the Canvas, and type *At ACB, You'll Get "360" Coverage*. Position the pointer and then press Return after "ACB," and after "Get" to create three lines of text.

Motion applies formatting identical to the last time you used the text tool, so the font, size, and color are the same, but the style is not. Furthermore, this text layer would look better if it were centered.

6  Press Esc to exit the Text tool. In the HUD, from the Alignment pop-up menu, choose Center, and reposition this text layer as you did the first.

7  Press Command-2 to open the Library, choose the Text Styles category, and locate the custom preset style that you saved. The small silhouette at the bottom right of the icon indicates that the preset was created by a user and is not part of the original Motion Library.

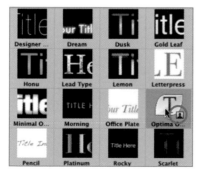

8  In the Timeline or the Canvas, drag the text style preset onto the text layer.

Because the preset contained characters with multiple formats, it has to guess which to use, and you may not get exactly the results you expect. That's OK, because you want to use a different size and color to better match this background. First, it's a good idea to turn on the safe zones to help align the text.

9   From the View and Overlay pop-up menu at the top right of the Canvas, choose Safe Zones, or press the ' (apostrophe) key.

The outer blue rectangle represents the action safe area, and all critical action should happen within it. The inner blue rectangle represents the title safe area, and text shouldn't extend outside it.

**NOTE** ▸ Although the safe zones were designed for analog television viewing, they ensure that you don't crowd the edge of the frame even if your viewing destination is the web only, where you know the full frame will be displayed.

10  In the HUD, change Size, Tracking, and Line Spacing as desired, and reposition the text as necessary. The off-white color doesn't work quite as well with this orange background.

11  In the Style pane of the Text Inspector, change the Face color to a dark blue, and change the Outline color to match the blue ring.

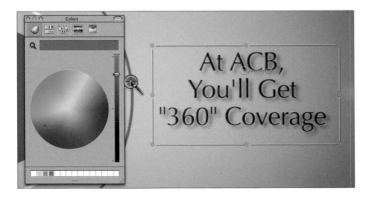

One final detail should be changed for this text layer. The apostrophe and the quotes look quite plain. You can replace them with more stylized versions.

**12** Double-click the text to select it, click after the opening quote glyph, and press Delete to delete the glyph.

**13** Choose Edit > Special Characters, and in the Characters Palette, choose the Punctuation category. Select the open quote mark, and click Insert.

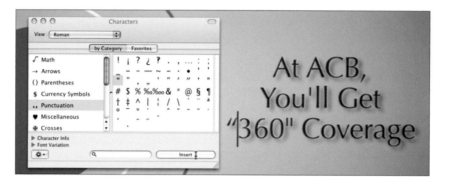

**14** Using the same method, delete and replace the close quote mark and the apostrophe. Close the Characters Palette, press Esc to exit the text tool, and press Shift-Z to view the text in the context of the entire frame. Make any final adjustments you desire, and save your work.

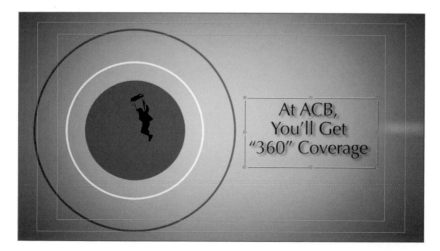

## Duplicating, Editing, and Aligning Text Layers

To create the last three text layers at the end of this project, you will copy the first text layer, modify it, and duplicate the result. First, though, let's trim the current text layer.

**1** With the *At ACB* text layer still selected, move the playhead to the *Investments* marker in the Timeline. Move the playhead back one frame, press O to trim the text layer's Out point to it, and return the playhead to the *At ACB* marker.

> **NOTE ▶** You may need to drag the Timeline's Zoom slider or double-click the marker to see the full marker name.

Rather than typing text and applying a text style, we'll copy a text layer that already has the correct style and move it to this marker.

**2** In the Timeline, select the *Are You Prepared?* text layer, and press Command-D to duplicate it. Then choose Mark > Move Selected In Point or press Shift-[ (left bracket) to move the In point of the copy to the *Investments* marker. The layer doesn't last to the end of the project, but you'll deal with that later.

**3** In the Canvas, drag the text to the left side of the screen, and double-click it to switch to the Text tool. Select the text, type *Investments.*, and press Esc to exit the Text tool. Change Alignment to Center, change the size as you like, and reposition the text a little above the horizontal middle of the frame to make room for two more text layers below it.

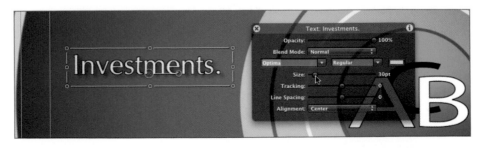

The other two text layers should start at the next two markers, but if you create them at this marker, you'll be able to align and distribute all of them without moving the playhead.

**4**   Option-drag the *Investments.* text layer downward to create and position a copy. Double-click the copy and change the text to "Insurance." Press Esc.

**TIP** ▶ If you press and hold down the Shift key after starting to Option-drag the layer, you will constrain the copy to horizontal or vertical movement.

**5**   Press Command-D to duplicate the *Insurance* layer. Drag it down, change it to read "Peace of Mind," and press Esc.

The three text layers don't need any formatting or styling work, but they may not be properly aligned or an unequal amount of space may exist between them. You can use Motion's Alignment commands to quickly rectify this situation. First, however, it's a good idea to lock groups of layers that you don't want to move accidentally.

**6**   In the Timeline, click the Lock icon for the *Vignette*, *Logo*, *Video*, and *Background* groups. The Lock icon closes, and slanted lines appear on the Timeline bars to indicate that the groups are locked. If you select a locked group or layer, or a layer inside a locked group, a red outline appears in the Canvas to warn you that it is locked. Locked layers and groups cannot be modified in any way.

 You can also press Control-L to lock selected layers or groups.

7 In the Canvas, with the *Peace of Mind* layer still selected, Shift-click the other two text layers to add them to the selection.

8 Choose Object > Alignment > Align Horizontal Centers.

9 Choose Object > Alignment > Distribute Vertical Centers.

The text layers are now precisely aligned and distributed. If you feel you have too much or too little space between the layers, select just the top layer, and drag it up or down. Then select all the layers, and once more choose Object > Alignment > Distribute Vertical Centers.

**10** With all three text layers selected, reposition them as necessary.

To finish up, move the In points of the copies to their respective markers and trim the Out points of all three layers to the end of the project.

**11** In the Timeline, move the playhead to the *Insurance* marker, select the *Insurance* layer (which will deselect the other layers), and press Shift-[ (left bracket) to move the layer's In point to the playhead.

**12** Move the playhead to the *Peace of Mind* marker, select the *Peace of Mind* layer, and press Shift-[ (left bracket) to move its In point to the playhead.

**13** Drag the playhead to the end of the project. Shift-select all three text layers, and press O to trim their Out points to the playhead.

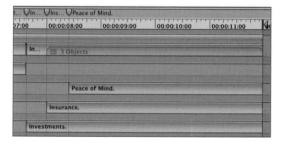

**14** Press the ' (apostrophe) key to turn off the safe zones, play the project to inspect your work, and save the file.

Each text layer appears at the appropriate time. However, the first two text layers stay on the screen too long, and the first two light streaks don't align with the text layers, but we'll address these issues shortly.

## Applying Text Behaviors

Now that your text is nicely formatted, styled, and positioned, it's time to animate it on and off the screen. In addition to the keyframing methods and behaviors that you already know, Motion includes a collection of Text behaviors. In this exercise, we'll start in the Layers tab and set a play range around the first text layer.

**1**    Press F6 to close the Timing pane, and press F5 to open the Project pane. Open the *Text* group and close all other groups, if necessary.

**2**    Select the *Are You Prepared?* text layer. Press Shift-O to move the playhead to its Out point, and press Command-Option-O to set a play range Out point. Press Shift-I to move the playhead to the layer's In point, press Command-Option-I to set a play range In point, and finally, press the Spacebar to start playback.

**3**    Press Command-2 to open the Library, and choose the Behaviors category. There are two folders of text behaviors: Text Animation and Text Sequence.

**4** Choose the Text Sequence folder. The folder contains six subfolders of Text Sequence behaviors. A Text Sequence behavior creates animation that ripples or *sequences* through the characters in the layer, animating each one in the same manner but at different points in time. Let's try a few.

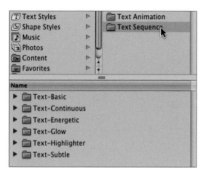

**5** Click the disclosure triangle next to the Text-Basic folder (or, if you are in icon view, double-click the folder). Locate Blur In, and drag that behavior to the *Are You Prepared?* text layer.

The behavior appears under the layer in the Layers tab and the mini-Timeline. The text in the Canvas animates onto the screen one letter at a time, with each letter starting very blurry and then coming into focus. The controls on the first character look similar to those you previously used with the Adjust Glyph tool.

Notice that the behavior duration is shorter than the text layer duration. All other behaviors, filters, and masks last as long as the layer to which they are applied, but because the text behaviors are designed to animate text onto or off of the screen, they have a shorter default duration.

**6** From the Library, drag the Blur Out behavior onto the same text layer, and in the mini-Timeline, drag it to the right so that its Out point aligns with the play range Out point. The text now animates on and off the screen.

**7** Delete the two behaviors, experiment with a few more from the other categories, and delete them all when you are done.

## Animating Text Using the Sequence Text Behavior

All of the behaviors in the Text Sequence folders are presets that were created using a single behavior called Sequence Text. You can use this behavior to create your own animations. The Sequence Text behavior also allows you to create character-by-character animation directly in the Canvas. Once you understand how it works, not only will you be able to make your own animations from scratch, you also will be able to quickly customize any of the presets that are based on this behavior.

**1** In the Library, choose the Text Animation folder. Hidden innocently among three other very useful behaviors (feel free to try them out) is the Sequence Text behavior.

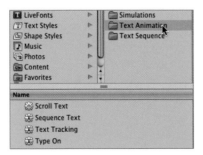

**2** Drag the Sequence Text behavior to the *Are You Prepared?* layer. Play the project. Because the behavior does nothing by default, it lasts for the duration of the layer, which is much too long for this project.

**3** In the mini-Timeline, drag the layer's Out point to the left. Using the information box as a guide, trim it a duration of 1:00.

Because the man in the video is falling, you'd like to make the text appear to fall into place, starting above the screen and rotating as it moves down.

**4**  If you have very little gray space around the Canvas, Command-Spacebar-drag to the left to create more.

**5**  In the Canvas, drag the green arrow to move the first character up and off the screen. This action sets the initial positions for *all* the characters. Immediately, all the letters animate from above the screen to their original positions, one after the other.

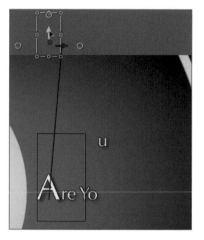

**6**  Drag the top rotation handle (the white circle) downward to set an initial x-rotation of at least 180 degrees. Now all the letters start upside down and spin into position. It's a little hard to see because they are animating so quickly.

You can increase the overlap of each character's animation using the Spread parameter.

**7**  In the HUD, increase Spread to about 14. Now, up to 14 characters on each side of the central animating character are either finishing or starting to animate, which creates a smoother, overlapping animation. The total duration of the animation, however, remains unchanged.

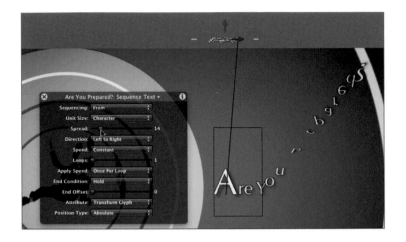

The tool that you are using to change the initial positions and rotations of the letters looks like the Adjust Glyph tool, and it is very similar; but it's actually the Adjust Item tool, and is available only when you have selected a Sequence Text behavior. While you can use this tool to interactively change the starting position, rotation, and scale of characters, there are additional parameters that you can change in the Inspector.

8    Press F2 to open the Behaviors tab of the Inspector. From the Parameter's Add pop-up menu, choose Format.

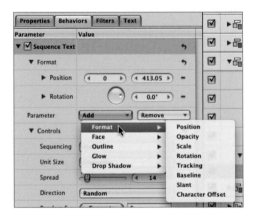

All of the parameters in the pop-up menu can be animated, which includes most of the parameters from both the Format and Style panes of the Text Inspector. You can start to see why this behavior is so powerful.

9    Choose Opacity and drag the Opacity slider that appears to 0.

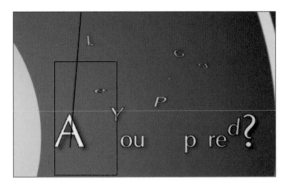

Each parameter that you choose appears in the Behaviors tab, where you can change its starting value. There are many other parameters you can also adjust.

**10** From the Direction pop-up menu, choose Random. The letters now appear to animate into position in a random order.

**11** Stop playback and save your work.

## Animating Using the Adjust Glyph Tool

Earlier in this lesson, you used the Adjust Glyph tool to change the style of individual characters: You enlarged the "A" and the "?" in the first text layer. You can also use this tool to animate individual characters using keyframes, even if those characters are already animated with a behavior. In this exercise, you will use the Adjust Glyph tool to keyframe the position of the question mark so that it floats into place along its own unique path and lands in place later than the rest of the characters.

**1** With the Sequence Text behavior still selected, press Shift-O to move the playhead to the behavior's Out point; then type *+12* and press Enter to move the playhead forward 12 frames, or half a second.

Remember when you inspected the Project Properties window at the beginning of the previous lesson? It told you that the project frame rate is 23.98 fps, so 12 frames is about half a second, enough time to bring attention to the question mark settling into place.

2   In the Layers tab, select the *Are You Prepared?* text layer (which switches the current Adjust Item tool to the Select/Transform tool). Then, in the Canvas, Control-click the text, choose Transform Glyph to select the Adjust Glyph tool, and select the question mark.

3   In the Format pane of the Text Inspector, Option-click the Animation menus for the Offset parameter and the Rotation parameter to set a keyframe for each, thereby locking the character in place on this frame.

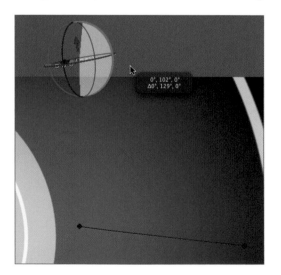

4   Press Shift-I to move the playhead to the layer's In point. Press A to turn on recording, and in the Canvas, drag the red x-axis arrow to move the character's starting position to the left. Change its rotation as you like. Because recording is enabled, these changes set keyframes and create a motion path.

**NOTE** ► When repositioning a character with the Adjust Glyph tool, remember that you are changing its Offset parameter in the Format pane of the Text Inspector, not changing the Position parameter in the Properties tab.

5    Move the playhead to the point where the character drops down low, at about 2:19, and then drag it higher in the Canvas and rotate it again.

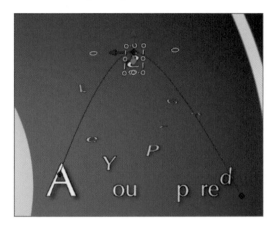

6    Play the play range, and add, adjust, or move keyframes as you like. Press A to disable recording, and press Tab to return to the Select/Transform tool. Note that the red motion path can be a bit confusing because it represents just the path of the keyframed Offset parameter before it is combined with the animation from the Sequence Text behavior.

**TIP** ► If you disable the Sequence Text behavior, the character will follow the red motion path.

You may have noticed that some of the letters look a little soft or jagged as they animate into position. Motion's default render quality is Normal, which is good for most projects, but you may want to change it when working with text that is not flat to the screen or is scaled up very large.

7    From the Render pop-up menu, choose Quality > Best.

The letters now look crisp and clear. This setting affects playback performance and render time, so it's best to leave it set to Normal until exporting, or to choose Render Quality > Best in the Output tab of the Export Options dialog when you export (which will override the default project setting).

8    In the Render pop-up menu, return the Quality setting to Normal.

It's time to turn our attention to animating this text layer off the screen.

9    In the mini-Timeline, move the playhead to 4:16, when the orange circle has moved to behind the last character, and press O to trim the layer's Out point to the playhead to end the text at this frame.

**NOTE ▶** The light streak should align to the bottom of the text. If it doesn't, open the *Light Streaks* group and select the *Line* layer. It is the only one that is not dimmed, because the other two layers do not exist at the current playhead location. Reposition the *Line* layer in the Canvas, close the *Light Streaks* group, and reselect the *Are You Prepared?* text layer.

Let's use another Sequence Text behavior to make it look as if the expanding circle is pushing the letters off the screen, following the light streak.

**10** In the Toolbar, click the Add Behavior icon and choose Text Animation > Sequence Text.

**11** Rename the original *Sequence Text* behavior to *Animate In*, and then rename the new *Sequence Text 1* behavior *to Animate Out*.

**12** Move the playhead to the point where the orange circle touches the first character, at about 4:03, and press I to trim the behavior's In point to the playhead. This is where the animation will start.

**13** In the HUD, from the Sequencing pop-up menu, choose To so that the characters animate *to* the new position and rotation.

**14** Using the Adjust Item tool, click the "A" character and drag it off the screen to the right and up, and then rotate it on two or three axes—as if it were blown off the screen.

**15** In the HUD, increase Spread to around 20, and then step through the animation, trimming the behavior's In and Out points to best match the timing of the animation to the expanding orange circle.

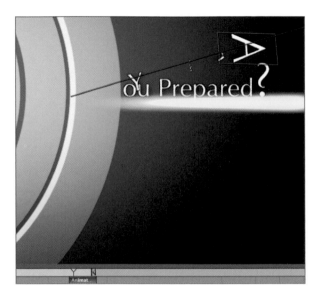

**16** Save your work.

## Saving a Text Animation Favorite

In this exercise, you will animate the next line of text using the Sequence Text behavior, but this time using different settings. Then you will save the behavior as a favorite so that it can be reapplied at any time and for any project. Finally, you will align the light streak, animate the last three text layers with copies of a preset, and experiment with motion blur. To start, let's set a play range around the next text layer.

**1**    In the Layers tab, select the *At ACB, you'll get 360 degree coverage* text layer. Press Shift-O to move the playhead to its Out point, and press Command-Option-O to set the play range Out point at the playhead. Press Shift-I to move the playhead to its In point, and press Command-Option-I to set the play range In point at the playhead. Finally, press the Spacebar to begin playback.

This process of setting a play range around a layer should be almost second nature by now.

**2**   In the Toolbar, click the Add Behavior icon and choose Text Animation > Sequence Text.

**3**   In the mini-Timeline, trim the behavior's Out point to 5:23 so that the duration is 1:00.

For this text animation, you will make the letters appear to emanate from the center of the video to enforce the idea that ACB is providing coverage to the man with the parachute.

**4**   Click inside the bounding box around the "A" (not on one of the arrows), and drag this letter to the center of the masked video. By clicking inside the box but not on an arrow, you can drag along both x and y axes at the same time.

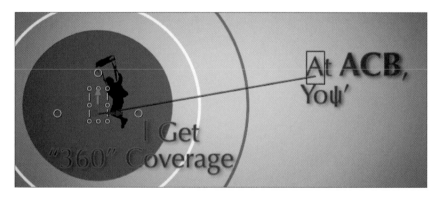

**5**   Shift-Option-drag a control handle to scale down the character to about 20%.

**6**   In the HUD, increase Spread to about 16.

In order to hide the characters before they begin to move, you will animate their opacity.

**7**   In the Behaviors tab of the Inspector, click the Parameter's Add pop-up menu and choose Format > Opacity. When the Opacity slider appears, drag it to 0.

To keep the letters from bunching up so much as they animate on, you will animate the Tracking parameter.

**8** From the Add pop-up menu, choose Format > Tracking, and set the Tracking value to -100%.

That's not bad, but let's look at an alternative. Each character animates on at a different time, but the animation is exactly the same for each. Earlier, you used the Adjust Glyph tool to keyframe an individual character's position and rotation, which animated it differently from the other characters. However, you can also adjust the Variance parameters to vary the animation of individual characters.

**9** In the Variance section of the Behaviors tab, increase the Variance value to about 50%, and then experiment with changing the other parameters.

The characters now assemble themselves from all over the screen, which could be another way to imply "360 degree coverage." Although keyframing a glyph gives you precise control, the Variance parameters let you vary the sequence text animation with a single slider.

If you think you might like to use this custom text animation in another project, you could save it as a favorite.

10  In the Library, select the Favorites folder. Rename the Sequence Text behavior to *Fly In with Variation,* and then drag it from the Layers tab to the stack area at the bottom of the Library. This custom preset will now be available to any Motion project on this computer.

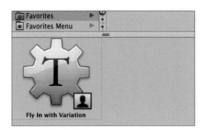

The next step is to adjust the light streak so that it loops around the "360."

11  Stop playback and move the playhead to a point where you can see the light streak loop.

12  Open the *Light Streaks* group, and select the *Light Streak 2* paint stroke layer (If you are working with the project you used inLesson 8, the layer name is *Bezier.*). Control-click the paint stroke in the Canvas, choose Edit Points, and adjust the control points and Bezier handles as necessary.

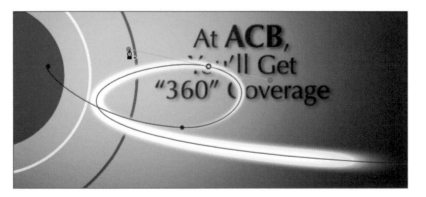

13  Press Shift-S to return to the Select/Transform tool. Close the *Light Streaks* group, and select the *Investments* text layer.

The transition to this next section is so fast that you don't need to animate the *At ACB* text off the screen. A straight cut will work just fine. To finish, we'll apply a preset text sequence behavior to the last three lines of text, starting with the *Investments* layer.

**14**   Set a play range around the *Investments* layer. Click the Add Behavior icon, and choose Text-Basic > Fade Characters Center In; then, in the mini-Timeline, trim the behavior to 1:00.

**15**   In the Layers tab, Option-drag the behavior from the *Investments* layer to the *Insurance* layer, and drag it again to the *Peace of Mind* layer. The copied behaviors automatically align to the In points of each text layer.

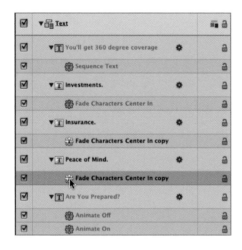

**16**   Press Option-X to reset the play range, deselect everything, close all groups, play the project, tweak as desired, and save your work.

## Adding Motion Blur

Sometimes, an animation's appearance can be improved by adding motion blur. As a final step, let's try enabling and adjusting motion blur for this project. In Motion, motion blur is a universal property; you turn it on or off for the entire project.

**1**   From the Render Options pop-up menu at the top right of the Canvas, choose Motion Blur, or press Option-M.

> **TIP**   You can also turn on motion blur by choosing View > Render Options > Motion Blur.

**NOTE ▶** Motion blur does not affect motion within a QuickTime movie or image sequence.

You can see how it affects both the animating rings and the characters. Motion blur works by creating subframes from the frames before and after the current frame and then adding them to the current frame with varying levels of opacity. Because each frame uses information from multiple subframes, the playback speed and render times are affected. You can adjust the number of samples and the shutter angle in the Project Properties window.

2   Choose Edit > Project Properties or press Command-J, and click the Render Settings tab.

The default number of samples is 8, and the shutter angle is 360 degrees. Samples refer to the number of subframes rendered for every 360 degrees of shutter angle. The shutter angle acts like the shutter of a film camera. Increasing the angle increases the number of frames over which the shutter is open, spreading out the samples.

3   Increase Samples to 16, decrease Shutter Angle to 180 degrees, and click OK. There are now more copies of each character, and they are spaced together more closely.

As with the Render Quality setting, it's a good idea to leave motion blur turned off while you are working, and then turn it on before exporting or turn it on as an Export option. If you plan to embed your Motion project in another Final Cut Studio application, turn it on before saving the project.

**4**  Press Option-M to turn off motion blur, and save your work.

Nice job. You've created, formatted, and styled text layers; learned how to change the format and style of an individual glyph; saved and applied text styles; animated text layers using preset behaviors and customized behaviors; animated individual glyphs; and worked with motion blur. To expand your knowledge, feel free to dig deeper into the text animation presets and the text options available in the Inspector.

## Lesson Review

1.  Name two of the three panes in the Text tab of the Inspector.
2.  Which tool do you use to change the scale, position, rotation, formatting, or style of an individual character in a text layer, and how do you select that tool?
3.  From which two locations can you apply a preset text style?
4.  Which behavior was used to create all the Text Sequence presets in the Library?
5.  Which parameters of a text layer can you animate directly in the Canvas using a Sequence Text behavior?
6.  How can you animate an individual character so that it behaves differently from the rest of a text layer that is animated with a text behavior?
7.  With the Adjust Glyph tool, you can change the offset, scale, and rotation of a character directly in the Canvas. Where are those parameters located in the Inspector?
8.  Describe one method for turning on motion blur, and identify where you can adjust its settings.

*Answers*

1.  Format, Style, and Layout.

2.  You use the Adjust Glyph tool, which you can select from the 2D transform tools in the Toolbar (the first of the three View tools) or by Control-clicking a text layer in the Canvas and choosing Transform Glyph.

3.  From the Style Preset pop-up menu in the Style pane of the Text Inspector, or from the Text Styles category in the Library.

4.  The Sequence Text behavior.

5.  Position, rotation, and scale.

6.  Set keyframes for that character using the Adjust Glyph tool.

7.  In the Format pane of the Text Inspector (as opposed to the Properties tab, which contains Position, Scale, and Rotation parameters for the entire text layer).

8.  You can turn on motion blur from the Render Options pop-up menu, by choosing View > Render Options > Motion Blur, or by pressing Option-M. To change its settings, open the Project Properties window by choosing Edit > Project Properties or pressing Command-J, and then select the Render Settings tab.

## Keyboard Shortcuts

| | |
|---|---|
| **T** | Select the Text tool |
| **Tab** | Rotate through each available tool for the selected object |
| **Esc (Escape)** | Exit text-entry mode |
| **Control-L** | Lock the selected layer(s) or group(s) |
| **Option-M** | Toggle motion blur off and on |
| **Shift-[** | Move selected In point to the playhead |
| **Shift-]** | Move selected Out point to the playhead |

# 10

**Lesson Files** Motion4_Book_Files > Lessons > Lesson_10

**Media** Motion4_Book_Files > Media > Rockumentary behaviors; Secret Agent

**Time** This lesson takes approximately 60 minutes to complete.

**Goals** Create and modify a particle emitter

Use an image sequence as a cell source

Browse, apply, and customize preset emitters and replicators

Create and modify a replicator

Lesson **10**

# Working with Particle Emitters and Replicators

If you've ever wanted to add chimney smoke and falling leaves to an autumn scene, or quickly create an animated background pattern, you are going to love particle emitters and replicators.

Particle emitters shoot out a continuous stream of objects and can be used to create almost anything: natural phenomena like fog, smoke, fire, and rain; a flock of birds; pulsing light fields; or a cascade of video clips.

Replicators create a fixed pattern of objects that you can animate to create an incredible variety of backgrounds, transitions, and moving elements such as video walls, splattering paint, or growing leaves.

You can use just about any object as a source for both emitters and replicators, including your own graphics, image sequences, movies, or elements from Motion's vast Library. And both emitters and replicators have their own unique behaviors for creating compelling animations.

Motion contains a huge number of preset emitters and replicators to get you started—you can use them as is, modify them, or make your own from scratch.

In this lesson, we'll use a particle emitter to re-create the shower of cascading photos that starts your Rockumentary DVD project. Then the replicator will be used to animate a pattern of video clips and create an animated background for a line of text.

## Using Emitters to Make Particle Systems

You create particle systems in Motion with an object called an *emitter*. The emitter uses a source image to create a "spray" of copies called *particles* that appear, move, and disappear. The particles can be created out of just about any object in Motion: a photo or graphic, a video clip, a text layer, or a shape—it's all fair game. In this exercise, we'll create particles using an image sequence, which is a sequentially numbered series of still images that Motion interprets as a movie. Then the particles will be animated to look as if they are falling back in space. Let's start by inspecting the image sequence.

1   Open Motion4_Book_Files > Lessons > Lesson_10 > Particles_Start. Save it to the Student_Saves folder, and press F5 to open the Project pane.

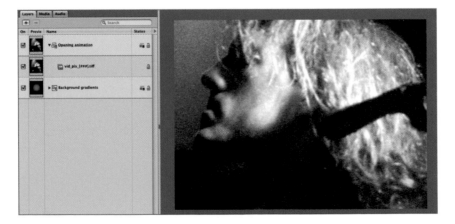

This project contains two groups: The *Background gradients* group contains the background elements you created in an earlier lesson, and the *Opening animation* group contains an image sequence.

2   Select the *vid_pix_[###].tiff* layer, and Command-Spacebar-drag left in the Canvas to zoom out far enough to see the layer's bounding box. Press Shift-V to see the full view area, and then play the project.

The photos play for one frame each. The first time you play the project, the photos load into RAM, so playback may be slow. After the photos have been cached in RAM, playback speed increases to real time. The large bounding box in the Canvas indicates that the photos are much larger than the project resolution. While viewing the full view area, you can see that some photos are tall and some are wide—something you wouldn't be able to determine by viewing only the bounding box, which represents the maximum size of every image.

**NOTE ▶** Although imported images are automatically scaled to fit the Canvas size, movies and image sequences are not. Before importing into Motion, it's a good idea to scale your media to the maximum size necessary for your project to improve playback performance and render times. In this exercise, the high resolution of the photos gives you the flexibility to start them at a size larger than project size before they appear to fall back into space.

Before making a particle system from this image sequence, let's determine how many images it contains.

3   Stop playback, and press Shift-O to move the playhead to the layer's Out point. Click the current frame icon at the bottom left of the Canvas to switch from timecode to frames.

Because the layer ends at frame 48 and an image sequence plays 1 image per frame, there must be 48 images. This information will be useful as you work with the particle emitter. Now let's make a particle system.

4   Resume playback, and in the Toolbar, click the Make Particles icon, or press E.

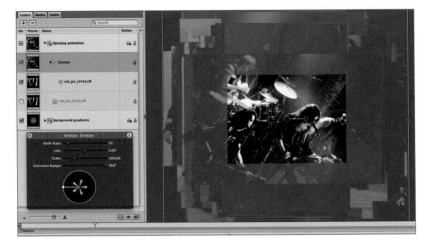

A lot happens when you click that icon. In the Layers tab, the *vid_pix_[###].tiff* layer is deactivated, so it no longer appears in the Canvas. Above it are two new objects: The layer named Emitter is, surprisingly enough, the emitter— the object that emits particles. Tucked underneath the emitter is the *cell,* which represents and controls the particles that are emitted. It takes on the name of the source for the particle system, our image sequence layer.

The Canvas fills with dozens of overlapping images, and new ones constantly appear. Finally, the HUD acquires several Emitter parameters.

As you can see, creating a particle system is easy, but modifying it to suit your project takes a few more steps. Let's start our modifications in the HUD (heads-up display).

5   In the HUD, reduce Birth Rate to 5 and Scale to 20.

6   Press Shift-V to turn off the full view area, and press Option-Z to display the Canvas at 100 percent size.

With only five new particles born every second—and each particle reduced to 20 percent of its original size—it's now easier to see what's going on in the animation. However, each particle is changing over time, from one photo to the next. Before you go cross-eyed, let's change that.

**7**   Press F4 to open the fourth tab of the Inspector, which is now the Emitter tab.

You have a lot of parameters to adjust here, but don't be overwhelmed. They are logically organized, so you can tackle them a few at a time.

8   Near the bottom of the tab, deselect the Play Frames checkbox. Leave the Random Start Frame checkbox selected. Now each particle is born with a randomly assigned image from the image sequence, and displays only that image for its short lifespan of 5 seconds (as indicated in the HUD). Then it "dies," never to be seen again.

The particles are born in the center of the Canvas and move out in all directions. Often, you will want to change the direction, the range, and the speed of the particles. The visual interface at the bottom of the HUD is called the *emission control*—and it lets you do just that.

9   In the HUD, drag the point that rests at the left edge of the circle to create an emission range of less than 360 degrees. Drag inside the "pie slice" to change the emission angle, and drag in and out on the arrow(s) to adjust the particle speed.

The particles now appear to spray out of the center and up to the right, as if you were holding your thumb on the end of a hose to control the width of the spray, its direction, and its speed.

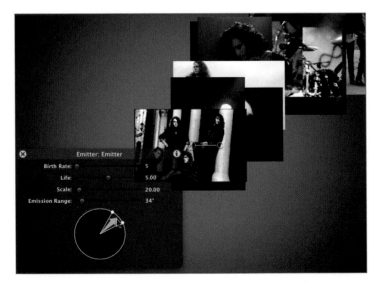

The controls in the HUD let you make some basic changes to the particles' behavior, but to really tailor the emitter to look the way you want will require working in the Inspector. Let's first see how the emitter and the particles are related to each other.

**NOTE ▶** While you have full control of the emission range and angle in the HUD, speed range adjustments are limited. You can make the particles go faster by using the Inspector.

**10** In the Layers tab, select the *vid_pix_[###].tiff* layer that is tucked under the *Emitter* layer, and look at the fourth tab of the Inspector.

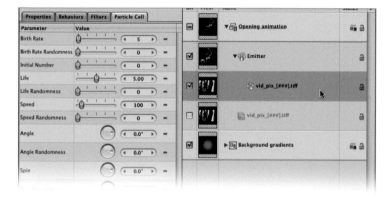

The layer you select is the *cell* of the emitter, which is why the context-sensitive Object tab is now named Particle Cell. Once again, think of the cell as representing the objects created by the emitter, and the emitter as the device that spits out those objects. Or, in terms of the hose-and-water analogy, the hose is the emitter, and the cell represents the water droplets.

**11** Now select the *Emitter* layer in the Layers tab, and examine the Inspector.

Below the parameters that control the emitter, you will see the Cell Controls, which include the same parameters found in the Particle Cell tab. As a convenience, Motion places the parameters for both the cell and the emitter in the Emitter tab. So, you can adjust both sets of parameters when the Emitter layer is selected.

**12** Save your work.

## Adjusting Emitter and Cell Controls in the Inspector

Now we'll alter the Emitter tab parameters to make the particles—the photographs— look as if they are falling back in space, spinning as they get smaller. Right now, all the particles emanate from a single point in the center of the Canvas. It would look better if they started from different positions—even outside the visible Canvas area— and fell into view.

**1** Continue to play the project. In the Emitter tab, from the Shape pop-up menu, choose Rectangle. You have many options for the shape of the emitter. When you choose a shape, parameters for that shape appear below. By default, the rectangle is 300 x 300 pixels with five columns and rows, and all particles are born in this five-by-five grid. This pattern is easier to see if you stop the particles' movement.

**2** In the middle of the Emitter tab, set Speed to 0.

The bounding box in the Canvas is a square, and the center of each photo aligns to the five-by-five grid. However, you want something larger and more random.

**3**   In the Emitter tab, click the disclosure triangle to open the Size parameter. Set Width to 1000 and Height to 600; then set Arrangement to Random Fill. Customizing a particle emitter is an iterative process, so you may later return to further adjust these settings. For now, the photos are born in random positions all over the Canvas.

To make the photos look as if they are moving away from you, you will use a behavior designed specifically for particles. The only tricky thing to remember about this behavior is that you apply it to the cell, not the emitter.

**4**   Near the bottom of the Emitter tab, use the slider to return Scale to 100%. The photos will start large and the behavior will make them grow smaller.

**5**   In the Layers tab, select the cell below the *Emitter* layer. In the Toolbar, click the Add Behavior icon, and choose Particles > Scale Over Life.

By default, the particles scale from 0% to 100% size, which actually looks quite interesting but isn't what you want here.

**6** In the HUD, change Scale At Birth to 100 and Scale At Death to 0.

> **TIP** To make smaller changes in the HUD, Option-click next to the slider.

The photos now start at full size and scale down, but the new ones cover the old ones so quickly that you never see them get small. Return to the Inspector for a few more adjustments.

**7** In the Layers tab, select the *Emitter* layer, and in the Emitter tab, change Birth Rate to 1. You can now see the photos changing scale, which creates the illusion that they are moving back in space. Remember, Speed is still set to 0, so the only movement is due to the particles' change in scale.

This is still not quite the effect you want, because each particle scales down around its anchor point and appears to move toward the edge of the screen. If the particles were falling back in space, they would appear to move toward the center of the screen.

Instead of changing the Scale Over Life parameter, you can make the particles move along the z-axis by turning the emitter into a 3D particle emitter.

**8** In the Layers tab, deselect the activation checkbox for the Scale Over Life parameter.

**9** In the Emitter tab, select the 3D checkbox. New emission parameters appear below the checkbox; but because the Speed parameter is set to 0, the particles aren't moving.

**10** Set Speed to 1,000, Emission Latitude to 0, Emission Longitude to 180, and Emission Range to 0.

The photos now appear to fall quickly back in 3D space. It would be less jarring if they faded into view rather than popping onto the screen.

**11** Near the bottom of the Emitter tab, click the Opacity Over Life disclosure triangle to reveal the gradient editor. Click the white bar to add three opacity tags, and set the opacity value for the outer two tags to 0. The photos now fade into view when they are born and fade out when they die.

**TIP** ▶ You can also Control-click (or right-click) an opacity tag and change its value by sampling from the pop-up grayscale chart.

A key aspect of particle systems is their ability to introduce particle variations, or randomness, to create a more natural, organic look. If you inspect the parameters in the Cell Controls section of the Emitter tab, you will see that many include a randomness parameter. For example, below Birth Rate is Birth Rate Randomness, below Life is Life Randomness, and so on. These randomness parameters are the keys to a more natural-looking particle system.

**12** Change Speed Randomness to 500, Angle Randomness to 90, Spin Randomness to 60, and Scale Randomness to 50. These values are added to and subtracted from to each parameter above to create a range of values. For example, the speed of each particle will vary between 500 and 1,500 pixels per second.

Each photo now has a different speed, angle, spin rate, and scale, which makes your composition more interesting. If you don't like the type of randomness or you are seeing too many repeating images, you can adjust the randomness using the Random Seed parameter. Because you have a total of 48 images to choose from and are seeing only about five onscreen at any one time, you should be able to avoid duplicates.

**13** At the bottom of the Emitter tab, click the Random Seed's Generate button repeatedly to change the particle pattern until you find one you like.

> **TIP** ▶ The number next to the Generate button lets you re-create the same randomness in different copies of the project: If you or someone else creates the same project with the same settings and enters the same random number, he or she will get an identical particle pattern.

Some of the photos are in black and white and some are in color. You can make them all black and white using a filter, and then tint them using the emitter's Color Mode parameter.

**14** In the Layers tab, select the original source layer, *vid_pix_[###].tiff*; then click the Add Filter icon in the Toolbar and choose Color Correction > Desaturate.

Effects applied to the source layer in the particle system are passed through to the particles—a powerful feature.

**15** Reselect the *Emitter* layer, and in the Emitter tab, from the Color Mode pop-up menu, choose Colorize. Use the eyedropper to sample the orange background color in the Canvas. The particles are shaded with the selected color.

**16** Experiment further by dramatically increasing the emitter shape's Width and Height settings and adjusting the other parameters. Save your work.

## Adding Cells

A particle emitter can have multiple cells, and each cell can be adjusted independently of the others, allowing you to create complex particle systems. You will add a cell to this particle emitter so that it also creates particles for the years the band was together. The first step is to add the new particle source to the project.

**1** In the File Browser, navigate to Motion4_Book_Files > Media > Rockumentary-behaviors. Click the List View button. With the project still playing, select and import the [####].psd:1984-1992 file into the Opening Animation group.

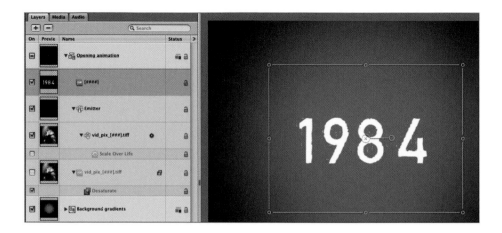

This file is another image sequence, in which the original filenames of each image are the years 1984 to 1992, so they've been interpreted by Motion as four-digit sequential file numbering and are therefore collapsed to #### in the image sequence filename.

One way to create a new cell in the current emitter from this layer is to drag it to the emitter.

2   In the Layers tab, rename the *[####]* layer to *Years*, deselect its activation checkbox, and drag it to the *Emitter* layer.

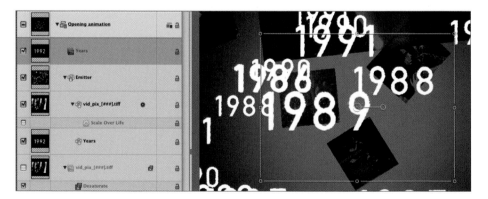

A new cell appears below the emitter, and the Canvas fills with animated dates. When you add a new cell in this manner, the cell starts with the default cell settings. Rather than customize this cell from scratch, let's duplicate the existing, customized cell and replace the source.

**3**   Press Command-Z to remove the cell you just created. Select the vid_pix_[###].tiff cell and press Command-D to duplicate it.

**4**   Drag the *Years* layer on top of the new *vid_pix_[###].tiff copy* cell layer. Wait for the hooked arrow icon before you release the mouse button. The year images now animate in exactly the same pattern as the photos, so a year image appears on top of every photo. It's not quite what we want, but it's close.

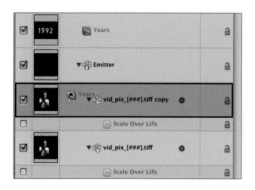

**5**   Press F4 to open the Particle Cell tab, and click the Generate button. The year images now mix nicely with the photos. But they could use a little more tweaking.

**6**   In the Emitter tab, use the Cell Controls to increase the scale, modify the color, and adjust the other settings of the particle cell to your liking.

**NOTE** ▶ If you select the Emitter tab, you will find that the Cell Controls are no longer available in that tab because you have more than one cell in the emitter.

**7** Stop playback and save your work.

## Using Emitters from the Library

The Motion Library includes a large, varied set of particle emitter presets. Now that you know more about how particle emitters work, it will be easier for you to modify the presets to suit your projects. Let's look through the presets, apply one, and modify it.

**1** Choose File > New, select the DVCPRO HD 720p24 preset, and click OK. You will experiment with particle emitters in a new project.

**NOTE** ▶ The other project is still open and can be selected from the Window menu.

**2** Press Command-2 to open the Library, and choose Particle Emitters. There are over 200 particle presets organized into eight categories.

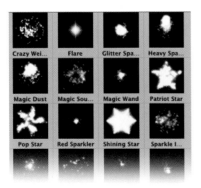

**3** Choose the Sparkles category, and make sure that the Icon View button is selected. There are 24 types of sparkle emitters.

**4**   Select the Magic Wand preset, and drag around in the Preview area.

The emitter follows your pointer movements, providing a preview of how it will look if animated. Let's try animating it.

**5**   Click Apply to bring the emitter into the Canvas, and start playback.

**6**   In the Toolbar, click the Add Behavior icon, and choose Basic Motion > Motion Path.

**7**   In the Canvas, drag the control points to reposition them. Double-click the red motion path line to add control points. Drag the points to adjust the Bezier handles and create a curving, overlapping path.

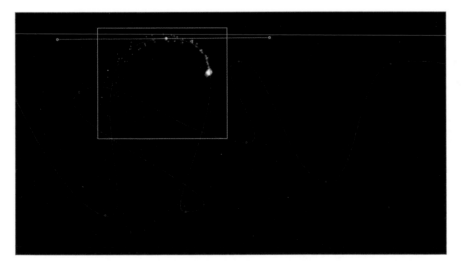

**8**   Press F5 to open the Project pane. This preset emitter contains two cells: one for the central flare and one for the stream of sparks. Because the emitter is moving so quickly, there don't seem to be many sparks.

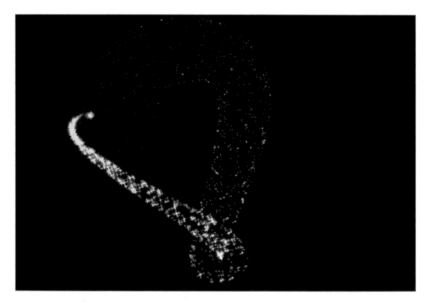

**9** Select the *Spark06* cell layer, and press F4 to open the Particle Cell tab. Increase Birth Rate to around 250 to create many more particles, and then increase Life to around 5 seconds to create a longer trail.

When you combine behaviors and filters with particles, the creative possibilities are almost infinite.

**10** Select and delete the group to start over. Browse, apply, and adjust some of the other particle presets. If you make something you like, drag it to the Favorites folder in the Library to make the customized preset available in future projects.

**11** In the Library, choose the Content folder, and then choose the Particle Images folder. This folder contains hundreds of images and movies that you can use to make particles for your projects.

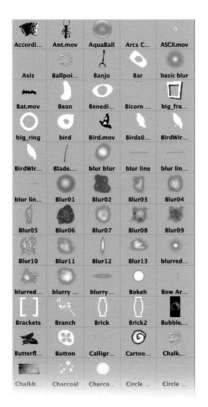

**12** Select a particle image. Add it to your project, and make a particle system out of it by clicking the Make Particles icon in the Toolbar or pressing E. Experiment with changing the parameters.

You should now understand the basics of particle systems. You can use this knowledge to modify a preset emitter to fit your project or to create your own particle emitter from scratch.

## Replicating Elements

The replicator creates patterns from copies of a source object. The structure of a replicator is very similar to that of a particle emitter. Unlike a particle emitter, however, a replicator creates a fixed number of copies in a static pattern. You can animate a replicator using keyframes, behaviors, and a dedicated behavior called the Sequence Replicator behavior.

In this exercise, we'll return to the ACB Financial promo project to create an alternative background design based on replicators.

1   Close any open projects, open Motion4_Book_Files > Lessons > Lesson_10 > Replicators_Start, and save it to the Student_Saves folder. Press F5 to open the Project pane, press Shift-Z to fit the Canvas to the window, and play the play range.

The animated circles are gone, the light streaks are gone, the video no longer shrinks and grows at the edit point, and there is a new empty *Replicators* group. Otherwise, the project is the same as the one you worked with in an earlier lesson. You will start designing a background by replicating the first video clip to create a pattern to animate.

2   Stop playback and move the playhead to 1:00. This is the frame where the circle mask on the video stops scaling down. It's a good place to bring on the replicated images.

3   Select the *Video* group, and in the Toolbar, click the Replicate icon, or press L.

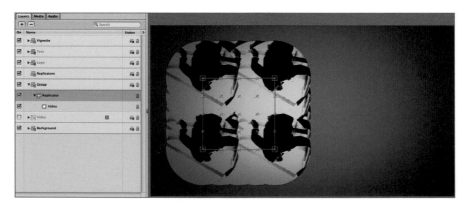

As with a particle emitter, several things happen at once. In the Layers tab, the *Video* group (the source for the replicator) is deactivated. A new *Replicator* layer appears above the *Video* group in its own new group, and below the replicator, the replicator cell appears with the same name as the source object, *Video*. In the Toolbar, the Adjust Item tool is selected, and a replicator bounding box appears in the Canvas. By default, the replicator creates 25 copies of the source object in the Canvas, in a five-by-five grid.

4    In the HUD, decrease Columns to 3 and Rows to 2, and drag a corner of the replicator bounding box to spread out the copies.

**NOTE ▶** This replicator bounding box is available only when the Adjust Item tool—also called the Replicator tool—is chosen.

Let's build on the circle theme of this project by changing the replicator shape.

5    In the HUD, from the Shape pop-up menu, choose Circle. From the Arrangement pop-up menu, choose Outline, and set Points to 8.

That's about all you can adjust in the HUD, so let's get busy in the Inspector.

6   Press F4 to open the Replicator tab. Many of these parameters are similar to ones you used with particle emitters.

**7** Set Radius to 250 and Scale to 52%, and then in the Layers tab, select the *Video* group's activation checkbox to turn it back on.

In this case, you want to see the original source object. With the pattern in place, you will use the behavior designed just for replicators to animate the pattern onto the screen.

**8** In the Toolbar, click the Add Behavior icon, and choose Replicator > Sequence Replicator.

If you recall the Sequence Text behavior from the last lesson, this behavior is very similar: It creates animation that *sequences* through each of the copies in the pattern. By default, it is applied to the full duration of the replicator, so you need to trim it.

**9** Press Command–Option–Right Arrow to move the playhead to the marker at 2:02 (indicated by a faint vertical line on the behavior bar in the mini-Timeline), and press O to trim the behavior's Out point to the playhead. Press Command-Option-O to set a play range Out point at the same frame, and start playback.

The replicated pattern will animate onscreen from 1:00 to 2:02, ending at the point where the video freezes. Just as with the Sequence Text behavior, you must choose the parameter (or parameters) you want to animate.

**10** In the Behaviors tab of the Inspector (which opened automatically when you added the behavior), from the Parameter's Add pop-up menu, choose Scale.

**11** In the Scale parameter that appears, change the value to 0, change the Sequencing parameter to From, and increase Spread to 3.

**12** From the Add pop-up menu, choose Rotation, and set the Rotation value to -180.

The copies now scale up and spin into place, one after the other. You can take the animation a little further by keyframing a couple of the replicator's parameters.

**13** Stop playback. Press Shift-O to move the playhead to the behavior's Out point. In the Replicator tab, Option-click the animation menus for Radius and Offset to set keyframes.

| Parameter | Value |
|---|---|
| Shape | Circle |
| Arrangement | Outline |
| Radius | 250 |
| Points | 8 |
| Offset | 0% |
| Build Style | Clockwise |

**14** Press Shift-I to move the playhead to the behavior's In point, and Option-click the Radius and Offset parameters once again to set keyframes. Change Radius to 0 and Offset to -30%, and then resume playback.

The copies scale up from the center of the circle. It would look better if they were behind the original video.

**15** In the Layers tab, drag the *Replicator* layer into the *Replicators* group, and delete the empty group. Select the *Replicators* group, and choose Object > Send Backward, or press Command-[ (left bracket), to move the *Replicator* group below the *Video* group. The replicated pattern now emerges from behind the original video. Save your work.

## Modifying Replicator Presets

As with particle emitters, Motion includes a large variety of preset replicators that you can use "out of the box" or modify to your heart's content. You will modify a preset replicator to create a background to frame the first text layer in the project.

**1** Stop playback. Move the playhead to the marker at 2:02, and press Command-Option-I to set a play range In point. Move the playhead to the next marker at 3:23, press Command-Option-O to set a play range Out point, and resume playback.

In this section of the project, the first text message animates onscreen. A subtle animated background could give the text more focus and weight.

**2** Press Command-2 to open the Library, and choose Replicators. You will find over 200 presets organized into categories based on their potential uses.

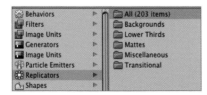

**3**  Choose the Lower Thirds folder and preview several of the presets.

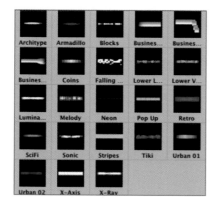

Because most of these presets were created with a replicator and animated with the Sequence Replicator behavior, it is easy to modify them and make them look quite different.

**4**  With the project still playing, locate the Lower Lounge preset and drag it into the *Replicators* group.

**5**  Select the *Lower Lounge* replicator layer, and in the Canvas, drag the layer to position it under the text.

The pattern is too wide, and the rounded squares don't work well with the circle theme you've established. This replicator uses the deactivated *Shape* layer in the *Replicators* group as its source, but you can replace that with a circle shape you already have in the project.

**6**  Open the *Lower Lounge* replicator layer to reveal the cell and behaviors below.

**7**  Open the *Logo* group. Drag the *Circle* layer onto the *Shape* cell layer below the *Lower Lounge* replicator layer. Wait for the hooked arrow icon to appear, and release the mouse button.

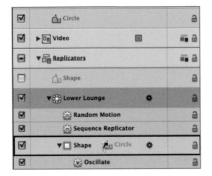

The circle shape replaces the rounded rectangle shape as the source of the replicator, so undulating circles now dance slowly behind the text. But they exist from the start of the project, don't animate on, and are too intense, which distracts from the text.

8  Stop playback. Press Shift-Home to move the playhead to the play range In point, select the Lower Lounge replicator layer, and press I to trim its In point to the playhead. Now move the playhead to a point where the text is visible.

9  To choose the Adjust Item tool, Control-click the replicator in the Canvas, and from the shortcut menu, choose Replicator. Resize and reposition the layer to fit behind the text, and then press Shift-S to return to the Select/Transform tool.

10 In the HUD, decrease Opacity to about 31%.

11 In the Layers tab, select the Sequence Replicator behavior below the Lower Lounge replicator, and in the mini-Timeline, move the playhead to 2:17. Press O to trim the behavior to a duration of 15 frames, and resume playback.

This behavior was used to animate the opacity of the copies, but you will repurpose it to animate the pattern onto the screen.

12 In the Behaviors tab, in the Sequence Replicator section, change Loops to 1, Scale to 0, and Spread to 4.

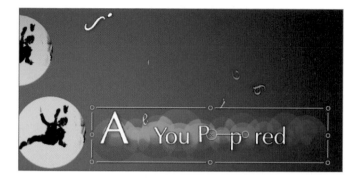

That looks good. Now you will animate the pattern off the screen using a copy of this behavior.

**13** Stop playback. Move the playhead to the point where the text has completely left the screen at 4:14, and set a play range Out point. Press Command-D to duplicate the Sequence Replicator behavior. Choose Mark > Move Selected Out Point to move the copy's Out point to the playhead. Rename the original behavior to *Animate On*, and rename the copy to *Animate Off*. Resume playback.

**14** In the Behaviors tab, in the Animate Off section, change Sequencing To and Opacity to 0; and from the Remove pop-up menu, choose Scale to remove that parameter.

Rather than animating scale to shrink the circles, let's have them follow the letters as they fly off the screen.

**15** From the Add pop-up menu, choose Position. Set the X-position to 1000 and the Y-position to 500; then save your work. The copies now fly up and to the right, following the characters off the screen.

You have worked with both particle emitters and replicators in this lesson, building each from scratch and modifying presets from the Library. You now have the know-how to leverage the incredible arsenal of presets in the Motion Library, or to build your own custom particle emitters and replicators for your next project.

## Lesson Review

1.  Name the two particle system components that appear in the Layers tab when you make a particle emitter.

2.  You've created particles from a leaf graphic you found in the Library, and made those particles spin by increasing the Spin value in the Emitter tab. But you now want each of them to spin at different rates. Which Emitter tab parameter do you adjust to do this?

3.  How do you change particles' size during their lifespan?

4.  Your particles appear at random locations on the screen, but you'd like to change those random locations. What button can you click to create a different random pattern?

5.  What's the primary difference between a particle emitter and a replicator?

6.  How can you animate a replicator's elements so that they fade onto the screen, one after the other?

7.  Name three shapes that can be chosen from the Shape parameter pop-up menu for a particle emitter or a replicator.

8.  True or false: You can use a QuickTime movie as the source for a particle emitter, but you can't use it as a replicator source.

### Answers

1.  The emitter and the cell.

2.  The Spin Randomness parameter.

3.  Apply the Scale Over Life behavior to the particles' cell.

4.  The Generate button for the Random Seed parameter.

5. A particle emitter creates a continuous stream of particles that are born, stay onscreen for some time, and then die. A replicator creates a fixed number of elements in a static pattern.

6. Use the Sequence Replicator behavior, add the Opacity parameter, set the parameter to 0, and set Sequencing to From.

7. Line, Rectangle, Circle, Burst, Spiral, Wave, Geometry, and Image. Particle emitters can also have a Point shape.

8. False. You can use images, image sequences, movies, or many of Motion's objects (text, generators, shapes) as sources for both emitters and replicators.

## Keyboard Shortcuts

| | |
|---|---|
| **E** | Create a particle emitter |
| **L** | Create a replicator |
| **Shift-End** | Move the playhead to the play range Out point |
| **Shift-Home** | Move the playhead to the play range In point |
| **Shift-V** | Show the full view area |

# 11

| | |
|---|---|
| **Lesson Files** | Motion4_Book_Files > Lessons > Lesson_11 |
| **Media** | Motion4_Book_Files > Media > Rockumentary-behaviors |
| **Time** | This lesson takes approximately 45 minutes to complete. |
| **Goals** | Work with audio in the Project pane, Audio Editor, and Timeline |
| | Create project and layer markers |
| | Use keyframes and behaviors to automate audio levels |
| | Edit to the beat of an audio track |
| | Sync animation to audio with the Audio Parameter behavior |

# Using Audio

Audio doesn't get the respect it deserves. Good-quality audio, used creatively, can make a decent motion graphics spot spectacular. On the other hand, low-quality audio—or audio that's poorly selected, edited, or mixed—can kill a good animation.

With more and more media being watched on portable devices and heard through tiny speakers, it's more important than ever to make your audio stand out.

In Motion, you have a host of tools for importing, mixing, and automating your audio—and for tightly integrating it with your motion graphics.

In this lesson, you will assemble the final Rockumentary DVD Menu project and use a music track to time your edits and create animation. You will explore Motion's audio interface, you will use markers to identify edit points, and you will set keyframes and use behaviors to change audio levels over time. You'll finish by working with Motion's powerful Audio Parameter behavior.

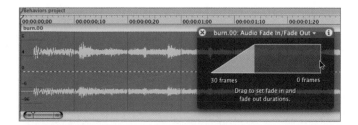

# Importing Audio

You can import audio into Motion just as you would a video clip or image; and if the audio file has multiple channels, you have the option of importing those channels separately or mixed down to a single track. To see and adjust the audio, you use the Audio tab.

**1** Navigate to Motion4_Book_Files > Lessons > Lesson_11, open *Rockumentary_Audio_ start*, choose File > Save As, and save the project to the Lesson_11 > Student_Saves folder.

**2** Press F5 to open the Project pane. The project currently has no content.

**3** Choose Edit > Project Properties or press Command-J.

The project settings are those required for a standard definition DVD menu: 720 x 480 with an NTSC D1/DV pixel aspect ratio. The duration is 37;14, just long enough for the audio that we'll add momentarily. Background Color is set to black, the default, but the Background setting has been changed to Solid to ensure that any transparency in the final DVD menu appears with a black background.

**4** Press OK to close the Project Properties window. Let's start building the project by importing the audio track.

**5** In the File Browser, navigate to Motion4_Book_Files > Media > Rockumentary and select **burn.00.aif**. The audio file plays, and in the Preview area you can see that its duration of 37.5 seconds matches the project's duration. You can also see that this file is a multichannel audio file.

6   Drag the file to the Canvas, and wait for the drop menu to appear before releasing the mouse button. You have the option to mix the file down to a two-channel stereo track or to import all the tracks individually.

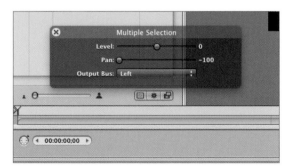

7   Choose Import All Tracks. A green indented bar appears in the mini-Timeline, and the HUD indicates that multiple objects are selected. However, the Layers tab is still empty because in the Project pane, audio tracks appear in their own Audio tab.

8   Click the Audio tab to open it or press Command-6.

**NOTE ▶** To see all the columns, you may need to increase the Project pane's width by dragging out the middle of the separator bar.

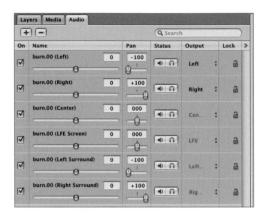

The audio file is a 5.1 surround sound file. In the Audio tab, you can view and modify the six individual tracks of the file, and the level, pan, and output channels. If your hardware does not support 5.1 surround sound, all outputs except Left and Right will be dimmed and will not be played.

**TIP** You can send your audio files from Motion to Soundtrack Pro to add effects or repair problems. Control-click (or right-click) the audio track and choose Send to Soundtrack Pro. The Motion project automatically updates with the changes you make in Soundtrack Pro.

The Audio tab is great for listening to and adjusting the mix of multiple tracks. For this project, a two-channel stereo mix in a single file is all you need. It will also make the audio easier to manage.

9   Shift-click the first and last audio tracks to select them all, and press Delete to delete them.

10  In the File Browser, click the Import button. The file now appears in the Audio tab as a single stereo track.

**11** In the transport controls at the bottom of the Canvas, make sure the Play/Mute Audio button is turned on, and play the project to hear the audio. This is the same audio from the final Rockumentary QuickTime movie that you watched in an earlier lesson.

**12** Stop playback, press Home, and save the project.

## Setting Markers and Keyframes in the Audio Editor

While the Audio tab is a good place to change the mix of multiple tracks, to work on an individual audio track, the Audio Editor is more useful. The Audio Editor displays a selected audio track and plays it *independently* of the project, with its own playhead. You won't hear other tracks or see any video play. In this exercise, you will use the Audio Editor to set a marker for the DVD menu's loop point, and then keyframe the volume of the audio to fade up at the beginning of the track.

**1** With the burn.00 track still selected, press F5 to close the Project pane, press F6 to open the Timing pane, and click the Audio Editor tab. You also can press Command-9 to open the Audio Editor.

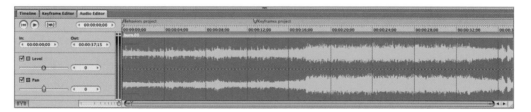

In addition to the Level and Pan controls that were available in the Audio tab, the Audio Editor displays a waveform for the track to help you spot changes in the audio level.

Two *project markers* are visible above the ruler area. Markers are a great way to flag and locate individual frames or a range of frames in a project, a layer, or a group. They're particularly useful when you want to add a layer, record a keyframe, or synchronize an action across multiple layers at a specific point in time. Markers can also be used to send information to other Final Cut Studio applications. You can create markers in the Timeline, Keyframe Editor, or the Audio Editor.

**2** In the Audio Editor, click the Play button in the Audio Editor to play the track. Stop the playhead where the music really kicks in at about 17;20, and then hold down the mouse button on the playhead and scrub back and forth a few frames. When you scrub the playhead in the Audio Editor, the audio at that frame repeats, so you can locate a specific musical change, such as a cymbal crash, bass note, drum hit, or guitar chord.

You've just located the frame where the DVD menu finishes animating together, and the highlights should appear to identify the selections that can be made by the viewer. It is also the frame from which the menu will repeat when it reaches its end. In other words, it is the *loop point* for the DVD menu. Motion uses a special marker to identify a loop point.

3   Press M to add a project marker at the playhead, and then double-click the marker to open the Edit Marker dialog.

> **NOTE ▸** Because the Audio Editor is independent of the project Timeline, markers work a little differently here. In the Timeline (or Keyframe Editor), pressing M adds a marker to the selected layer or group or, if nothing is selected, adds a project marker. Pressing Shift-M creates a project marker in the Timeline (or Keyframe Editor), even when a layer is selected. In the Audio Editor, you can press M to set a project marker. To edit a marker in the Timeline or Keyframe Editor, double-click the marker, or press Command-Option-M. In the Audio Editor, double-click the marker. Finally, if you try to move to a marker in the Audio Editor using the Mark > Go to Previous Marker or Next Marker commands, or the keyboard shortcuts, the Timeline playhead will move to a marker but the Audio Editor playhead, which is independent, will remain stationary.

4   In the Edit Marker dialog, from the Type pop-up menu, choose DVD Menu Loop.

5   Click the Color pop-up menu, and choose a different marker color to set this marker apart from the other markers.

If you import this Motion project into DVD Studio Pro and apply it as a menu, DVD Studio Pro will automatically set a loop point for the menu at the marker. Note that the Name field for the marker is dimmed. You can't change the name of a DVD Menu Loop marker.

**6** Click OK to close the Edit Marker dialog. The new marker appears in the Audio Editor, along with its name.

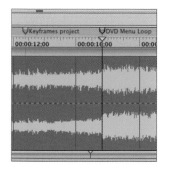

Next, we'll adjust the audio's volume, or level, to start very low and increase over the first second of the project. When you change a video parameter over time, it's called *animation*, but when you change audio over time, it's called *automation*. Whatever you want to call it, Motion offers two approaches for automating audio: keyframes and behaviors. We'll try each one.

The pink and blue dashed lines in the middle of the Audio Editor represent the level and pan settings of the track, respectively. They are flat because neither currently changes. To work on the level, you'll first hide the pan.

**7** Deselect the Pan checkbox.

**8** Adjust the Zoom slider to focus on the beginning of the track, and then move the playhead to 1;00.

**9** Double-click the dashed pink line at the playhead to add a keyframe.

**10** At 0;00, double-click the dashed pink line to add another keyframe, and then drag the keyframe down as far as it will go. Click the Jump to Start button; then click the Play/Pause button. The audio now fades up over the first second.

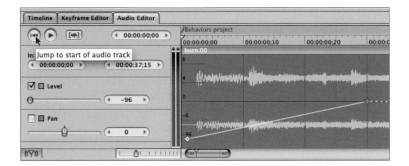

You can accomplish the same result using an Audio behavior.

**11** Press Command-Z three times to delete the keyframes.

**12** In the Toolbar, click the Add Behavior icon and choose Audio > Audio Fade In/Fade Out.

**13** In the HUD, set Fade In to 30 frames and Fade Out to 0 frames. A slanted pink line in the Audio Editor shows the effect of the behavior.

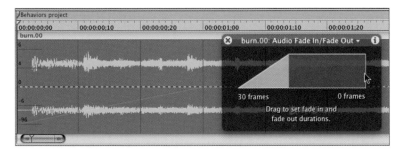

In this example, either method yields the same result. However, if you wanted the audio level to change during the middle of the track, you could use only keyframes.

**14** Save your work.

You are ready to add the video elements and create animation based on the audio track.

## Working with Audio and Video

In earlier lessons, you created the three sections of the Rockumentary DVD menu. In Lesson 2, you composited the menu elements: everything that happens after the loop point. In Lesson 6, you used behaviors to animate the opening dates and pictures in space.

And in Lesson 7, you used keyframes to create the middle section, in which the DVD menu elements animate into position.

Now you will import each of those completed projects as groups, using markers to line them up. Then you will set up your workspace to view the audio and video layers at the same time to help you set markers and edit to the beat of the music.

1   Press Command-7 or click the Timeline tab to select it. The markers are visible in both the Timeline and the Audio Editor.

2   At the bottom left of the Timeline, click the Show/Hide Audio button to display all audio tracks in the project.

Now both audio and video layers are visible in one window. You are going to be importing many layers, so you will need to make some room.

3   Close the *burn.00* layer to hide the behavior applied to it, drag up on the middle of the Timing pane separator bar to make the window much larger, drag down on the separator bar above the audio to make more room for video layers, and then press Shift-Z to fit the Canvas to the smaller window.

4   Near the top of the File Browser and to the left of the Path pop-up menu, click the Back arrow three times to return to the Lesson_11 folder. Select the **A_Behaviors** file, and with the playhead at the start of the project, click the Import button.

This file contains a group of Motion layers that were dragged from a Motion project to the Finder. It comes into this project as a group that ends at the DVD Menu Loop marker.

5   Click in the empty area below the *A_Behaviors* group to deselect it. Then start dragging the **B_Keyframes** project file from the File Browser to the Timeline. While dragging, press the Shift key to snap the In point to the Keyframes project marker.

This group overlaps the *A_Behaviors* group so that the background elements in that group will be visible.

**NOTE** ▶ If the *B_Keyframes* group imports inside the *A_Behaviors* group, undo, press Command-Shift-A to deselect everything, and try again.

6   Choose Edit > Deselect All. In the File Browser, select the **C_Compositing** file, and Shift-drag the group in the Timeline to snap its In point to the DVD Menu Loop marker.

**7**   Play the project.

The music plays, the photos and dates fall back in space, and the DVD menu elements animate into position. However, the photos in the upper right corner of the DVD menu don't change at all. You will address that next, editing them to change based on the beats in the music.

**NOTE ▶** Depending on your hardware, playback may appear jumpy. When audio is enabled in the transport controls, by default Motion skips video frames as necessary to sync the audio with the video and play in real time. If you turn off the audio, Motion will revert to what you are used to seeing: It will play every frame, taking as long as necessary to do so, with the result that the frame rate can vary. You can change this default behavior in the Project section of Motion > Preferences > Project > Playback Control.

## Editing to the Beat

One way to more tightly integrate audio into your project is to time your edits to match audio cues, such as the beats of a music track. Because Motion lets you set markers as the project plays, or "on the fly," you can quickly identify key audio cues for your edit points.

In this exercise, you will set a play range and add markers to the audio layer, tapping out the beats as the music plays. Then you will trim each photo layer to a marker.

**1**   With the playhead placed anywhere to the right of the DVD Menu Loop marker, Control-click in the gray band containing the marker names. From the shortcut menu, choose Previous Marker, and press Command-Option-I to set a play range In point. You will be doing all your editing and animation work in this play range.

**2**   Press Command–Option–Left Arrow to move the playhead to the Keyframes project marker, and then select the *burn.00* audio layer.

**TIP ▶** Press Command–Option–Left Arrow to move the playhead to the previous marker or Command–Option–Right Arrow to move the playhead to the next marker.

You are going to add markers to the audio layer as the project is playing, so it's helpful to have a little "preroll" to get ready to start placing markers right after the DVD Menu Loop marker.

**3**   Start playback. As the playhead hits the DVD Menu Loop marker, start tapping the M key on every other beat to lay down markers on the audio layer.

A few tips:

▶ The music is in 4/4 time, or four beats to a measure. Try to place markers when you hear the drum hit on beats 1 and 3—not on beats 2 and 4.

▶ If you want to start over, choose Mark > Markers > Delete All Markers.

▶ Add markers for the last beats 3 and 4 (with the drum hits).

▶ If the playback is choppy, turn off the *C_Compositing* group.

▶ You should end up with about 19 markers.

▶ Play back the project. If some of your markers are a bit late, simply drag them to the left to more precisely match the beat.

▶ To remove a marker, drag it up off the bar, where it will disappear in a puff of smoke.

You can now trim each photo layer to a marker.

4  Open the *C_Compositing* group. (Turn it back on if you turned it off.)

5  Open the *Menu Graphics and Stills* group.

6  Open the *Stills* group and scroll down so that you can see the bottom layer in the group *vid_pix_001*.

   **NOTE** ▶ Because some layers reference the same media, they may have an additional number in the layer name, such as *vid_pix_001 2*. You can delete or ignore the extra digit.

7  Control-click in the ruler area and choose "Zoom to Play Range."

![Timeline window showing Stills group layers vid_pix_001 through vid_pix_013]

The In point for the *vid_pix_001* layer is already at the first marker on the audio layer.

8   Starting with the *vid_pix_002* layer, move the pointer over the layer's In point, and when the pointer changes to a resize cursor, drag to trim the In point of the layer to the next marker. Hold down the Shift key as you drag to snap to the marker.

9   Continue moving up, adjusting each layer in the group, trimming its In point to the next marker, which will create a stair-step pattern.

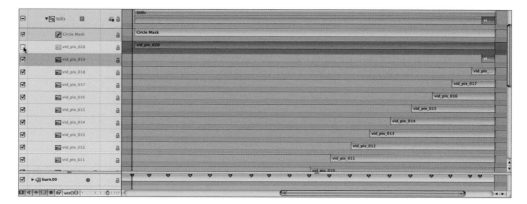

10  Work your way up to the *vid_pix_19* layer. The vid_pix_20 layer is extra, so you can turn it off.

**11**  Close the *Stills* and the *Menu Graphics and Stills* groups. Drag down on the separator bar to reduce the Timeline and enlarge the Canvas; then play the play range. The pictures now change to the beat of the music.

**12**  Save your work.

Great job! For the final task in this lesson, we'll use Motion's powerful Audio Parameter behavior to automatically animate layers to the music.

## Animating with Audio

In addition to *editing* to audio cues, *animating* to audio is a powerful way to combine your audio and video. While you could turn on recording and set keyframes to animate a layer to an audio track, Motion contains a powerful behavior that automates this process. It's called the Audio Parameter behavior, and it lets you animate any keyframeable parameter of any layer, group, or effect based on an audio track. (A keyframeable parameter is one that contains an Animation menu, which appears as a small dash, a hollow diamond, or a solid diamond to the right of the parameter in the Inspector.)

To apply the Audio Parameter behavior, you select a layer and then choose the parameter that you want to animate. For this project, you will animate the scale of the *OnE* layers so that they pulsate to the music.

**1**  In the Timeline, open the *Menu Graphics and Stills* group, then the *Graphics Over 1* group, and select the top *OnE_title copy* layer.

**2**   Press F1 to open the Properties tab of the Inspector. In the Parameter column, Control-click the word "Scale," and choose Audio from the list of Parameter behaviors.

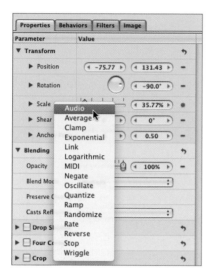

The Behaviors tab comes forward, displaying the parameters for the Audio Parameter behavior. Now you need to tell the behavior what audio track to use for the animation.

**3**   In the Behaviors tab, from the To pop-up menu, choose burn.00.

Motion analyzes the audio, and a bar graph appears in the Audio Graph window. The graph represents the levels of different frequencies of the audio track, from the low frequencies on the left to the high frequencies on the right.

You can use the sliders underneath and to the right of the Audio Graph to limit the animation to a specific frequency and level range—the very loud notes of a low-frequency bass drum, for example.

**4** Drag the sliders to set a range for the middle to lower frequencies at all but the lowest volumes.

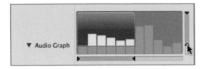

**5** Press the Spacebar to play the project and see the animation.

The *OnE* layer animates, but it gets much too large. To make the animation subtler, you change the Scale parameter—not the scale of the layer, but the Scale parameter for the behavior, which controls how dramatically the parameter you've selected changes as it animates.

**6** In the Behaviors tab, drag in the Scale field to set a value of about 0.05. The layer now pulses nicely to the music, but it appears to animate just a tiny bit late, which is most noticeable on the last two beats.

**TIP** ▶ Hold down the Option key while dragging in a parameter's value field to make finer adjustments.

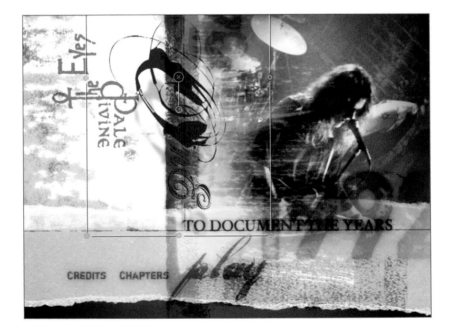

**7**  In the Behaviors tab, set the Delay value to -1. The animation now plays one frame sooner and more closely matches the music.

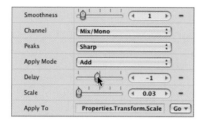

**8**  Experiment using different volume and frequency ranges in the Audio Graph to see how the animation changes. Play with the other parameters as well, such as Smoothness, Peaks, and Apply Mode.

**9**  When you are satisfied with the results, in the Timeline, Option-drag the Audio behavior from the *OnE_title copy* layer to the *OnE_title* layer beneath it so that both layers animate together.

The Audio Parameter behavior is very powerful because it can be applied to any keyframeable parameter of a layer, filter, or behavior.

**10**  At the bottom of the Behaviors tab, click the Go pop-up menu to view a list of all available parameters, and try applying the behavior to a few of them.

**11**  When you have finished experimenting, save your work.

Congratulations—you've learned how to import and work with audio in the Project pane, the Audio Editor, and the Timeline; how to use keyframes and behaviors to automate levels; how to use markers to edit to the beat; and how to use the Audio Parameter behavior to automatically animate a layer to audio. Audio is a crucial component for enhancing motion graphics, and you now have some powerful tools at your disposal for molding it to your needs.

## Lesson Review

1. How can you import a 5.1 surround sound file as six individual tracks?
2. Name three locations in the Motion interface where you can work with audio.
3. What are two ways that you can make the audio level of a track fade in?
4. What is the difference between project markers and layer markers?
5. If you can't remember the keyboard shortcuts to create, edit, jump to, and delete markers, what is the menu containing all these commands?
6. True or false: The Audio Parameter behavior lets you animate any keyframeable parameter of any group, layer, or effect to an audio track's specific frequency range and volume range.

### Answers

1. Drag the file from the File Browser to the Canvas, wait for the drop menu, and choose Import All Tracks.
2. The Audio tab of the Project pane, the Audio Editor in the Timing pane, and the Timeline in the Timing pane.
3. You can either set keyframes in the Audio Editor or use the Audio Fade In/Fade Out behavior.
4. Project markers appear over the ruler area of the Audio Editor and Timeline, while layer markers are applied directly to a selected layer, group, or effect.
5. The Mark menu.
6. True.

### Keyboard Shortcuts

| | |
|---|---|
| **M or ` (grave)** | Add a marker |
| **Command-Option-M** | Edit a marker |
| **Command-6** | Open the Audio tab in the Project pane |
| **Command-9** | Open the Audio Editor in the Timing pane |
| **Command–Option–Left Arrow** | Move the playhead to the previous marker |
| **Command–Option–Right Arrow** | Move the playhead to the next marker |

# Visual Effects Design

# 12

**Lesson Files**     Motion4_Book_Files > Lessons > Lesson_12

**Media**     Motion4_Book_Files > Media > Retiming

**Time**     This lesson takes approximately 30 minutes to complete.

**Goals**     Speed up and slow down a video clip

Apply optical flow frame blending

Use keyframes to create a variable speed ramp

Apply, trim, and combine Retiming behaviors

Use and modify Time filters

# Speed Changes and Optical Flow

It's rare to see a title sequence or an advertisement where the video hasn't been sped up, slowed down, or both: A car races toward the camera and suddenly slows to a crawl as it passes by; a skateboarder flies off the edge of a ramp and freezes at his apex; a new laptop spins around in a blur, slows down suddenly so that it's barely moving, and speeds up again just as suddenly.

These retiming effects can be created "in camera" by shooting at a higher frame rate, or "in post" by manipulating the footage—or some combination of the two.

In Motion, you can change and animate the frame rate of a video clip using either keyframes or behaviors. You can even combine the two methods for the greatest flexibility.

When you slow down a clip, you can control how the slow motion looks by choosing from several frame blending options. One method in particular, called *optical flow*, can create beautiful slow-motion effects previously achievable only with high-speed film cameras.

In this lesson, using a video clip that was shot at a high frame rate to create in-camera slow motion, we'll apply a constant speed change to speed it up and slow it down. You'll also work with the frame blending options, including Optical Flow, to create smooth slow motion.

We'll then vary the speed of the clip over time, creating *ramping* effects—first by using keyframes and then by using retiming behaviors. Finally, Motion's Time filters will be used to create time-based special effects.

## Creating Constant Speed Changes

The simplest way to change the speed of a clip is to apply a constant speed change—for example, slowing a clip down to 50 percent of its original speed or speeding it up to 200 percent. Constant speed changes are great for adjusting a clip's length to fit within a sequence, creating a time-lapse effect, or playing a clip in slow motion.

1   Navigate to Motion4_Book_Files > Lessons > Lesson_12. Open the Retiming_Start project, save it to the Student_Saves folder, and play it.

The project contains one of the surfing clips you've worked with in earlier lessons. It was shot at a high frame rate, probably 60 frames per second (fps), so that when it's played at a standard frame rate (in this case, 23.98 fps), the action appears in slow motion. You can return the clip to normal speed or slow it down further by using the Inspector. Notice that the project duration is longer than the duration of the clip. This extra time will come in handy when you slow down the clip.

2    With the project still playing, select the clip, press F1 to open the Properties tab of the Inspector, and at the bottom of the window, click the disclosure triangle for the Timing section.

In the Timing section, you can control the clip timing. The Speed parameter is currently set to the default value of 100%. Notice that the clip Duration is 8:01.

3    Drag in the Speed value field to change the Speed value to 200%. The clip now plays closer to real time. Notice that the bar in the mini-Timeline has become shorter, and the duration field now reads about 4:01. Because the clip plays twice as fast, it now lasts half as long.

4    Change the Speed value to 50%. The bar in the mini-Timeline now extends past the end of the project, and the project field indicates that the clip lasts about 16:02, or twice as long. The clip plays more slowly, but the motion is not very smooth.

When you slow down a clip, you are extending the existing frames over a longer time period, so frames are repeated. So when a clip is slowed down by 50 percent, every frame is played twice so that half the original frames can be played in the same amount of time. This repeating of frames can create a steplike effect that can be distracting. Motion gives you other options for how it handles clips that play at less than 100 percent speed.

## Using Frame Blending and Optical Flow

You change the way Motion handles clips that have been slowed down with the Frame Blending pop-up menu. By applying Optical Flow, you can turn jerky, steplike slow motion into smooth, fluid slow-motion effects with certain types of footage.

**1** In the Properties tabs Timing section, click the Frame Blending pop-up menu and choose Blending. Rather than repeating each frame, blending creates new frames by combining the original adjacent frames with varying levels of opacity to smooth out the transition from one frame to the next.

**2** Stop playback, and press the Left and Right Arrow keys to step through the clip. Between every original frame you can see a frame that blends the preceding and following frames.

**3** Locate the playhead on a frame in which you can see two blended images. Then, from the Frame Blending pop-up menu, choose Motion-Blur Blending.

Motion-Blur Blending creates blur between frames when a clip's frame rate is higher than the project's frame rate. Since this clip has been slowed down, blending has no impact.

**NOTE** ▶ Motion-Blur Blending is unrelated to Motion Blur, which is chosen in the Render pop-up menu and is adjusted in the Render Settings tab of Project Properties. Motion-Blur Blending creates blur within a video frame, while Motion Blur affects only animated objects.

The remaining Frame Blending option, Optical Flow, needs some time to do its magic because it first analyzes movement from frame to frame in order to generate entirely new frames in real time.

4   From the Frame Blending pop-up menu, choose Optical Flow. Then play the clip. Nothing seems to change, but an animated icon appears near the transport controls. This icon is the *analysis indicator*. It tells you that Motion is determining which pixels are moving from frame to frame.

5   Double-click the analysis indicator. The Background Task List dialog opens and displays the analysis progress. In this dialog, you also can pause and restart the analysis. The process runs as a *background task*, and you can continue to work in Motion while it is performed.

**NOTE** ▶ The more movement in a clip, the longer the analysis will take.

**TIP** ▶ You can batch-process multiple clips. Each clip is analyzed in the order in which it was added to the queue. You can reorder clips by dragging them up and down in the window.

**6** After the analysis is complete, play the project. The clip now plays much more smoothly.

**NOTE ▶** Depending on the source material, you may see artifacts in individual frames where Optical Flow has attempted to interpret the motion. Optical Flow works best on clips with little or no camera movement and a primary subject moving in the scene. A panning camera can create a tearing effect in the background.

When you perform the optical flow analysis, Motion creates a *cache* file that contains information about the clip. Once this cache has been created, you can make as many changes to the speed of the clip as you want, including adding keyframes and behaviors, and the clip never needs to be analyzed again. The cache file is large because it contains information to enable all possible speed changes.

You have some options on how the cache file is handled in Motion's Preferences window.

**7** Choose Motion > Preferences or press Command-, (comma).

**8** Click the Cache icon. In the Optical Flow Retiming section, you can choose a different location in which to store the cache file, and delete the cache file.

**TIP ▶** When your project is complete, consider deleting the cache files to free up disk space.

9    To see how large the cache file is, click the "Reveal in Finder" button, and then select the cache file to view its properties. This cache file is 135 MB.

The cache file includes the optical flow analysis of only the portion of the clip used in the project. The longer the clip's duration and the greater its resolution, the larger the cache file will be. If you are analyzing long HD-resolution clips, make sure you have adequate disk space to store the cache files.

> **TIP** ▶ You can send clips from Final Cut Pro to Motion to apply optical flow frame blending. Any constant or variable speed changes you made in Final Cut Pro and all keyframes will be retained in Motion.

**10** Return to Motion and close the Preferences window.

> **NOTE** ▶ If you extend a clip's In or Out points, Motion will analyze the added media as a background task.

**11** Change the Speed value from 50% to 25%. The clip immediately plays at the new speed with optical flow frame blending applied.

> **TIP** ▶ At the top left of the Canvas, keep an eye on the project's frame rate (displayed only when the project is playing). Optical flow processing during playback is GPU intensive, and you may need to render the clip to play at a full frame rate.

Next, you'll work with ways to change speed over time. Because the optical flow analysis was performed, the results of your changes with optical flow frame blending will be visible immediately. You can return the Frame Blending type to one of the other options at any time. If you later return to Optical Flow, it will read from the existing cache file.

## Creating Speed Ramps with Keyframes

The real fun of retiming clips starts when you change the speed over time. For example, a clip can start in slow motion, suddenly speed up, stop in a freeze frame, and speed up again.

**1** Stop playback and press Home to move the playhead to the start of the project.

**2** In the Properties tab's Timing section, click the Time Remap pop-up menu and choose Variable Speed. A Retime Value field appears with a value of 1. A solid diamond appears in the Animation menu to indicate that a keyframe is located at the playhead.

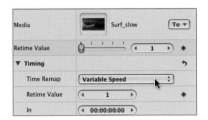

**3**   Next to the current time field, click the watch icon to toggle from timecode to frames. The Retime Value of 1 refers to Frame 1, which is the current playhead location. Working in frames will clarify the relationship between the current time field and the Retime Value field.

**4**   Drag the playhead to another frame, and look at the Retime Value field. No matter where you move the playhead, the frame under the playhead is the same as the frame in the Retime Value field. This indicates that the clip will play at its native speed: At any given frame in the project, the same frame of the video will be seen.

**5**   Press Command-8 to open the Keyframe Editor, and play the project. If necessary, drag the zoom slider to view the full curve in the window.

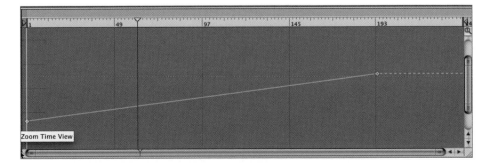

The project plays at 100 percent speed. The curve in the Keyframe Editor contains keyframes at the beginning and end of the clip. The first keyframe tells Motion to play the first frame of the clip at the beginning of the project, and the second keyframe tells Motion to play the last frame of the clip when the playhead reaches the corresponding frame in the Timeline. Between those keyframes, Motion interpolates a straight line, and therefore the project plays at normal speed.

Now that you have a curve, you can manipulate which frames of the video play and at what times. You'll create a freeze frame by adding two keyframes to the curve that have the same value.

**NOTE ▶** At the end of the clip, the last frame repeats as a freeze frame because you previously applied a constant slow-motion speed change and increased the clip duration. Changing to variable speed does not change the overall clip duration.

6   Move the playhead to frame 54, and double-click the keyframe curve directly under the playhead to add a keyframe. This is the frame in which the surfer is at his apex, a good frame to freeze.

7   Move the playhead to frame 90, and double-click to add a keyframe on the curve. Then select the keyframe, and in the Value field, enter *54*. Play the project. Because both of the new keyframes are playing the same frame of the video clip, the curve between them is flat, and the video appears to freeze between them.

The surfer stops and starts again rather suddenly. You can slow him to a stop and speed him up again by changing the interpolation of the keyframes.

8   Control-click (or right-click) the first new keyframe and choose Interpolation > Ease In.

9   Control-click the second keyframe and change its interpolation to Ease Out. The combination of the eased keyframes and optical flow frame blending creates a very smooth freeze-frame effect.

**10** Experiment by dragging the keyframes, adding more keyframes, and applying Bezier interpolation to keyframes to create your own speed ramp effects. Notice that a downward-facing curve means that the video will play backward.

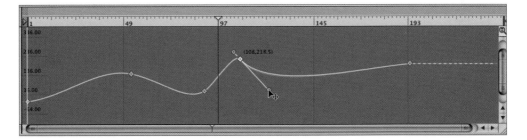

**TIP** ▶ If you just want to change the location of a keyframe without changing its value, drag it in the Timeline instead of dragging it in the Keyframe Editor, where you could accidentally drag it up or down, thereby changing its value. (You may need to click the Show/Hide Keyframes button at the bottom left of the Timeline.)

**11** Stop playback, press F6 to close the Timing pane, and save your work.

Using keyframes to change clip speed lets you precisely control which frame of video plays at any point in time.

## Creating Speed Effects with Retiming Behaviors

If you can animate an element in Motion using keyframes, it's likely that you can also animate it using behaviors. Time remapping is no exception. While keyframes allow great animation precision, Retiming behaviors have their own strengths. They can be added and adjusted quickly; they can be duplicated and stacked; they can be combined with keyframes; and they can create effects that would be difficult or time-consuming using keyframes.

Also, Retiming behaviors will not change those parts of a clip that they are not applied to. If you slow down the first half of a clip with a behavior, the rest of the clip will still play at 100 percent, and the clip will become longer. If you use keyframes to slow down the first half of a clip, the second half will speed up so that the total clip length remains the same.

You will start this exercise by building the same freeze-frame effect using a Retiming behavior. Then you'll modify the behavior, duplicate it, and try a few variations.

**1**   Return the Time Remap parameter to Constant Speed.

**2**   Return the Speed value to 100%.

**3**   In the mini-Timeline, drag the Out point of the clip as far as it will go.

These actions reset the clip to its default settings. However, if you were to return the Time Remap value to Variable Speed, the keyframes you created would still be intact. And the Optical Flow frame blending also would be intact.

Let's create a speed ramp effect using the Set Speed behavior.

**4**   Press Command-2 to open the Library, choose Behaviors, and then choose the Retiming folder.

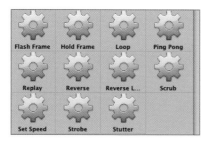

You have 11 Retiming behaviors available. Selecting a behavior displays a sample movie and written description in the Preview area.

5    Move the playhead to frame 54. Let's start the speed ramp at the same point as the freeze frame in the previous exercise.

6    Drag the Set Speed behavior from the Library onto the video clip in the Canvas, and then press I to trim the behavior's In point to the playhead.

7    Move the playhead to frame 90, and press O to trim the Out point. We'll end the speed ramp at the same point the freeze frame ended in the previous exercise.

8    Set the play range In and Out points a little before and after the behavior by dragging the blue arrows in the mini-Timeline, or press Command-Option-I to set the play range In point and Command-Option-O to set the play range Out point.

9    Start playback, and in the HUD drag the Speed slider to 0 to create a freeze-frame effect.

The Ease In Time and Ease Out Time parameters determine how many frames it takes to get from full speed to the Speed value. The curve parameters set acceleration and deceleration over the Time values and work much like the Bezier handles on keyframes.

10    Adjust the Time and Curve values in the HUD as you like.

One of the advantages to Retiming behaviors is that you can change their locations and durations right in the mini-Timeline.

**11**  Try dragging the Set Speed behavior earlier and later in time, and drag the In and/or Out points to change their durations. Adjust the play range as needed.

You can also quickly duplicate, add, and stack Retiming behaviors.

**12**  Press Command-D to duplicate the Set Speed behavior, press Command-7 to open the Timeline, and then reposition and trim each behavior to create two separate speed ramp effects.

Finally, you can combine Retiming behaviors and keyframes.

**13**  Press F1 to open the Properties tab of the Inspector, and in the Timing section, change the Time Remap parameter to Variable Speed. The keyframe curve you previously created is added to the Retiming behaviors (look at the Keyframe Editor to see the curve), and as the clip plays, both keyframes and behaviors manipulate its playback speed.

The other Retiming behaviors in the Library create a variety of time-related effects and can be freely mixed and matched in the Timeline.

**14**  Return the Time Remap parameter to Constant so that the keyframes no longer affect the animation.

**15** At the top of the Toolbar, click the Add Behavior icon and try several of the behaviors in the Retiming group. Trim them, move them, and adjust them in the HUD or the Behaviors tab to understand how they work.

## Using Time Filters

Time filters are designed to create time-based effects that you can use alone or in combination with time remapping and optical flow frame blending.

**1** In the Timing pane, deselect the activation checkboxes to disable all the Retiming behaviors you applied to your clip. It will be easier to see the effects of the Time filters if you use the speed of the original footage.

**2** Press F6 to close the Timing pane.

**3** Press Command-2 to go to the Library, choose Filters, and then choose the Time folder, which contains five Time filters.

**4** Select each filter and watch its preview. Most of the filters work by holding and/or combining frames on top of each other.

**5** Drag the Trails filter to the clip.

**6** In the HUD, increase Duration to .5 and Echoes to 8, and deselect the Decay checkbox.

The filter selects the lighter parts of each frame to create a series of images trailing the surfer. You can combine this effect with Retiming behaviors or keyframes.

**7** Enable the Retiming behaviors.

**8** Adjust the filter and Retiming behaviors as you like.

> **TIP** ▶ You can also keyframe the Trails filter parameters. For example, you could set a Duration of 0 until immediately after a freeze frame, and then increase the value to create a "spray" of copies that shoot out of the freeze frame.

With constant and variable time remapping, frame blending options such as Optical Flow, retiming behaviors, and time-based filters, Motion provides you with a vast arsenal of time-manipulation tools.

## Lesson Review

1. In which tab and section do you change the speed of a clip?
2. Name the two kinds of Time Remap speed changes.
3. Identify three of the four frame blending options.
4. True or false: You can continue working on a Motion project while the optical flow analysis is performed.
5. What does a downward-sloping Retime Value graph indicate?
6. Which Retiming behavior lets you create a speed ramp effect?
7. True or false: Retiming behaviors can be combined with keyframes.
8. Name two of the Time filters.

### Answers

1. The Properties tab of the Inspector in the Timing section.
2. Constant Speed and Variable Speed.
3. None, Blending, Motion-Blur Blending, and Optical Flow.
4. True—it's a background task.
5. The video will play backward.

6. The Set Speed behavior.

7. True.

8. Echo, Scrub, Strobe, Trails, Wide Time.

# 13

| | |
|---|---|
| Lesson Files | Motion4_Book_Files > Lessons > Lesson_13 |
| Media | Motion4_Book_Files > Media > Traitor |
| Time | This lesson takes approximately 60 minutes to complete. |
| Goals | Match project settings to footage |
| | Use shapes and masks to create a wide-screen matte |
| | Use markers to match shots |
| | Stabilize a shot |
| | Match-move one shot to another |
| | Create and animate a Bezier mask |
| | Combine masks |
| | Color-correct one shot to match another |

Lesson **13**

# Stabilizing and Tracking

The proliferation of lightweight handheld video cameras has been a boon to filmmakers, but it also has resulted in countless hours of shaky footage. While avoiding camera shake is best addressed in production—using a tripod or a mobile stabilizing device—you can smooth or eliminate it in Motion with a behavior designed specifically to stabilize camera movement.

Visual effects artists frequently stabilize footage when building a composite image—combining several shots into a single, integrated scene. To combine the shots, they frequently need to match the movement in one shot to the movement in another.

While most editors may not have the time to finesse a final visual effects shot, they can accomplish a lot with temporary effects. For instance, the editor can use a temp effects shot to communicate exact timing to the visual effects department. Further, when rough cuts are created that are good enough for screenings and don't have to involve the effects department, only final effects shots need to be rebuilt—saving countless hours and dollars.

Los Angeles–based editor Billy Fox (*Band of Brothers, Hustle & Flow*) uses all the applications in Final Cut Studio when he edits a film. He edits with Final Cut Pro, creates a temp soundtrack in Soundtrack Pro, and uses Motion to create temporary visual effects that are often so close to the final effects shot that they are used in screenings.

In this lesson, we'll create a visual effects shot using the tools and techniques that Fox used on Overture Films' international thriller *Traitor*, directed by Jeff Nachmanoff and starring Don Cheadle and Guy Pearce.

You'll combine two shots from the film to create the illusion of a car exploding immediately after someone climbs into it. First, the project will be set up and the clips will be synced with markers. Then, one shot will be stabilized and match-moved to a second shot so that both appear to have been captured with the same camera movement. Next, you'll apply and animate an *articulated*, or hand-drawn, mask to reveal just the portion of the clip that is changing. Finally, you will color-correct the shots to match each other.

## Setting Up the Project

We'll build this project from scratch, so the first thing to do is to create a new project. To make sure the settings of your project matches the properties of the video clips, let's inspect the footage.

1   Close any open projects.

2   In the File Browser, navigate to Motion4_Book_Files > Media > Traitor.

3   Select one video clip, check the settings in the Preview area, and then select the other and check its settings.

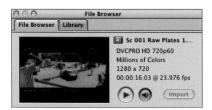

These clips have a resolution of 1280 x 720 pixels and a frame rate of 23.976 frames per second (fps), and are compressed with the DVCPRO HD codec. You will create a new project using these settings.

**4**   Choose File > New. From the Preset pop-up menu, choose the DVCPRO HD 720p24 preset, and click OK.

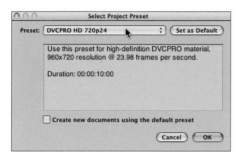

**NOTE** ▶ The frame rate of 23.976 fps is often rounded to 23.98 or 24 fps.

**5**   In the File Browser, double-click the **Sc 001 Raw Plates 1.2a.mov** clip to open it in a separate viewer, and press the Spacebar to play the clip.

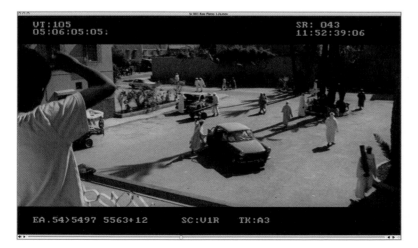

Opening a clip in a separate viewer allows you to see the video at full size and full duration. In this shot, the boy walks to the balcony and waves to his father, who gets into the back of the car.

**6** Press Command-W to close the viewer window. In the File Browser, click the Import button to import the clip and center it in the Canvas; then play the project.

The clip is over 16 seconds long, but the default project duration is just 10 seconds, so you don't see the full clip. Rather than extend the duration of the project, you can move the clip so that the last 10 seconds are visible.

**7** Stop playback, press End to move the playhead to the end of the project, and then choose Mark > Move Selected Out Point, or press Shift-] (right bracket).

The clip now ends at the end of the project. You no longer see the first 6 seconds of the clip, which is fine because we'll only be working on the part of the clip in which you can see the car. Now, import the second clip and use markers to align it with the first clip.

**8** In the File Browser, double-click the **Sc 001 Raw Plates 1.2b.mov** clip to open it in a separate viewer and play the clip. In this shot, the car was removed and replaced by a similar car rigged with explosives that are detonated. You want to match the explosion in the second clip to the first clip so that it occurs right after the man gets in and closes the door.

**9** Press Command-W to close the viewer, press Home to move the playhead back to the start of the project, and then click the Import button to import the **Sc 001 Raw Plates 1.2b.mov** clip.

To use markers to line up the shots, we'll work in the Timeline.

**10** Press F6 to open the Timing pane, and in the Timeline, move the playhead to the frame just before the fireball shoots out of the car door (at 00:21). Press M to add a marker to the layer. You want to match this frame to the frame on the first clip when the man closes the door.

**11** Deselect the activation checkbox for the *Sc 001 Raw Plates 1.2b* layer so that you can see the first clip below.

**12** Select the Sc 001 Raw Plates 1.2a layer, move the playhead to the frame just after the man closes the door (at 03:16), and press M to add a marker to the layer.

Now you're ready to line up the markers and trim the explosion shot.

**13** Drag the upper *Sc 001 Raw Plates 1.2b* layer to the right, holding down the Shift key, until the markers snap to each other. Press I to trim the layer's In point to the playhead, turn the visibility of the layer back on, and play the project. The car now explodes right after the man gets in and closes the door. However, the upper clip ends before the end of the play range.

**14** Stop playback. Press Shift-O to move the playhead to the Out point of the *Sc 001 Raw Plates 1.2b* layer, and then press Command-Option-O to move the play range Out point to the playhead.

**15** Save the project to Lessons > Lesson_13 > Student_Saves.

The shots are nicely edited together, but the numbers on the black bars above and below are distracting. A matte will cover them up.

## Creating a Wide-Screen Matte

As you can see, the aspect ratio of the original film does not match that of the video, which is why black bars appear along the top and bottom of the film frame. The video clips were created by transferring the original film frames to video. The aspect ratio of the project is 16:9, which is the standard HD aspect ratio. In the film world, you would call this ratio 1.78, which is the result of dividing 16 by 9. The aspect ratio of the film is 2.35. The process of placing a shot with one aspect ratio into a frame with a narrower aspect ratio is called *letterboxing*.

The numbers in the black bars represent time codes and key codes of the video transfer and original film frames, and are critical for the editor when matching the video frames back to the film frames. For now, however, they are a distraction. So we'll mask them out using a shape and an inverted mask.

1   Press Home to move the playhead to the start of the project.

2   Press Command-Spacebar, and drag left in the Canvas to create some extra space around the shot. The extra space will make the next steps easier.

3   In the Toolbar, choose the Rectangle tool.

4   In the Canvas, start dragging outside the top left corner of the frame and continue to drag down to the right to draw a rectangle that completely hides the frame.

5   Press the Esc (Escape) key to return to the Select/Transform tool.

6   In the HUD (press F7 if it isn't visible), click the arrow by the Fill color well, and choose a solid black color. To reveal the video underneath this black shape, you can add a mask. But first turn on the Film Zone as a guide.

**7** At the top right of the Canvas, from the View and Overlay pop-up menu, choose Film Zone. Two orange horizontal lines appear in the Canvas, indicating the top and bottom of the film frame.

**8** In the Toolbar, choose the Rectangle Mask tool.

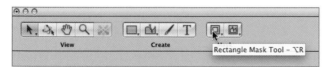

**9** Starting outside the visible frame in the Canvas, draw out a rectangle a little larger than the Film Zone guides. By default, the mask reveals everything inside the rectangle and hides everything outside, but you want to do the opposite.

**10** In the HUD, select the Invert Mask checkbox.

**11** Drag the top and bottom bounding box handles to align the horizontal edges of the mask to the Film Zone guides.

12 Click the View and Overlay pop-up menu and choose Film Zone or press Shift-'
   (apostrophe) to turn off the guides. Then press Command-S to save your work.

Terrific! Your project has the correct settings, the timing of the two shots matches, the play
range covers just the action you are interested in, and you've masked the distracting timecode and keycode elements. You can now match movement in the two shots.

## Stabilizing a Shot

To make these two shots look as if they are really one shot, the framing and camera movement in each shot need to match, especially at the edit point. To accomplish this,
let's first remove all camera movement from the second clip using the Stabilize behavior.

Before stabilizing the shot, however, you should more closely examine the differences between
the two shots. Renaming the clips will make it easier to refer to them going forward.

1 Continuing to work in the Timeline, rename the *Sc 001 Raw Plates 1.2b* layer to *Car
   Explodes*, and the *Sc 001 Raw Plates 1.2a* layer to *Man Gets In Car*. Also rename the
   *Rectangle* layer to *Widescreen Matte* and close the layer.

**2**   Select the Car Explodes layer. Press Shift-I to move the playhead to the layer's In point, and then press the Left Arrow and Right Arrow keys to toggle between the two clips at the edit point.

Ideally, you want a seamless transition between these two frames, but right now there are many differences between them:

▶   The camera is tilted down more in the first shot, so the car is higher in the frame.

▶   The car in the second shot has markings on the roof and hood that are not on the car in the first shot.

▶   The extras and the car in the background are in different locations.

▶   The second shot was made much later in the day, so the colors are different and the shadows have moved.

You won't be able to completely eliminate all these differences, but your goal is to match the shots closely enough so that they don't distract viewers of a rough cut of the movie. To do so, we'll stabilize the explosion shot, match it to the first shot, and then mask it to cut out everything but the exploding car. Stabilizing a shot is a surprisingly simple process.

**3**   Press Command-2 to go to the Library, and select Behaviors, then Motion Tracking. You use the four behaviors in this category to perform a variety of tracking-related operations.

**4**  Drag the Stabilize behavior onto the *Car Explodes* layer.

The behavior has several parameters that you can adjust in the HUD. Since you want to completely remove all camera movement from this shot, you'll leave Method set to Stabilize. You also need to tell the behavior to include Scale and Rotation because the camera may be moving back and forth and tilting.

> **TIP** ▶ Setting Method to Smooth is a great way to reduce shaky moving camera footage, such as when the camera is on a dolly or attached to a car. And with Zoom chosen in the Borders pop-up menu, Motion will automatically scale up the clip as much as necessary so that black borders won't appear in the Canvas.

**5**  In the HUD, click the Scale and Rotation buttons, click the Analyze button, and play the project when the analysis is done.

Motion analyzes the clip and attempts to remove all movement by changing the layer's position, rotation, and scale at every frame to keep the car in the same location. In the Canvas, the bounding box of the layer jumps around, and a jagged red line indicates the motion path of the layer as it moves while the car now appears to stay still. The next step is to match the stabilized car to the movement in the first shot.

## Creating a Match Move

The Match Move behavior is aptly named: It matches the movement of one layer to another. Here, you can match the stabilized exploding car to the car in the first video clip so that it follows the camera movement of the first clip only. To ensure that the match move is applied after the stabilization, you want to place the video layer in a group and apply the match move to the group.

1    Select the *Car Explodes* layer, choose Object > Group, and name the new group *Match Move*.

2    From the Library, drag the Match Move behavior onto the *Match Move* group.

In the HUD, the Source well already contains a layer because Motion has guessed, correctly, that you want to match the movement of this layer to the movement in the layer below it.

In the Canvas, a red circle with a crosshair appears. This is a *tracker*. By default, the behavior will only match the position of the layer, so there is only one tracker. You also want to track the layer's scale and rotation.

3    In the HUD, click Scale and Rotation. A second tracker appears at the far right of the Canvas.

For the match move to work, you use the trackers to identify what Motion should track to match the movement. While the location of the playhead didn't matter for the Stabilize behavior, it's critical for the Match Move behavior because you are placing trackers.

**4** Press Shift-I to move the playhead to the In point of the layer.

**5** Drag the center tracker around the Canvas.

When you click a tracker, Motion shows a zoomed-in view—not of the *Car Explosion* layer that is visible in the Canvas, but of *the layer you are match-moving to*. In this case, the zoomed-in area shows the *Man Gets In Car* layer below the *Car Explosion* layer.

You are matching the second clip to the first clip, so you need to select which part of the first clip to track. That is why you don't see any smoke in the zoomed-in area of the tracker. But what should you select to track? The tracker works best on an area of high contrast that stays in the frame. A good candidate here is the car itself—specifically, the specular highlights above the headlights.

**6**    Drag the center tracker to the bright spot on the right headlight (screen left).

The Inspector provides a close-up view and some additional information.

**7**    Press F2 to open the Behaviors tab of the Inspector, and then drag the second tracker to the highlight on top of the left headlight (screen right).

**8**   In the Behaviors tab, click the disclosure triangles for Anchor and Rotation, and increase the Search Size setting of each to 200%. A larger search size helps ensure that the tracker won't get lost if there is a lot of movement from one frame to the next.

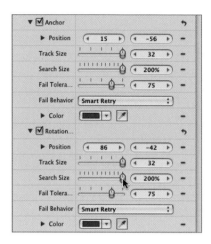

**9**   In the Behaviors tab or in the HUD, click the Analyze button.

**NOTE** ▶ If you want to see the layer being tracked, turn off the visibility of the upper layer. Turn it back on when the analysis completes successfully.

In the Canvas, white dots indicate the path of the trackers over the duration of the clip. In the Timeline, blue keyframe diamonds appear inside the Match Move bar.

**NOTE** ▶ You may need to click the Show/Hide Keyframes button near the bottom left of the Timeline to display the keyframes. You can also see them (and adjust them if necessary) in the Keyframe Editor.

**10** Play the project.

The *Car Explodes* clip now appears to jump all over the place. You removed the original camera movement and have essentially replaced it with the camera movement in the first clip. You can view the layers at the same time to reposition the exploding car over the first car.

**11** Stop playback and select the *Car Explodes* layer. Press Shift-I to move the playhead to the layer's In point. In the HUD, reduce the layer's opacity to about 60%, and then in the Canvas, align it to the car showing through underneath.

> **TIP** ▸ Press N to turn off snapping and make it easier to precisely position the layer. Hold down Command and tap the arrow keys to nudge the layer.

**12** Play the project. The cars in each clip start out aligned and remain aligned during the camera movement.

**13** Return the opacity of the *Car Explodes* layer to 100% and save your work.

The next step is to mask out the nonessential elements from the car explosion shot and animate the mask to change over time.

## Animating a Mask

Because there are so many differences between these two clips, the Bezier Mask tool can be used to create a rough mask around the exploding car so that the final shot uses only the background from the first clip. The mask will need to expand as the car explodes, so you will animate its control points by moving them on certain frames while recording is enabled, which will create keyframes.

When animating a mask, keep a couple of things in mind: First, you want to create as few control points as possible, but still have enough to make the mask as accurate as needed. Remember that the more control points you have, the more time it will take to animate them. Second, you may not need to animate every control point on every frame. You can save time if you animate just the first and last frames, then animate the frame right in the middle of those keyframes, and keep "splitting the difference"—animating the frame in the middle of two existing keyframes—until you are satisfied with the result.

Remember that in this exercise you are just trying to remove distracting elements, not make the perfect final shot.

1   If necessary, select the *Car Explodes* layer, and press Shift-I to move the playhead to the layer's In point.

2   In the Toolbar, choose the Bezier Mask tool.

3   In the Canvas, click around the car to create a mask with seven or eight control points that roughly enclose the car. Place the control points at the front of the car very close to the fender to avoid revealing the shadows in the *Car Explodes* layer.

**NOTE** ▶ As an alternative to using the Bezier Mask tool, you could create the mask with the B-Spline Mask tool, which you access by holding down the mouse button on the Bezier Mask tool and choosing it from the pop-up menu. B-Splines create smooth curves through control points without any Bezier handles to adjust.

**4**    In the HUD, increase the Feather amount to about 30 to blend the shots together. You may need to tighten up the mask by moving a few control points. Don't worry about the difference in asphalt color; we'll work on that later.

**TIP** ▶ Press Command-/ (slash) to turn the Canvas overlays off and on. This will hide the red mask lines and control points so that you can better see the final result.

Use recording to animate the mask.

**5**    Press A to turn on recording, press Shift-O to move the playhead to the layer's Out point, drag the mask to reposition it, and then reposition each control point to encompass the smoke and fire. Adjust the Feather amount as well to get the best blend between the elements.

Because recording is enabled, any changes you make to the mask are recorded as key-frames: not only each control point's position, but also the position, rotation, scale, and feathering of the mask.

**6**   Play the project. The mask expands with the explosion, but not quickly enough.

> **TIP** ▶ You can move the play range In point closer to the start of the second clip to play only the section you are working on.

**7**   Stop playback, and with recording still enabled, move the playhead to the middle of the *Car Explodes* layer and adjust the control points and Feather amount.

**8**   Play the project, and continue to split the difference: Place the playhead midway between two keyframes and adjust the mask as necessary.

A few techniques can speed the adjustment process:

▶   Press Option-Z to view the shot at full resolution (100% scale).

▶   Shift-click multiple control points to select them all and move them at the same time.

▶   Command-drag a control point to change the curve passing through it from linear to Bezier, and then adjust the Bezier handles to expand the mask near the control point.

▶   Click anywhere inside the mask to move the entire mask.

▶   If you find you need more points, double-click a mask line to add a control point. The new point will be added from the beginning of the mask to the end.

Try to get a tight mask animation with no more than six keyframe locations on the Bezier Mask bar in the Timeline, with most of them placed near the beginning of the explosion. Don't worry about including the hood as it flies off the car. Just let it disappear outside the mask.

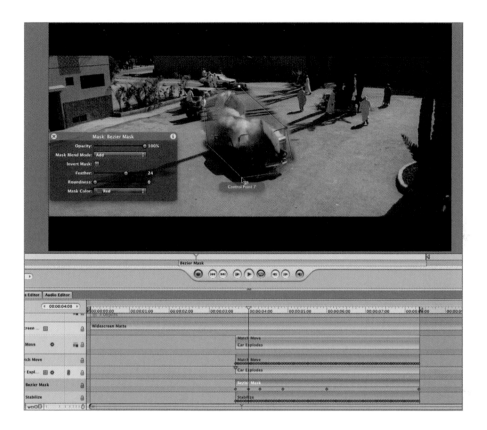

**9**   Press A to turn off recording and save your work.

## Color-Correcting a Shot

You've managed to hide most of the shadows from the second shot, but the change in time of day has also changed the color of the asphalt in the sunlight. You can match the brightness and color levels of the second shot to the first with the judicious application of a few color-correction filters.

The mask is so close to the car on the first frame that it's difficult to compare the shots. You can add another mask and change its blend mode to better compare the shots.

**1**   Select the *Car Explodes* layer, and press Shift-I to move the playhead to the beginning of the layer.

**2**  In the Toolbar, choose the Rectangle Mask tool. Draw a rectangle that covers the car, and then drag it to the right until it covers only half of the car. In the Timeline, rename the *Rectangle Mask* to *Temp Mask*.

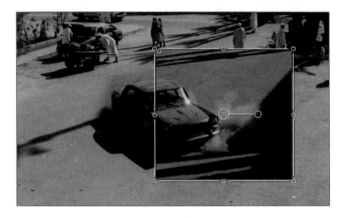

By default, a new mask is added to any existing masks. Here, you want to see the *Car Explodes* layer *only* in this new mask.

**3**  In the HUD, click the Mask Blend Mode pop-up menu and choose Replace. Now you can clearly see the difference in brightness and color of the asphalt and the difference in the brightness of the car. Let's brighten up the explosion layer with the Levels filter.

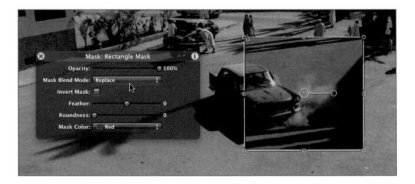

**4**  Select the *Car Explodes* layer, and then, in the Toolbar, click the Add Filter icon and choose Color Correction > Levels.

**NOTE ▸** If you don't select the layer first, the filter will be applied to the Rectangle mask and will have no effect.

**5**    Press F3 to open the Filters tab of the Inspector, and drag the white input triangle to the left until the brightness levels of the two clips match, at about 200.

**NOTE ▶** The Levels filter doesn't have any parameters in the HUD, so you need to adjust it in the Inspector.

**6**    Click the Add Filter icon and choose Color Correction > HSV Adjust.

**7**    In the HUD, adjust the Hue, Saturation, and Value sliders to best match the color between the clips. It's OK if the car color doesn't match perfectly, because you won't see both cars at the same time as you do with the asphalt.

It's a good idea to see if the color correction works over the entire clip.

**8**    In the Timeline, turn off the Temp Mask and scrub through the *Car Explodes* layer. Press Command-/ (slash) to turn the mask off and on. The color should stay consistent. If it didn't, you could turn on recording and keyframe the Levels and HSV Adjust filters to change them over time.

A short fade-in should complete the effect.

**9**   In the Toolbar, click the Add Behavior icon and choose Basic Motion > Fade In. In the HUD, set the Fade In time to 3 frames and the Fade Out time to 0 frames.

**10**   Press F6 to close the Timing pane, and press Option-X to reset the play range. Play the project, make any adjustments you like, and save your work.

Good job. You've created a temporary visual effects shot that's good enough for screening purposes and will give the visual effects department the exact timing information it needs to re-create the shot, saving time and money for everyone.

## Lesson Review

1.   You want to create a hole in a layer to reveal the layers underneath. You add a mask with the Circle Mask tool, but instead of creating a hole in the layer, it restricts the layer's visibility to the area inside the circle. How can you make it do the opposite?

2.   What parameters of a layer can you stabilize using the Stabilize behavior?

3.   When using the Match Move behavior to track the position and rotation of one layer to another, what is the minimum number of trackers you need to place?

4.   You are creating a mask with the Bezier Mask tool. You know that the mask must be animated to change over time. How many control points should you create?

5.   When animating a mask with recording enabled, name two other parameters you can change on the mask in addition to changing the positions of individual control points.

6.   You've applied the Levels filter to a layer but the HUD is empty. Where can you adjust the filter?

7.   The mask outline is making it difficult to see the edge of the layer and how it blends into the layer underneath. How can you hide the outline without deselecting the mask?

### Answers

1.   In the HUD or the Mask tab of the Inspector, select the Invert checkbox.

2.   Position, Rotation, and Scale.

3.   Two.

4.   Create as few control points as possible but enough to create an accurate mask.

5.   You can change any of the mask's Feather amount and its Transform properties, such as Position, Scale, and Rotation, and all will be recorded as keyframes.

6.  You can adjust the filter in the Filters tab of the Inspector.

7.  Choose Show Overlays from either the View and Overlay pop-up menu or from the View menu. Or, press Command-/ (slash) to turn off all the overlays.

**Keyboard Shortcuts**

| | |
|---|---|
| **Option-B** | Choose the Bezier Mask tool |
| **Option-BB** | Choose the B-Spline Mask tool |
| **R** | Choose the Rectangle tool |
| **Option-R** | Choose the Rectangle Mask tool |
| **Command-/** | Turn on and off the visibility of Canvas overlays |

# 14

# Lesson **14**
# Keying

When producers want an actor to hang off the edge of a cliff, blast aliens on a distant planet, or read a book at a Parisian outdoor café, they'll frequently save time and money, and keep everyone safe, by shooting the actor in a studio and then compositing that *foreground plate* onto a scene, the *background plate.*

To make it easier to place subjects into a new background, they are shot against a flat, bright, smooth, and uniformly colored surface, usually green. This color is used, in part, because there is so little of it in skin tones. This primary color can then be removed using a process called *keying.* The result of keying is a *key.* How easy or difficult it is to create a clean key is dependent upon the way the subject was shot: how brightly and evenly the background screen was lit; how far the subject was from that background; what colors the subject was wearing; how much movement and detail were in the shot; and the type of camera, recording media, and compression in use.

In this lesson, you will prepare a background for the composite and then key a green-screen shot with a keying filter. After optimizing the key, you will animate a mask to cut out potential problem areas, and finish by changing the brightness and color of the foreground plate to match the background.

## Preparing the Background Plate

To make the background plate less distracting, we'll delete the audio, choose a section of the video, and then blur it to make it appear out of focus.

1   Close any open projects, and press Command-N to create a new project. Choose the DVCPRO HD 720p24 preset, click OK, and save the project to the Lesson_14 > Student_Saves folder.

> **NOTE** ▸ Make sure that Correct for Aspect Ratio is checked under the View and Overlay pop-up menu.

2   In the File Browser, navigate to Motion4_Book_Files > Media > Keying and select the **public square.mov** file. This video clip is an afternoon shot of an outdoor public square. The DVCPRO HD codec and frame rate match those of the project you just created.

3   Click the Import button to center the clip in the Canvas.

You won't need the audio that is part of this shot, so let's delete it. You will need to first unlink it from the video.

4   Press F5 to open the Project pane, click the Audio tab, and click the link icon to unlink the audio from the video.

> **TIP** ▸ You can also link and unlink audio and video in the Layers tab.

5   Press the Delete key to delete the audio, return to the Layers tab, select the public square layer, press Shift-Z to fit the Canvas to the window, and play the project. The woman crossing the frame in the background might catch the viewer's eye. You'll need to see only a few seconds of this clip, so you can start the clip later.

6   Click in the Canvas to select the layer, and then, in the mini-Timeline, drag the layer bar left to move it back in time -3:15 until the woman has moved to about the center of the frame.

The foreground plate will cover her at this point. However, all the detail in the background can be distracting as well. A blur filter will make the background look out of focus.

7   In the Toolbar, click the Add Filter icon, and choose Blur > Gaussian Blur.

NOTE ▶ Motion also has a Defocus filter, designed to simulate an out-of-focus shot. It's more processor intensive and not necessary for this project.

The default Amount of 4 is fine for now. However, the blur has created a soft black edge around the shot's frame because the filter blurs beyond the boundary of the Canvas and brings in black pixels. Fortunately, there's an easy way to get rid of them.

8   Press F3 to open the Filters tab of the Inspector, and select the Crop checkbox. The filter's effect is now cropped to just the Canvas, and the soft black edge is eliminated.

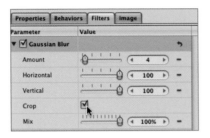

With the background plate prepared, it's time to add the foreground.

9   Press Command-1 to open the File Browser, and select the **turn and look.mov** file. This video clip was shot against a bright green wall in a studio. It was compressed with Apple's ProRes 4444 codec, a different codec than that of the background plate, in order to retain as much detail as possible with a relatively low data rate. It also has a larger frame size than the background clip, which will give you some flexibility for scaling and framing. Fortunately, the frame rate matches the background clip's frame rate.

TIP ▶ You can mix and match codecs and frame sizes in a composition, but it's a good idea to match frame rates if possible to avoid any skipped or repeating frames.

10  Click the Import button to center the clip in the Canvas.

The layer is so large that its bounding box may not be visible in the Canvas. Rather than zooming out on the Canvas to be able to scale the layer with the bounding box, you're going to adjust the layer's scale in the Inspector.

**11**  Press F1 to open the Properties tab of the Inspector, set the scale to 75%, and then, in the Canvas, drag the layer to the left a bit.

Dead-center framing can pull energy out of a shot, so reframing the woman to a side makes the composition a bit more dynamic. Let's set a play range and take a look at the clip.

**12**  Press Shift-O to move the playhead to the layer's Out point, press Command-Option-O to set a play range Out point at the playhead, and play the project.

Now that's you've set everything up, you're ready to remove the greenscreen.

## Keying the Shot

Motion includes several keying filters for compositing a greenscreen or bluescreen shot onto a background. The Primatte RT filter is a good first choice because it combines multiple keying functions into one filter and can work in real time.

Creating a good key is all about sweating the details, so it's a good idea to make sure you are looking at the image at its correct size.

**1**  Press Option-Z to scale the Canvas to 100%. If necessary, press F5 to close the Project pane so that you can see the full Canvas.

2   With the *turn and look* layer still selected, in the Toolbar, click the Add Filter icon, and choose Keying > Primatte RT.

Immediately, the filter knocks out the greenscreen, and the background plate shows through. However, this first-pass key is less than ideal. Before you begin to refine it, it's a good idea to find the most challenging frame.

3   Scrub through the shot to a point where the woman's hair is in the air, at about 0:13. At this frame, you can see how chunky the key is on her hair, and how much green remains.

You'll begin by sampling the greenscreen to tell the filter precisely what color to remove.

**4**   In the HUD (press F7 if it isn't visible), change Output Type to Foreground.

The full foreground plate returns to view. You want to sample a representative color of the greenscreen. It's quite evenly lit, but notice how it gets darker near the right edge. You want to sample close to the subject.

**5**   In the HUD, click the eyedropper icon next to the Backing Color setting to select it, and then click the greenscreen near the woman's right shoulder. Selecting any green pixels close to the subject should work well.

Now you can examine and refine the matte.

**6** From the Output Type pop-up menu, choose Matte.

The matte is a grayscale representation of your key. Areas of white are visible, areas of black are completely transparent, and areas of gray are partially transparent. Ideally, the background is completely black and the subject is completely white up to the edges, which should be smooth, without any stairstepping.

The Noise Removal and Matte Density sliders in the HUD let you refine the matte.

**7** Drag the Noise Removal slider to 0; then drag the Matte Density slider to a point where the interior of the matte is all white and there is good detail in the hair, at about .56.

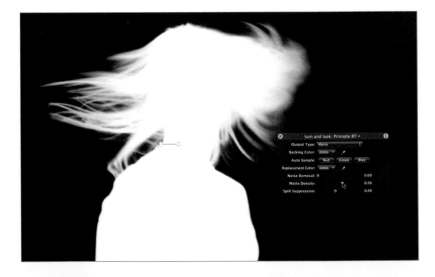

Perfecting the matte has introduced some noise at the edge of the greenscreen—gray speckles indicating that part of the greenscreen will be visible. The far edge doesn't matter because you will mask it off, but a little noise removal will ensure that the greenscreen is completely transparent.

**8**  Adjust the Noise Removal slider to about .02. Too much noise removal begins to contract the matte, so a little is all that is needed.

The next step is to mask off the extraneous parts of the greenscreen. Called a *garbage matte*, this matte is meant to hide mike booms, C-stands, clamps, gaffer's tape, or any other objects that shouldn't be in the shot. By making a tight mask around your subject, you also make the keying process easier, because you don't have to worry about parts of the greenscreen that may not be optimally lit and are more difficult to key. You will use the Bezier Mask tool to create a mask, and then you will animate that mask to move with the subject.

**9**  Move the playhead to the start of the project, from the Toolbar choose the Bezier Mask tool, and use just a few points to draw a rough mask around the subject.

**10** Press A to enable recording. Move the playhead to the frame where the woman's hair is farthest to the left (about 0:10), and adjust the control points to keep all her hair visible.

**TIP** ▶ Command-drag a control point to create a smooth curve through the point, and adjust the curve with the Bezier handles.

**11** Move the playhead to the frame where the woman's hair is farthest to the right (about 0:14), and move the control points as necessary.

**12** Move the playhead to the frame where her hair has settled down (about 0:21), and move the control points to tighten up the mask.

**13** Press the Right and Left Arrow keys to step through the clip frame by frame, adjusting control points as necessary. As you do so, you may notice that the matte has some imperfections that weren't apparent on the frame in which you adjusted the keying filter.

**14** Press A to turn off recording, use the HUD to add some Feather to the mask to create a smoother transition, and move the playhead to 1:21. Here, you can see some gray areas near the sleeve of the woman's shirt that indicate partial transparency.

**15** Press F5 to open the Project pane, and select the Primatte RT filter; in the HUD, decrease Matte Density to 0.53. Save your work.

Excellent. You now have a clean, tight matte on the subject. It's time to check out the final composite and make it match the background.

## Refining the Composite

Making a greenscreen shot appear as if it were really part of a background plate depends on many factors that are outside your control. In particular, if the studio lighting didn't exactly match the outdoor lighting of the background plate, it can be very difficult to pull off a convincing composite. However, if the lighting is fairly even in both shots, you can adjust the foreground's overall brightness and color balance to better match that of the background.

**1** With the Primatte RT filter still selected, use the HUD to change Output Type to Processed Foreground, and move the playhead to a frame where the woman's hair is flying.

There's lots of nice hair detail, but why is it so green? When a subject is shot in front of a greenscreen, the light from the screen bounces back and hits him or her from behind, wrapping around the edges of the subject. You can see this effect not only in her hair, but also along her shoulders and arm. This green fringing is called *spill*, and one way to get rid of it is using a spill suppressor.

2   In the HUD, move the Spill Suppression slider to about 0.58. Don't go too far, or you'll introduce a magenta cast to the image. The spill suppressor takes advantage of your computer's additive RGB color space, in which complementary colors added together create shades of gray. Because the complement of green is magenta, if you add in just the right amount of magenta to green, you completely remove all of the color cast.

The green is gone, but the woman still doesn't look as if she's actually standing in the town square. Part of the reason for this is that the lighting in the sunny outdoor shot doesn't match the studio lighting of the greenscreen shot, which you can't do much about. However, the overall brightness or *luminance* and color balance on the woman don't match those of the background, which you *can* do something about.

**3**    In the Toolbar, click the Add Filter icon, and choose Color Correction > Levels.

**4**    In the Filters tab of the Inspector, drag the middle gray triangle under the Histogram to about 0.71 to darken the midtones of the image.

Adjusting the midtones, or gamma, darkens the overall image without affecting the brightest or darkest areas, and more closely matches the clip's brightness levels to the background. But the subject still appears quite a bit redder than the background. To more precisely examine the differences, you can compare the red, green, and blue values of the background pixels to the foreground pixels.

**5**    Control-click just below the bank of tools at the left side of the Toolbar, and choose Color to display red, green, and blue (RGB) pixel values. Now, as you move the pointer over the Canvas, these values update to reflect the RGB values of the pixel under the pointer.

**6**   Move the pointer over the white umbrellas in the background. The RGB values are all close to the same value of about 200, indicating that the umbrellas are a neutral shade of bright gray with little to no color.

> **NOTE** ▸ The values are displayed based on the bit depth of the project, which is 8-bit, or 255 levels of gray for each channel. A value of 0 means no color in that channel, and a value of 255 means full color for that channel. If you work in a project with a different bit depth (which you can change in Edit > Project Properties), the color values will appear based on a scale of 0 to 1.

**7**   Move the pointer over the lightest area of the woman's shirt. Here, the red values are consistently higher—about 190 or so—while green and blue are about 160. You can use the Levels filter to reduce the red.

**8**   In the Filters tab, from the RGB pop-up menu, choose Red. Any changes you make to the histogram will now affect only the Red channel.

**9**   Drag the white output triangle to the left, going back and forth between the Canvas and the Inspector to check the RGB values in the woman's shirt until they are roughly equal, when the slider is at about 213.

**10** Play the project and save your work.

You've prepared a background shot, keyed a greenscreen shot, and adjusted the luminance and color balance to match the shots together. You now have a solid grounding in the fundamentals of creating a key.

## Lesson Review

1.  How can you stop a blur filter from including pixels outside of the Canvas?
2.  When adding clips to a Motion project, which characteristic of a video clip is best kept consistent between clips: resolution, codec, or frame rate?
3.  Where is the best place to sample a representative greenscreen pixel when using the Primatte RT filter?
4.  You are looking at a keyed shot with Output Type set to Matte. The subject is mostly white, but a few areas of gray are present inside the matte. Which parameter of the Primatte RT filter do you adjust?
5.  You've perfected the matte on your subject, but noise remains near the edges of the matte where the greenscreen lighting was darker. If you adjust the Noise Removal amount, it adversely affects your subject's matte. What approach can you use to remove the noise?
6.  Your key looks great, but a green halo appears around your subject. How can you neutralize it using the Primatte RT filter?
7.  How can you check the actual RGB values of an area that should be white in the background plate and compare it with the foreground plate?
8.  Identify one filter that you can use to adjust luminance and color balance separately.

### Answers

1.  Select the Crop checkbox in the Filters tab of the Inspector.
2.  Using clips with the same frame rate (that also match the project frame rate) will ensure that no frames are skipped or repeated.
3.  Sample somewhere close to the subject being keyed, particularly near areas of detail like hair.

4. The Matte Density parameter.

5. Create a garbage matte to mask off the noise, and animate it as necessary.

6. Increase the Spill Suppression setting to add enough magenta to cancel out the green.

7. Turn on the Color indicators in the Toolbar, and move the pointer over pixels in the image.

8. The Levels filter lets you adjust the overall RGB brightness values, and also select and adjust the individual red, green, and blue channels.

# An Introduction to 3D

# 15

## Lesson 15
# Building a 3D Scene

We live in a three-dimensional world, but Motion's world takes place on a flat, two-dimensional computer screen.

Yet even on this flat screen, Motion lets you create a virtual 3D world in which you can move and rotate layers in three-dimensional space and use cameras to look at the world. You can even step away from the camera to look at scenes from multiple angles.

You can create a world filled with layers of text, video, and animated graphics, and animate a camera to fly through the world, stopping to look at anything you wish.

In this lesson, you will learn the basics of manipulating layers and groups in 3D space, how to add a camera, and how to use the various 3D controls as you arrange scenes in 3D space.

## Making 3D Transformations in the Canvas

At its most basic, working in 3D means that you can change the position and rotation of layers along three axes: the horizontal, or x-axis; the vertical, or y-axis; and the depth, or z-axis, which points straight out of your computer screen. You can transform layers using the Inspector or the HUD, or do so directly in the Canvas. You will use all these tools to arrange each layer of a group so that they form a "set." As on a Hollywood film set, the performers—Motion's layers—can be arranged on your 3D stage.

**1** In the File Browser, navigate to Lessons > Lesson_15, double-click the Top Surfers 3D Start project to open it, and press F5 to open the Project pane.

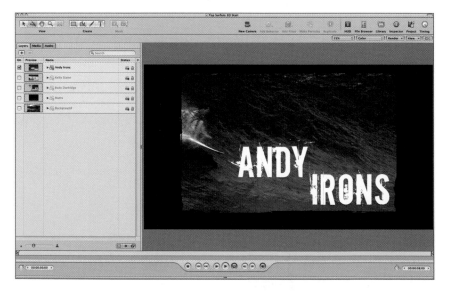

This project contains several layers organized into groups. It is similar to projects you worked with in earlier lessons but has some important differences that make it more effective for setup as a 3D scene. To see all the layers in the Layers tab without scrolling, you can resize the layers.

**2**    In the Layers tab, drag up between any two layers or groups to shrink the size of each layer, and then open all the groups and layers to inspect the project's structure.

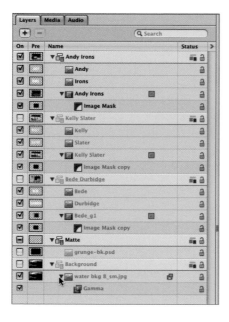

In previous projects, the title graphics were organized into one group, and all the video layers were in another group.

In this project, we'll find a group for each surfer that contains the title graphics and video for that surfer. This arrangement allows you to treat each video/text combination as a "set" made up of layers that you can move and rotate individually, and then move and rotate together by transforming the group that contains them.

The *Kelly Slater* and *Bede Durbidge* groups are turned off, so you see only the *Andy Irons* group in the Canvas.

Each surfing video has an image mask applied, and all three image masks are using the same source to create the mask: the *grunge-bk.psd* layer in the *Matte* group.

The last group contains the background graphic and is also currently turned off so that you can focus on the surfer groups.

**3**    Press F6 to open the Timing pane, and in the Timeline, open each of the surfer groups. At the top middle of the Timing pane, drag up on the resizing bar until you can see all the layers of these three groups.

**NOTE** ▶ If you can't see the ends of all the layer bars, drag the resize slider at the lower left of the Timeline.

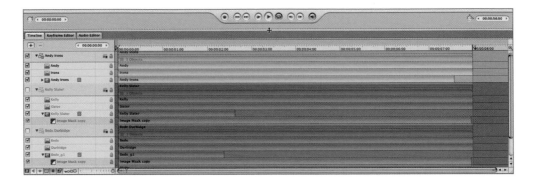

In previous projects, the surfer video and title graphic layers were trimmed to start and end at different points in time; here, the graphics last for the full project, and each video has its own fixed length. However, all layers start on the first frame of the project. This setup will come in handy when you arrange the layers and groups in 3D space, because you'll be able to see them all without moving the playhead.

4 Press F6 to close the Timing pane, and then save the project to the Lesson_15 > Student_Saves folder.

Now that you understand the structure of the project, you can create depth in the scene by moving and rotating the layers in 3D space.

5 In the *Andy Irons* group, select the *Andy* graphic layer, press F1 to open the Properties tab of the Inspector, and click the disclosure triangles for both Position and Rotation to display all three X, Y, and Z parameters.

In earlier lessons, you saw that you can use the Inspector controls to move a layer forward or backward along the z-axis, and tilt it along its x-axis, like opening a lid, or swing it along its y-axis, like opening a door.

**6**  For each of the Position and Rotation properties, drag in the value fields to see how these values affect the layer. Undo after each change.

You can also make these 3D position and rotation changes in the HUD and directly in the Canvas. To do so, you use a special tool.

**7**  In the Toolbar, choose the Adjust 3D Transform tool, or press Q.

The HUD populates with the 3D Transform tools, and the center of the selected layer in the Canvas now contains three colored arrows and three hollow white circles.

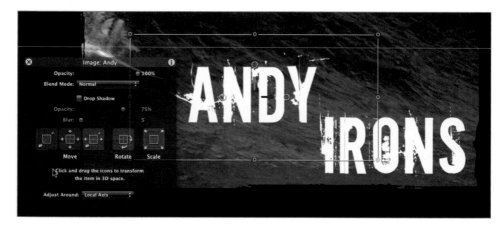

**8**  In the left Move control in the HUD, drag left to move the *Andy* layer forward (toward you) along the z-axis. Keep your eye on the Inspector to set a value of about 150 pixels.

**9**  In the HUD, drag in the middle Move control to slide the layer up and over to the right a little, again watching the Inspector to see exactly which parameters are changing.

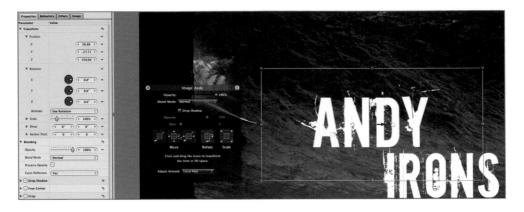

The right Move control in the HUD moves the selected layer along either the x-axis or z-axis, but you don't need it here. This control is useful when you want to spread layers out in space and keep them all on the same horizontal plane, like actors on a stage.

**10**  In the HUD, try dragging in the Rotate control, watching both the Canvas and the Inspector. The layer rotates along the x, y, and z axes, but in this exercise you just want to swing the layer on its y-axis.

**11**  In the Inspector, drag right on the Rotate control to set the Y Rotation value to 35 degrees.

You can make these same types of 3D transformations directly in the Canvas with the Adjust 3D Transform tool. Let's position and rotate the *Irons* layer to offset it from the *Andy* layer.

**12**  Select the *Irons* layer.

The colors of the three axis arrows —red, green, and blue, or RGB—map to the three axes of 3D space. The red arrow represents the x, or horizontal, axis; the green arrow represents the y, or vertical, axis; and the blue arrow represents the z, or depth, axis. The blue arrow is pointing almost directly at you, so it looks more like a dot than an arrow.

You drag an arrow to constrain movement to that axis alone.

**13** Drag the blue arrow to the right and watch the tooltip to move the layer about 150 pixels forward along the z-axis. The selected arrow turns yellow. Notice that the tooltip value matches what is shown in the Inspector.

**14** Drag the red arrow to the left to move this layer partially underneath the *Andy* layer, and then drag the green arrow up to move the layers closer together.

> **TIP** You can also drag anywhere inside the bounding box to move along both x and y axes at the same time.

The hollow white circles at the 12, 3, and 9 o'clock positions are rotation handles.

**15** Drag the 9 o'clock rotation handle to the left to rotate the layer -35 degrees around the y-axis. Colored rotation bands appear to indicate the axis of rotation.

> **TIP** Layers and groups rotate around their anchor points. Therefore, changing the location of the anchor point can have a dramatic impact on the rotation. For example, if you wanted to swing a graphic of a door from the edge rather than from its center, you would move the anchor point to that edge.

You can see how easy it is to change the position and rotation of layers in 3D space using the Inspector, the HUD, and the Canvas. One more crucial step remains for making layers behave as though they live in a 3D world: converting the groups that contain them into 3D groups.

## Converting 2D Groups to 3D

Layers won't interact with each other—and won't respond to cameras or lights—unless they are contained inside 3D groups. Fortunately, it's quite easy to switch a group from 2D to 3D.

Before you do so, however, you will work with the various axis modes in the HUD and Canvas. They can be handy when manipulating layers and groups.

Let's say you want to push the *Irons* layer straight back in z-space, to move it behind the video clip.

**1**   In the HUD, drag left and right on the left-hand Move control; then undo the change.

**2**   In the Canvas, drag left and right on the blue z-axis arrow.

Notice that in both cases the layer does not move straight toward you or away from you. Rather, it moves along the layer's own z-axis, which is perpendicular to the surface of the layer.

**3**   In the HUD, drag around in the Rotate control; then undo the change.

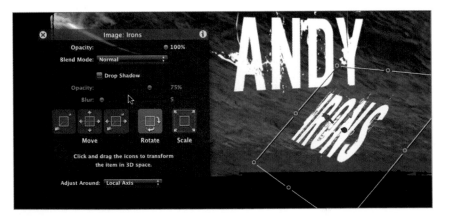

Notice in the Canvas that the colored arrows move as the layer moves: The red arrow stays horizontal with respect to the layer, the green arrow stays vertical with respect to the layer, and the blue arrow always points straight out from the plane of the layer. This is called Local Axis mode. You are adjusting the layer around its own, local set of axes.

4   In the HUD, from the Adjust Around pop-up menu, choose View Axis. In the Canvas, the blue arrow now points directly at you, even though the layer is rotated.

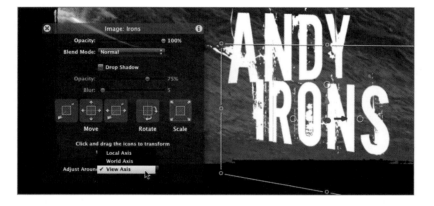

5   In the HUD, once again drag around in the Rotate control, watch the results, and then undo the change. This time, no matter how the layer moves, the axes remain fixed: Red is always horizontal, green is always vertical, and blue is always pointing straight out—with respect to the computer screen, or *your view* of the project.

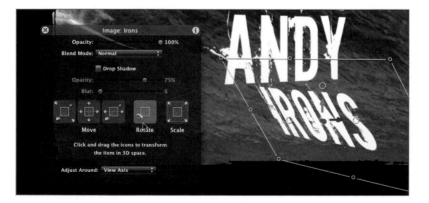

**NOTE ▶** The other option, World Axis, is currently the same as View Axis. That will change after you add a camera and begin to move in 3D space. The Inspector's Position and Rotation values are always based on the World Axis.

This axis mode makes it easier to push the layer directly away from you.

**6**   In the HUD, drag the left Move control to the right; or, in the Canvas, drag the blue arrow to the left to move the *Irons* layer back in z-space to about -15 pixels.

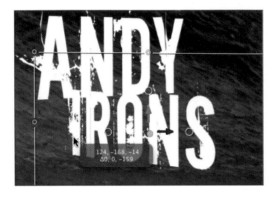

The *Andy Irons* video layer is located at 0 pixels along the z-axis (you can select it and check that value in the Inspector), so the *Irons* layer should be at least partially behind the video now, but it still appears completely in front. This is because you are working in a 2D group, and layers in 2D groups do not interact with each other.

The compositing order of 2D group layers in the Canvas is dictated entirely by the layer order in the Layers tab. Because the *Irons* graphic layer is above the *Andy Irons* video layer in the Layers tab, it will always appear above the video in the Canvas.

Another way to see that the layers aren't yet truly 3D is to rotate the group.

**7**   Select the *Andy Irons* group, and then, in the Canvas, drag the top rotation handle down to tilt the group around its x-axis.

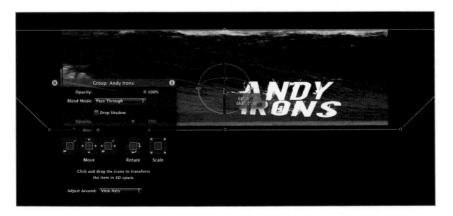

All the layers appear completely flat, and the mask doesn't tilt with the layers. To make layers interact with each other based on their positions in z-space rather than their layer order, you need to switch the group containing them to 3D.

**8**   Undo the group rotation, and then, in the Layers tab, click the 2D/3D icon for the *Andy Irons* group.

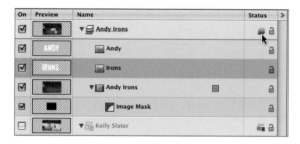

The icon changes from a group of three flat rectangles to a stack of rectangles to indicate that it is now a 3D group. Notice the difference between it and the icon on the *Kelly Slater* group below.

In the Canvas, the Irons graphic now intersects with the video layer.

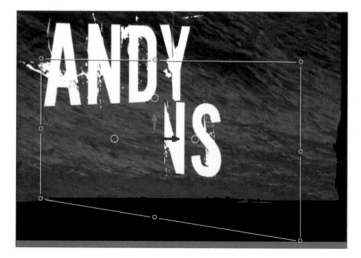

Let's return it to its previous location.

**9**  Use the HUD or Canvas to move the Irons graphic forward to about 150 pixels along the z-axis.

**10**  Once again, rotate the group down around the x-axis. The layers remain rotated and spread out in z-space when you look at them from a different angle.

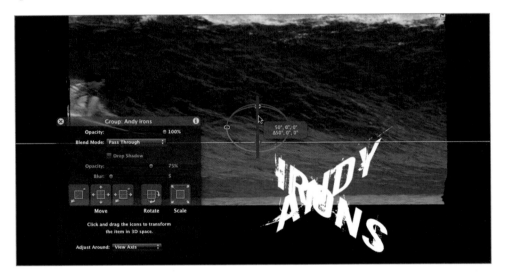

You are finished building your first scene. You will use these same tools to arrange the other two scenes in a similar fashion.

**11**  Undo the group rotation, and turn off the *Andy Irons* group.

**12**  Turn on the *Kelly Slater* group and make it a 3D group.

> **TIP** You can also make a selected 2D group into a 3D group by choosing Object > 3D group or pressing Control-D.

To make sure these text graphics have the same rotations and z-positions as the ones in the first set, you can copy the values from the layers in the *Andy Irons* group.

**13**  Select the *Andy* layer. You want the *Kelly* layer to start with the same position and rotation as the *Andy* layer.

**14**  Drag the word "Transform" from the Properties tab onto the *Kelly* layer in the Layers tab.

The *Kelly* layer takes on all the values from the Transform group of parameters. It is now about 150 pixels forward in z-space and rotated 35 degrees on the y-axis. Let's do the same for the *Slater* layer.

**15** Select the *Irons* layer, and drag the word "Transform" to the *Slater* layer.

With both graphics layers properly positioned and rotated with respect to each other, you only need to reposition them with respect to the video.

**16** Shift-click both the *Kelly* and *Slater* layers to select them, and in the Canvas, drag them up and to the left so that they don't obscure the surfer in the video. Now you just need to repeat the same process on the last set.

**17** Turn off the *Kelly Slater* group; then turn on the *Bede Durbidge* group and make it 3D. Drag the Transform properties from *Kelly* to *Bede* and from *Slater* to *Durbidge*, and then reposition the layers as necessary. Save your work.

Terrific! Your 3D "sets" are now built. The next step is to spread them out in 3D space. For that task, it's very helpful to have a camera in the project.

## Adding and Working with Cameras

A 3D environment without a camera is like a fast car without the keys. You can sit in it and look around, but you can't go anywhere.

When you add a camera to a Motion project, a whole set of new tools, or *3D overlays*, become available. You can use these tools to manipulate the camera or to step away from the camera to get a different perspective on your 3D scene. You can even fly into the virtual air to get a bird's-eye view as you build your scene.

If you don't have any 3D groups in your project, adding a camera will automatically switch all your groups to 3D. Let's try it.

**1** Close all the groups in the Layers tab. You don't need to see the individual layers for the next steps.

**2**    Command-click each of the three 3D groups to select them, and then press Control-D to revert them to 2D groups.

**3**    In the Toolbar, choose the New Camera icon. A dialog appears to warn you that cameras affect only 3D groups.

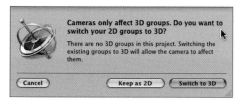

**4**    Click "Switch to 3D."

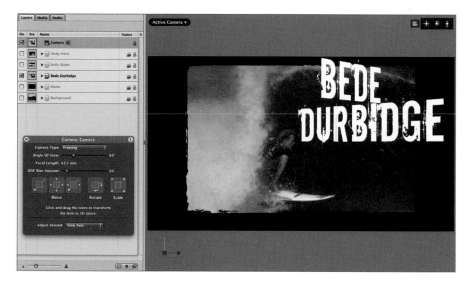

Several things happen:

▶  All the groups in the project are automatically switched to 3D.

▶  A new Camera layer appears at the top of the Layers tab.

▶  The HUD Transform controls now affect the camera.

▶  New tools appear in three corners of the Canvas. These tools are part of a group of five tools called *3D overlays*. They are available only when a camera is in the scene. You can choose specific 3D overlays to turn on or off, and you can toggle the visibility of all the 3D overlays.

**5**   At the right of the Toolbar, click the View and Overlay pop-up menu.

The five 3D overlays are listed underneath the Show 3D Overlays command. The Inset view and 3D grid are not visible in the Canvas because they appear only under certain conditions.

**NOTE** ▸ If you do not see checkmarks next to every 3D overlay and Show 3D Overlays, choose each one until all 3D overlays are turned on.

You are now looking at the scene through the camera, as indicated by the words "Active Camera" at the top left of the Canvas. By default, the camera is placed so that your view of the scene did not change. Now that you have a camera, you can move it around.

**6**   In the HUD, use the 3D transform tools to move and rotate the camera. Notice that the changes are also made in the Inspector. Undo after each change.

When you move the camera up and down or rotate it, notice that a 3D grid appears in the Canvas. The grid represents the "floor" of the virtual world, with a red x-axis and a blue z-axis intersecting at 0,0,0—your virtual "home base." This grid can help you stay oriented as you move around in 3D space.

At the top right of the Canvas is a set of three icons with a camera icon to the left. The three icons are the 3D View tools—Pan, Orbit, and Dolly. You can use them to manipulate the camera as you did when using the HUD.

**NOTE** ▶ If you can use the HUD to manipulate the camera, why would you need the 3D View tools? In the HUD, the camera can be manipulated only if it is the selected layer. Often, a different layer or group will be selected because you are working on it (transforming it, animating it, or adding effects) and you'd like to move the camera to change your view of the scene. The 3D View tools allow you to move and rotate the camera even when the camera layer is not selected.

7  Drag the Pan, Orbit, and Dolly controls to see how they work. Notice the changes reflected in the Inspector. This time, do not undo your changes.

These tools include a handy feature to quickly reset the camera.

8  Double-click any one of the 3D View tools and look at the Inspector.

Double-clicking a 3D View tool resets the camera to 0,0,0 for both Position and Rotation, so it is once again looking at the center of your virtual world. Like Dorothy clicking the heels of her ruby slippers, no matter how far afield you may stray in 3D space, you can always come home with a simple double-click.

But what does it mean when the camera is at 0,0,0? You know the video layer is at 0,0,0, so doesn't the camera have to back up a distance from the very center of the z-axis to "look at" the video and have it fill the screen?

To understand where the camera is in relationship to the layers in your scene, you need to step away from the camera, or even fly above it. And that's the purpose of the 3D overlay at the bottom left of the Canvas, the Compass.

**9**   Move your pointer over the arrows around the Compass but don't press the mouse button. The arrow under the mouse lights up, and text appears, identifying the name of the view you will be taken to if you click that part of the Compass.

**10**   Click the top of the green arrow to go to the Top view. The scene rotates as you "fly" above it. You are now looking straight down the world's y-axis.

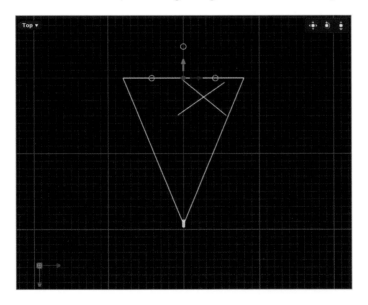

**NOTE** ▸ If you don't see the full camera outline, press Shift-Z to fit the scene to the Canvas.

Layers in Motion are always 2D—like playing cards—which is why the two rotated graphics layers look like a white X in the Canvas. You can't see a line for the video layer because it aligns with the focal plane of the camera as represented by the base of the yellow isosceles triangle.

The red, green, and blue arrows are located at the center of the focal plane, which is why the camera's location is 0,0,0. In other words, the position of the camera is determined by its focal plane, not by its body.

**11** In the HUD, drag the Rotate control.

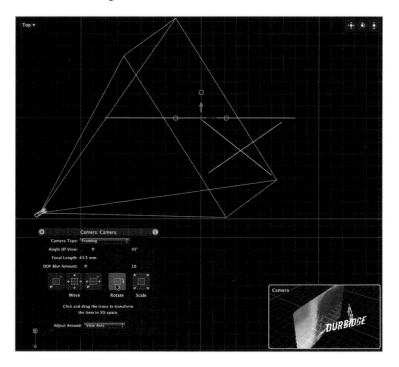

Notice that the camera rotates around the center of its focal plane. No matter how much you rotate the camera, it stays focused on the center of your virtual world. This behavior will come in handy when you animate your camera in the next lesson.

Notice also that a small window appears at the bottom right, the Inset view. It shows you how the scene looks from the camera's point of view—so you can adjust the camera from a different view, and still see the results from the camera's view.

You may wonder why the axes' arrow colors for the camera don't match the grid colors: The green arrow lines up with the blue grid line. If you look in the HUD, you can see that you are in View Axis mode—the mode in which z (blue) is always pointing straight at you.

**12** Undo the camera rotation, and then, in the HUD, change the View Axis to World Axis. The axes of the camera and the 3D grid now match.

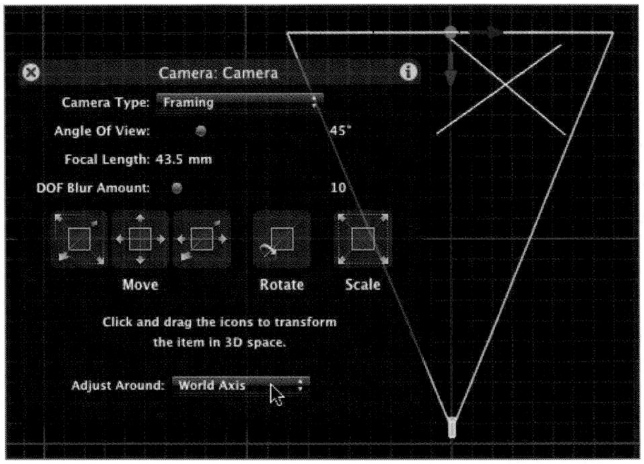

Look at the 3D View tools at the top right of the Canvas. Now that you are not in the Active Camera view, the camera icon no longer appears next to these tools. Therefore, these tools will pan, orbit, and dolly the current view without moving the camera.

**13** Use the 3D View tools to pan, orbit, and dolly the view.

Notice that the camera has not moved, and neither have any of the layers. You have changed only your view of the scene.

The menu at the top left of the Canvas is the Camera menu, and it indicates the current view. An asterisk has been added next to Top because you modified the Top view.

**14** From the Camera menu, choose Reset View. The asterisk disappears and the view once again looks straight down the world's y-axis.

To go to the view looking through the camera, you use the Camera menu.

**15** From the Camera menu, choose Active Camera, or press Control-A. Your view rotates from the Top view back to the original camera view.

Now that you know how to turn on and use the 3D overlays to change your view of the scene and to manipulate the camera, you can arrange the groups in 3D space.

## Arranging and Modifying Groups and Layers in 3D Space

In the next lesson, we will animate the camera to fly from one set to the next. But right now, all the groups are located at the same place: the center of the virtual world. So you'll spread them apart, and rotate them so that the camera must twist and turn as it moves from one group to the next.

To move groups in 3D space, you can use the 3D overlays and the Adjust 3D Transform tool. To see the impact of your changes from more than one angle, we'll use a view layout to add another window to the Canvas.

After you have spread out the groups and layers in 3D space, you may still need to do some work on them—transforming layers, and adding masks, filters, or behaviors. The Frame Objects commands will help you quickly find and modify elements. Finally, you will use a 2D group to add a background that stays put, no matter where the camera moves.

## Arranging the Groups

The first task is to move two of the groups away from the camera and then rotate them to face it. Facing the camera isn't required, but it can create a pleasing arrangement that makes it easy for the camera to turn and see each group.

**1**   In the Layers tab, select the activation checkboxes of the *Andy Irons* and *Kelly Slater* layers so that you can see them as you move them in 3D space.

The groups of layers are currently stacked on top of each other. To spread them apart, use different views to get a broader perspective.

**2**   Click the Compass to go to the Top view; then, in the 3D View tools, use the Dolly and Pan controls to move your view higher and down to the left, so that the camera and groups are near the upper right of the Canvas.

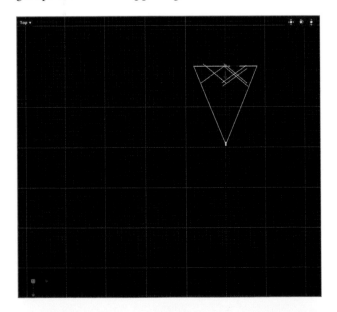

We'll leave the *Andy Irons* group in front of the camera, move the *Kelly Slater* group to the left and down, and move the *Bede Durbidge* group directly behind the camera.

**3** In the Layers tab, select the *Kelly Slater* group, and in the Canvas, drag the red x-axis arrow to the left, using the tooltip as a guide to move the group about 3000 pixels.

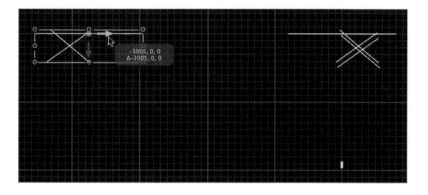

**4** Drag the blue z-axis arrow down to move the group about 1500 pixels, until it is even with the camera.

**5** Move your pointer near the top left of the group's bounding box, until the green rotation band appears, and then Shift-drag down and to the right to rotate the group 90 degrees counterclockwise around its y-axis.

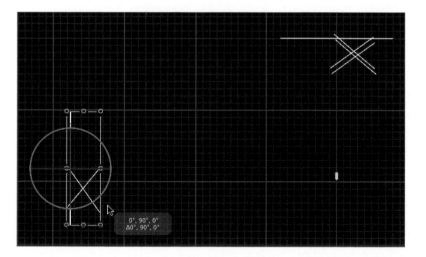

**TIP** It can be a little difficult to locate the rotation handles in this view. You could also go to the Properties tab of the Inspector and set the Rotation Y value to 90.

The *Kelly Slater* group is now off-camera to the left, and facing the camera; so if the camera turned to look, it would see the elements of the group face-on.

Let's now move and rotate the *Bede Durbidge* group. To keep the Inset view from getting in the way, you will turn it off.

6  From the View and Overlay pop-up menu, choose Inset View to deactivate it.

7  Select the *Bede Durbidge* group. Drag the blue arrow down to move the group about 3000 pixels; then drag the green rotation band to rotate the group 180 degrees to face the camera. This is your preliminary set arrangement. You can adjust it as you wish, after you see how it looks with the camera animation.

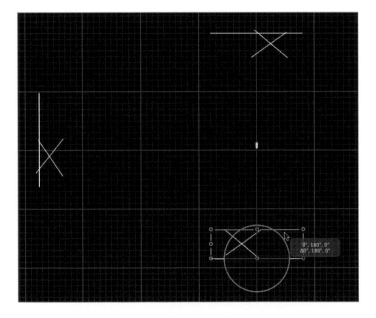

Now, you'd like to see what these groups look like from closer to the "ground," but you'd like to keep this view onscreen as well, in case you want to use it to make changes.

8  At the upper right of the Canvas, from the View Layouts pop-up menu, choose the split horizontal view—the third option.

The Canvas splits into two windows of the scene. The upper window shows the Top view you were working in, and it has a yellow border around it to indicate that it is the active view. The lower window shows the Right view by default, but you can change either window to whichever view you want.

**NOTE** ▶ The active window is the one that animates during playback. You can make a window active by clicking inside it.

**9**   Use the Camera menu to set the upper window to the Active Camera view.

**10**  In the lower window, click the center of the Compass to go to the Perspective view, and then use the 3D View tools to pan, orbit, and dolly the view until you can see all three sets in the window.

The text graphics for the other sets are visible, but the video is not. This is because all three video clips are masked by the same graphic in the Matte group, and the graphic is still located at 0,0,0. So, it masks the *Andy Irons* video layer, but it's no longer aligned with the other two video layers.

To align the masks, we want a separate copy of the graphic to mask each video layer, and we'll move each copy to the exact same location as each video layer.

## Modifying Layers in 3D Space

In this exercise, we will create copies of the graphic that was used as a mask and copy it to each of the three surfer groups. Then each copy will be aligned with the video layer in that group. While you could drag the layers in the different Canvas windows to align them, there is a much faster way to move a layer to a precise location in 3D space.

1   Open the *Matte* group. Option-drag a copy of the **grunge-bk.psd** layer to each of the three surfer groups, and then delete the *Matte* group.

The surfer groups open, and a copy of the graphic is now located in the top layer of each group. In the lower viewport of the Canvas, all the video clips appear without masks.

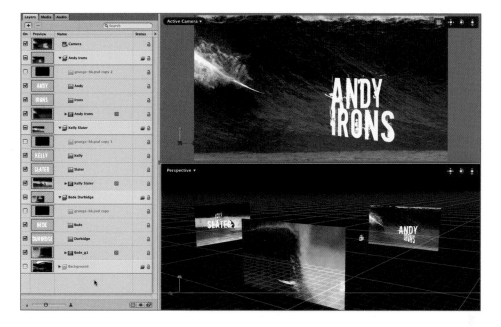

To move each *grunge* graphic layer to the same position and rotation of each video clip, let's copy the parameters from the video clip to the graphic.

2   In the *Andy Irons* group, select and activate the *grunge-bk.psd copy 2* layer and look at the Properties tab of the Inspector. In the Perspective view, the layer is clearly in the wrong position; in the Inspector, you can see that it's nowhere close to 0,0,0—the location of the *Andy Irons* video clip.

While you could click the Transform properties reset arrow to return the layer to 0,0,0 for both position and rotation, you would also be resetting the scale, which you don't want to do. Besides, that approach won't work if the layer you want to match the graphic to isn't at 0,0,0.

3   Select the *Andy Irons* video layer.

4   In the Properties tab, Shift-click the words *Position* and *Rotation* to select them both, and then drag them onto the *grunge-bk.psd copy 2* layer. The Position and Rotation

values are copied to the graphic, and in the Active Camera view it lines up with the video. Now you just need to apply it as the source for the image mask.

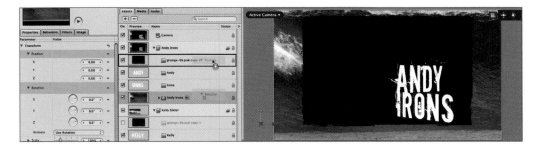

**5**   Open the *Andy Irons* video layer to reveal the image mask, and then drag the *grunge-bk .psd copy 2* layer onto the image mask. The video in the Active Camera view is now properly masked by the graphic.

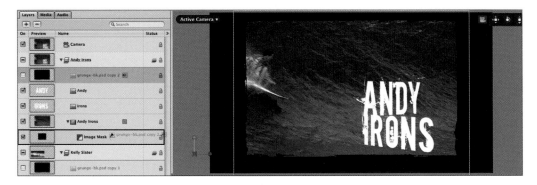

**NOTE ▶** In earlier lessons, you set the source of the image mask by first selecting the image mask, and then dragging the source layer to the well in the HUD. Dragging directly to the image mask in the Layers tab is a shortcut method for achieving the same result.

This process of dragging parameters from the Inspector to a layer can be used to move any layer to align with any other layer in 3D space. It's quite powerful, and we'll use it again for the *Kelly Slater* group. However, this group is a bit difficult to see in the Perspective view. It's on an angle and far away. You could use the 3D View tools to move closer, but there's a faster way to move the camera to frame any group or layer in 3D space.

**6**    Close the *Andy Irons* group, and select the *Kelly Slater* video layer inside the *Kelly Slater* group.

**7**    In the upper viewport, from the Camera menu, choose Frame Object. The camera rotates to face the selected layer, and pans and dollies until its focal plane touches the layer, thereby framing the layer.

NOTE ▸ This command changes the position and orientation of the camera itself—not just a view—so be cautious when using it if the camera is already in a specific location that you want to preserve, or if you have already animated the camera with behaviors or keyframes. In this case, the starting position of the camera is 0,0,0, so it's very easy to return "home" by double-clicking one of the 3D View tools or resetting the camera's Transform parameters in the Properties tab.

**8**    In the Properties tab, Shift-click the Position and Rotation parameters, and drag them inside the *Kelly Slater* group onto the *grunge-bk.psd copy 1* layer.

NOTE ▸ The position and rotation of the *Kelly Slater* video layer is 0,0,0—even though the layer isn't close to the center of the virtual world. This is because the coordinates are relative to the group containing the layer. Although you moved the entire group and changed its position and rotation, you haven't changed the position or rotation of this layer with respect to the group that contains it.

**9**    Open the *Kelly Slater* video layer, and drag the *grunge-bk.psd copy 1* layer onto the image mask. The video now appears masked in the Active Camera view. There's just one more group to go.

**10** Close the *Kelly Slater* group, select the *Bede_g1* video layer, and choose Frame Object from the Camera menu or press Command-F to frame the layer with the camera.

**11** In the Properties tab, Shift-click the Position and Rotation parameters, and drag them inside the *Bede Durbidge* group onto the *grunge-bk.psd copy* layer.

**12** Open the *Bede_g1* video layer, and drag the *grunge-bk.psd copy* layer onto the image mask. All three video groups should now appear properly masked.

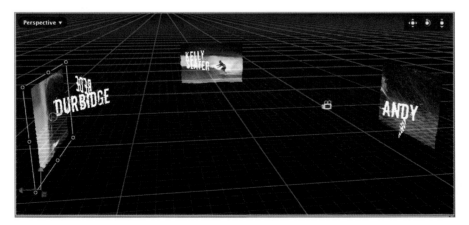

**NOTE ▶** Feel free to adjust the Perspective view to look at all the sets.

To finish setting up the 3D scene, let's add a background.

## Mixing 2D and 3D Groups

Motion lets you freely mix 2D and 3D groups in a 3D project. Because 2D groups aren't affected by the camera, they can be used to add elements that you always want to see, such as a watermark, station ID, or background element.

**1**   Close the *Bede Durbidge* group and turn on the visibility of the *Background* group.

In the Active Camera view, where the camera is framing Bede's group, nothing changes. But in the Perspective view, the background wave graphic appears behind Andy's group.

Because the *Background* group is a 3D group, the camera sees it in 3D space at a fixed location. But you want to see the background no matter where the camera moves.

**2**   Click the 2D/3D icon for the *Background* group to switch it to a 2D group. Now the wave graphic appears in the upper Active Camera window behind the Bede video, and also appears in the Perspective view, flat to the screen.

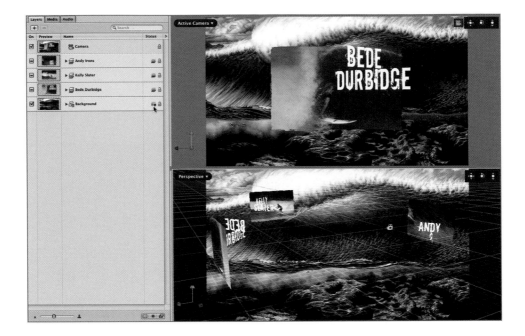

3   Try orbiting the camera with the 3D View tool in the Active Camera view.

    No matter where the camera looks, the wave graphic stays still and always faces the
    viewer. However, you can still manipulate the position and rotation of 2D groups and
    their layers.

4   In the upper Active Camera window, double-click one of the 3D View tools to reset
    the camera to its default location at 0,0,0, framing the *Andy* group.

5   Open the *Background* group and select the *water bkg B_sm.jpg* layer.

6   Look at the top left of the Toolbar. If the Adjust 3D Transform tool is not selected,
    press Q to select it.

7   In the HUD, drag in the Move, Rotate, and Scale controls to transform the layer. After
    each adjustment, press Command-Z to undo it.

    The layer moves and rotates in the Active Camera and Perspective views. This means
    that you can position and rotate a layer in a 2D group as needed to set it up, but it
    won't move from that orientation when the camera moves.

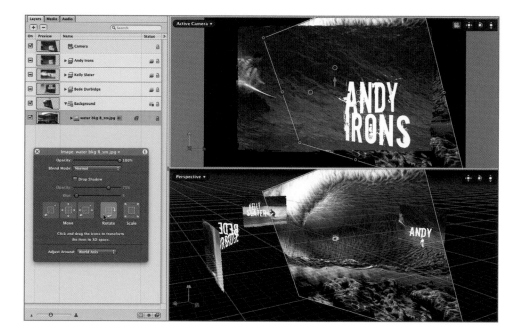

Notice that no matter how far forward you move the layer along the z-axis, it never moves in front of the surfing video. This is because 2D groups respect the layer order in the Layers tab.

**8**   Close the *Background* group, select it, and choose Object > Bring to Front. The wave now obscures all other groups because it's a 2D group at the top of the layer stack. If this group contained a small semitransparent watermark, corporate logo, or station ID in the corner of the screen, it would stay there as the camera moved.

**9**   Choose Object > Send to Back to return the *Background* group to the bottom of the layer stack and the back of the composition.

**10**   Save the project.

Good work. You now know how to turn on and use the 3D overlays, manipulate a camera, arrange layers and groups in 3D space, quickly move the camera to specific locations in 3D space to modify elements, and mix 2D and 3D groups. Your scene is arranged, and you are ready to animate the camera.

## Lesson Review

1.  How can you automatically switch all groups in your project to 3D?

2.  Name three locations in which you can change the position and rotation of a layer or group in 3D space.

3.  What's the difference between layers in a 2D group and in a 3D group?

4.  Do the 3D View tools always control the camera?

5.  Which tool is used to make 3D transformations directly in the Canvas, and which keyboard shortcut selects it?

6.  How can you quickly move a camera to look at and frame a specific layer in 3D space?

7.  In the HUD, how would you set the Adjust Around pop-up menu if you wanted the z-axis of a layer to always point straight at you, no matter how the layer or the camera was oriented?

8.  You have two layers in different locations and rotations in 3D space. You add an image mask to each layer, and you apply the same source layer to both image masks. One layer is masked and one is not. How can you make it mask both layers?

### Answers

1.  By adding a camera.

2.  In the Inspector, the HUD, or the Canvas.

3.  Layers in 2D groups are not affected by the camera, and are composited based on stacking order in the Layers tab.

4.  No. The 3D View tools control the camera only when the window is set to a Camera view.

5.  The Adjust 3D Transform tool allows you to transform the position and rotation of layers and groups in both the HUD and the Canvas. Press Q to select the Adjust 3D Transform tool.

6.  Select the layer, and from the Camera menu, choose Frame Object, or press Command-F.

7.  Set the Adjust Around pop-up menu to View Axis mode to orient the axes so that they reflect the orientation of your computer screen.

8.  The image mask uses the location and rotation of the source layer to mask the target layer. So you need separate copies of each image mask source, each aligned to the layer you are masking.

**Keyboard Shortcuts**

| | |
|---|---|
| **Q** | Select the Adjust 3D Transform tool |
| **Control-A** | Select the Active Camera view from the Camera menu |
| **Control-D** | Toggle a group between 2D and 3D |
| **Command-F** | Frame the selected object |
| **Control-P** | Choose the Perspective view from the Camera menu |
| **Control-R** | Reset an orthogonal view |
| **Command-Option-/ (slash)** | Toggle visibility of the 3D overlays |

# 16

Lesson Files     Motion4_Book_Files > Lessons > Lesson_16

Media     Motion4_Book_Files > Media > Pipeline; Rockumentary-Behaviors

Time     This lesson takes approximately 90 minutes to complete.

Goals     Animate a camera with behaviors

Animate a camera with keyframes

Work with depth of field

Turn on and adjust reflections

Understand light types

Work with casting and receiving shadows

Lesson **16**

# Animating Cameras and Using Advanced 3D Features

Now that you've learned how to arrange layers and groups into virtual sets in 3D, the real fun begins: animating the camera to fly from set to set, examining each one before moving to the next.

In this lesson, you will animate your camera using two methods—behaviors and keyframes—and explore several of the advanced 3D features of Motion, including limiting the camera's depth of field, turning on reflections, adding lights, and casting shadows.

## Animating a Camera with Behaviors

In the previous lesson, you created a 3D scene with the surfing videos and text graphics. In this exercise, two camera behaviors—Framing and Sweep—will animate the camera through that scene. The Framing behavior flies the camera to a new location in 3D space, and the Sweep behavior orbits the camera around its point of interest.

### Using the Framing Behavior

The Framing behavior makes it fast and easy to fly the camera right to a specific layer. It even orients the camera to face the layer.

1   Navigate to Motion4_Book_Files > Lessons > Lesson_16 and open the Camera Animation – Behaviors Start project. Then save it in the Student_Saves folder. This project is the same as the project you completed in Lesson 15. Let's take a quick look at its structure.

    **NOTE ▸** You can open this project from the Finder or directly from the File Browser in Motion.

2   Open the Layers tab (F5), select the camera, and use the Compass to go to the Top view.

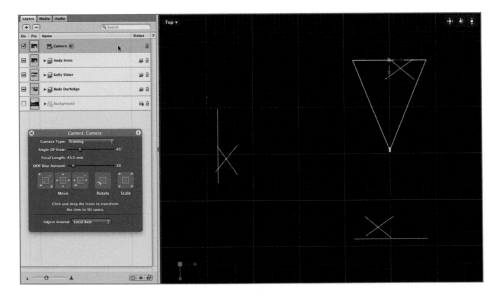

The three surfing groups are spread out in 3D space, each one containing a video layer and layers for the first and last name graphics, which have been rotated and positioned in front of the video. The camera is located at 0,0,0—the center of the virtual world—framing the *Andy Irons* group.

We'll animate the camera from this Top view. You want to move the camera from its current location to the *Kelly Slater* group. But when should the move start?

**3** Play the project, and stop just after the voiceover says, "Andy Irons, four-time Triple Crown Champion"—at about 3:02. Because the voiceover has finished introducing Andy but has not yet introduced Kelly, this is a great time to move the camera to look at Kelly, using the Framing behavior.

**4** In the Library, choose Behaviors, then Camera. The six different behaviors in this folder animate a camera in different ways. The Preview area displays information and a sample animation that shows how each behavior works.

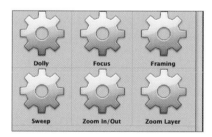

**TIP** In addition to the Camera behaviors, cameras can be animated using Basic Motion behaviors like Throw, Spin, Motion Path, and Point At. Parameter behaviors will also animate cameras. For example, try adding a Wriggle Parameter behavior to the camera's position to create some camera shake.

**5** Drag the Framing behavior onto the *Camera* layer in the Layers tab. Click the framing behavior now under the Camera layer to make the Canvas to make it the active window, and then press I to trim the behavior's In point to the playhead.

The behavior appears under the *Camera* layer, and like most behaviors, it is applied to the entire duration of the layer, so you also need to trim the Out point.

**6** Play the project and stop just after the voiceover says, "Kelly." Then press O to trim the behavior's Out point to the playhead.

**7**  Set a play range around the behavior, starting a little before the In point and ending a little after the Out point. Resume playback to see the animation.

> **TIP** ▶ You can drag the play range In and Out points, but it may be faster to press Command-Option-I to set the play range In point and Command-Option-O to set the Out point.

> **TIP** ▶ While looping a short playback range, you may want to mute the audio by clicking the Play/Mute Audio button at the bottom of the Canvas.

The camera doesn't move, because you need to give the Framing behavior a target for it to frame.

**8**  Drag the *Kelly Slater* group from the Layers tab to the well in the HUD.

> **TIP** ▶ You can also drag the target layer or group directly onto the Framing behavior underneath the *Camera* layer.

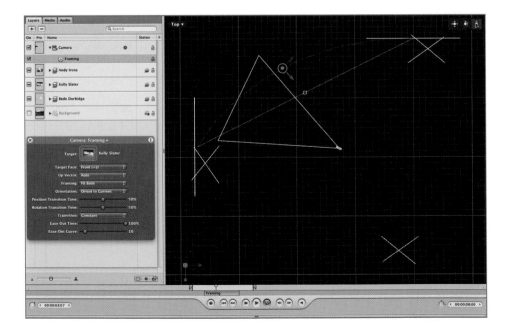

The camera now moves to the *Kelly Slater* group, rotating as it moves so that when it arrives, it's squarely facing the front of the group. It moves quite quickly because, by default, it completes its position and rotation changes halfway through the behavior. It also starts and stops rather suddenly. You can adjust these default settings in the HUD.

9   In the HUD, drag the Position Transition Time and the Rotation Transition Time sliders to 100%. The camera now lands on the *Kelly Slater* group at the end of the behavior.

10  From the Transition pop-up menu, choose Ease Both.

The camera now accelerates and decelerates more naturally. Let's see how things look from the camera's point of view.

11  Press Control-A to display the Active Camera view.

The camera move works well, but if you drag the playhead a bit beyond the play range, the video suddenly disappears. That's because all the video clips start at the first frame of the project. It was helpful to build the project this way so that you could see all the layers in 3D space without moving the playhead, but now you need to shift the layers in time so that each video is playing when the camera arrives to view that layer.

12  Stop playback, and press D, if necessary, to select the Framing behavior. The D key changes which element is selected by rotating through a selected layer and any effects applied to it.

13  Press Shift-I to move the playhead to the In point of the behavior.

14  Select the *Kelly Slater* group and press Shift-[ (left bracket) to move the group's In point to the playhead.

15  Press Option-X to reset the play range, unmute the audio if necessary, and play the project. The Kelly Slater video now lasts until after the voiceover introduces Bede Durbidge, at which point the camera will have moved on to Bede. To move the camera, we'll duplicate the Framing behavior we just adjusted.

**16**  Move the playhead to just after Kelly Slater's voiceover intro is complete, at about 6:07. This is where you want the next Framing behavior to begin.

**17**  Rename the Framing behavior to *Frame Kelly*, press Command-D to duplicate it, and rename the copy to *Frame Bede*. Drag the *Bede Durbidge* group into the HUD well, and then press Shift-[ (left bracket) to move the behavior's In point to the playhead.

Because you copied the existing behavior, it already has the right duration and animation properties. All you need to do is move the *Bede* group to start when the behavior starts.

**18**  Select the *Bede Durbidge* group, and press Shift-[ (left bracket) to move its In point to the playhead. Play the project.

The camera now animates quickly and smoothly to each of the surfers as they are introduced. It works well, but nothing is moving during the time that the camera is looking at each surfer. You can make things more dynamic by applying a Sweep behavior to keep the camera in motion as it looks at the layer or group that it is framing.

### Using the Sweep behavior

The Sweep behavior animates a camera to rotate or "sweep" around the scene that it is framing—its point of interest—as if it were attached to the scene with a string and can't look away.

1   While playing the project with the camera or one of its Framing behaviors selected, click the Add Behavior icon and choose Camera > Sweep.

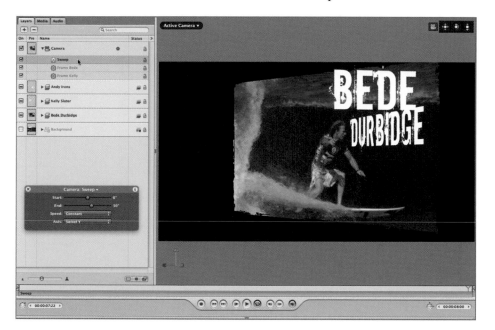

The behavior is applied to the full project duration, and the HUD indicates that the camera rotates from 0 to 30 degrees over the length of the behavior. This means that the camera looks at the first group straight on, and then rotates as it frames each group. Because you added the Sweep after the Framing behaviors, the rotation is continuous, which you can best see in the Top view.

2   Use the Compass to switch to the Top view, and continue playback.

The animation might look better if the camera were to start with a slight rotation in the opposite direction.

3   In the HUD, set the Start slider to -15 degrees and the End slider to 15 degrees.

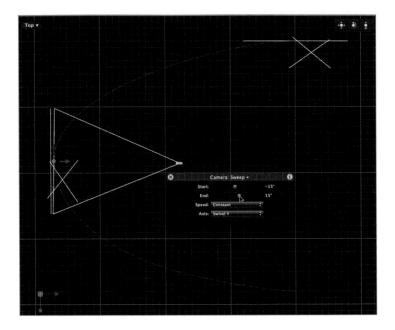

The camera now reaches 0 degrees when it is directly facing the *Kelly Slater* group, creating a more balanced look. If the Sweep were applied *before* the Framing behaviors, you would get a different result.

4   Reset the Start and End values to 0 and 30, respectively, and in the Layers tab, drag the Sweep behavior under the two Framing behaviors.

Because the Framing behaviors are now applied *after* the Sweep, they force the camera to frame each group face-on with no rotation, and the Sweep restarts the rotation from 0 degrees. As a result, each group gets the same look: starting face-on and then rotating in the same direction.

Let's say that you'd like the camera to sweep in the opposite direction on the middle *Kelly Slater* group. To do so, use separate Sweep behaviors.

5   Press F6 to open the Timing pane. We'll rename, duplicate, and trim the behaviors in the Timeline.

6   Rename the Sweep behavior to *Sweep Andy*. Then duplicate it and rename the copy to *Sweep Kelly*.

7   Duplicate *Sweep Kelly* and rename the copy to *Sweep Bede*.

**8**   Drag to trim each of the Sweep behaviors to fill the gaps between each Framing behavior.

**TIP** ▶ Shift-drag to snap the In or Out point of the behavior to the In or Out point of the Framing behaviors.

**9**   Make sure the Start value for all the Sweep behaviors is set to 0, and then set the End value to 15 for Andy, -15 for Kelly, and 6 for Bede.

Because the Framing behavior is on top in the Layers tab, the camera is forced to face each group. So, if you use a nonzero Start value for the Sweep, the animation will jump. The negative value for Kelly causes the camera to sweep in the opposite direction. And the lower value for Bede is needed because the final sweep doesn't last as long.

**NOTE** ▶ If you move the Sweep behaviors above the Framing behaviors in the Layers tab, you can set a nonzero starting value for each sweep to create an initial rotation. However, that stacking order may change the animation if you move the groups, as you will do shortly.

**10**   Press Control-A to return to the Active Camera view, and play the project. The animation is looking more interesting. A few tweaks should finish it off.

**11**   Press F6 to close the Timing pane, and save your work.

**Finessing Behaviors**

In this exercise, we'll set an initial rotation of the first set so that it starts at an angle rather than squarely facing the camera. Then we will change the location and orientation of an entire group. Because the camera is animated with behaviors, it will still find and frame a target group no matter how you move it or rotate it.

**1**   Select the *Sweep Andy* behavior, and set the Start slider to -15 and the End slider to 0. The video now turns to face the camera in a subtle reveal move.

For the *Kelly Slater* group, you can't adjust the Start value because the Framing behavior forces the camera to view the group face-on. However, you can rotate elements *inside* the group.

**2**   Select the *Sweep Kelly* behavior, press Shift-I to move the playhead to the In point of the behavior, and open the group.

You want to rotate the video, but keep it aligned with the mask, so you also need to rotate the mask source.

**3**   Command-click the *Kelly Slater* video layer and the *grunge-bk.psd copy 1* layer to select them, and in the Properties tab of the Inspector, set the Rotation Y value field to about -15 degrees.

This action rotates the video and its mask while keeping the group framed in the camera. We'll do the same for the Bede video, but in the opposite direction.

**4**   Select the *Sweep Bede* behavior, press Shift-I to move the playhead to its In point, and open the *Bede Durbidge* group. Command-click the *Bede_g1* and *grunge-bk.psd copy* layers, and in the Inspector, rotate them 15 degrees.

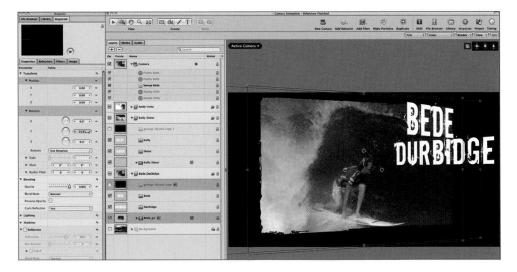

**5**   Save your work and play the project. Each group now starts a little off-axis, and the camera sweeps in the opposite direction on the middle group.

The overall camera movement is a little repetitive: It sweeps, moves to the left, stops and sweeps, moves to the left, stops and sweeps. The result is that the video and text graphics always appear to fly off to the right.

Because you framed each group using the Framing behavior, you can freely change the position and rotation of a group, and the camera will still frame it, which forces the camera to take a different route to the new destination. Moving a group can be a quick way to spice up the camera animation.

**6** Stop playback, and move the playhead to about 7:00. Close all open groups, and use the Compass to display the Right view.

> **TIP** Press Shift-Z to fit any view to the Canvas.

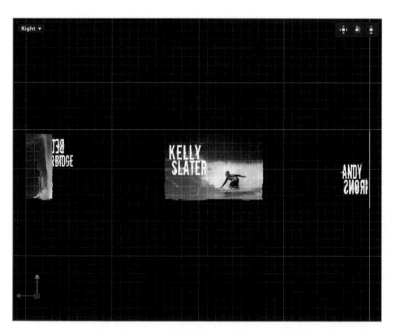

At 7:00, all the videos in the project are visible. In the Right view, you can see that each group is on a single horizontal plane and standing upright. Now let's transform the *Kelly Slater* group.

**7** Select the *Kelly Slater* group. In the Canvas, use the z-rotation handle to rotate the group 90 degrees clockwise, and move it up about 800 pixels.

**NOTE ▶** Make sure that the Adjust Around pop-up menu in the HUD is set to Local before rotating the group.

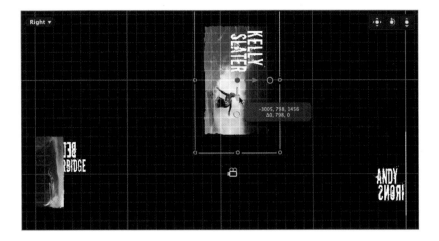

8 Select the camera so that you can see the focal plane outline; then play the project in the Right view. The red line indicates the new motion path of the camera, which rotates on both its y and z axes as it moves up to frame the *Kelly Slater* group. It then rotates again to frame the *Bede Durbidge* group.

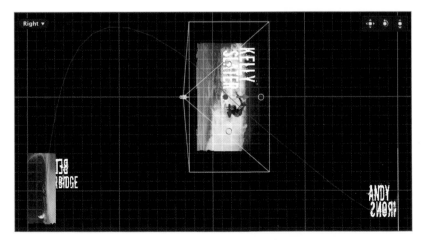

9 Press Control-A to return to the Active Camera view and see the result. The new camera animation creates a more dynamic transition between the groups, but the camera is now sweeping around the wrong axis for the *Kelly Slater* group.

Also, the gridlines can be distracting because they won't appear in the final rendered animation.

**10** To turn off the grid, from the View and Overlay pop-up menu, choose 3D Grid, or press Command-Shift-' (apostrophe).

**11** Select the *Sweep Kelly* behavior, and in the HUD, set Axis to Tilt X.

The Axis pop-up menu refers to the camera's axis of rotation. Because the camera had to rotate 90 degrees to frame the group, you needed to change the axis of rotation for the Sweep behavior.

The final step is to turn on the background.

**12** In the Layers tab, select the activation checkbox for the *Background* group, and play the project.

The *Background* group is a 2D group, so it is not affected by the camera and remains fixed in place as the camera moves, providing a consistent frame for the animation.

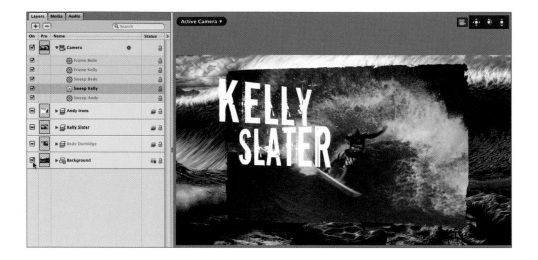

Well done. You've created and adjusted a camera animation in 3D space using behaviors. Next, you will animate a camera using keyframes.

## Animating a Camera with Keyframes

Behaviors are great for quickly framing a layer, sweeping around layers, zooming, and dollying (moving forward or backward). However, at other times, you may want precise control over where and how the camera moves. You can use keyframes to specify the exact location and orientation of the camera at any point in time, and you can change the interpolation of the keyframe curve to adjust the animation as the camera settles into position and then takes off toward its next destination.

### Adding a Second Camera

You can have multiple cameras in a Motion project. In this exercise, we will use the original camera as a reference and add a second camera to animate with keyframes.

1   Navigate to Motion4_Book_Files > Lessons > Lesson_16, open the Camera Animation – Keyframes Start project, and save it to the Student_Saves folder.

2   Play the play range.

This is a completed version of the Rockumentary DVD menu project that you started in an earlier lesson. In the first half, the camera pulls back through a series of pictures and graphics that spin and fall through space until the DVD menu elements assemble. While some of the layers are animated with Spin behaviors, most of the motion is due to the camera movement.

In the second half, the camera is stationary and only the photos change, so that the viewer can choose which part of the DVD to play.

The play range includes the first part of the project in which the camera animates.

3    Select the *Camera* layer, and press Command-8 to open the Keyframe Editor. The camera's Z-position (the blue curve) and Z-rotation (the pink curve) were animated with keyframes.

4   Press F1 to view the Properties tab of the Inspector. Open the Position and Rotation sections, if necessary, and watch the values change as the project plays.

The camera starts in z-space at about -6000 pixels, rotated -90 degrees. It pulls back toward the viewer until the top of the blue curve, when it reverses direction and pushes quickly forward and slams to a stop at 0,0,0. Throughout the move, the camera is slowly rotating back to 0 degrees.

5   Stop playback, press Home, and then press Shift-K repeatedly until the playhead lands on the last set of keyframes at the DVD Menu Loop marker. In the Inspector, notice that the camera's Position and Rotation values are both 0,0,0. In other words, the camera ends up back at the center of the virtual world.

6   Press F4 to view the Camera tab of the Inspector.

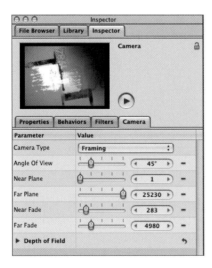

The Near Plane and Far Plane parameters determine how closely layers can approach the camera before disappearing and how deeply the camera can "see" into z-space. The Fade parameters allow layers to fade in and out rather than just popping on and off the screen. In this project, these parameters already have been adjusted to make the layers fade into and out of view at the proper distances.

7   In the Toolbar, click the New Camera icon.

8   Rename the new Camera 1 to *My Camera*. Rename the original camera to *Original Camera*, and then turn it off.

**9**   Select the My Camera layer, and in the Properties tab, select the *My Camera* layer, and confirm that the Position and Rotation values are set to zero. You now have a fresh new camera located at the center of the virtual world, and you can always turn on the original camera as a reference.

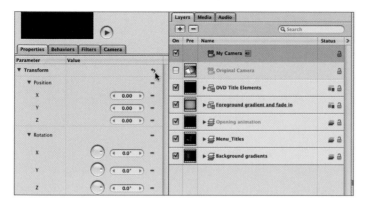

**NOTE ▶** When you add a camera, it is placed at the same location as the active camera based on the current playhead location. That is why you created the new camera with the playhead positioned at the last set of keyframes, where the original camera had returned to 0,0,0.

**10**   Go to the Camera tab of the Inspector. Your new camera has automatically taken all the values from the original camera.

**TIP ▶** You could also leave the Original Camera turned on, and toggle between the cameras by selecting either one from the Camera menu at the top left of the Canvas. If both cameras are turned on and the view is set to Active Camera, you can see the view from the top camera in the Layers tab.

### Keyframing the Camera

With your new camera in place, it's time to animate it. No matter how the camera animates through the pictures and graphics, when it reaches the marker for the DVD menu loop point, you always want it to end at 0,0,0 for both position and rotation. So, the first order of business is to set a keyframe at that marker.

**1**   Place the playhead at the marker (17;22) and select the *My Camera* layer. Go to the Properties tab and Option-click the top Animation menus for Position and Rotation to set keyframes for all three axes of each property.

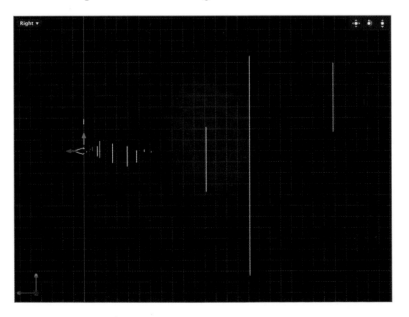

You can now work backward from this point, knowing that no matter where you start or where you wander, the camera will always end at the center of its virtual world.

Let's set the next keyframe at the beginning of the project.

2   Press Home, and turn off the *Foreground gradient and fade in* group so that you can see all the layers. Select the *My Camera* layer.

To better see how the layers are arranged in 3D space, change your view.

3   Use the Compass to choose the Right view.

From this view, you can see the camera's ending position, viewing all the layers in the project. You want to start the animation with the camera pushed forward into z-space (to the right in this view), past all the picture layers. But from this view, you can't see the content of the layers, only their positions.

4    At the top right of the Canvas, from the View Layouts pop-up menu, choose the split-horizontal view. Set the lower window to Active Camera, and then press Shift-Z to fit the view to the window. Now the camera can be moved along its z-axis in the Right view, and the results are visible in the Active Camera view.

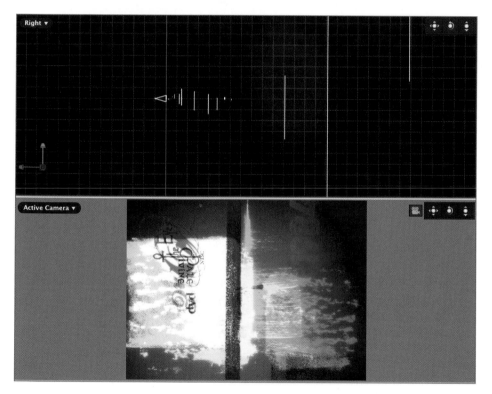

5    Press A to turn on recording. Click in the upper window to make it active. Select the *My Camera* layer, and drag right on the blue z-axis arrow until you pass the last photo, where the tooltip reads about -6200 pixels.

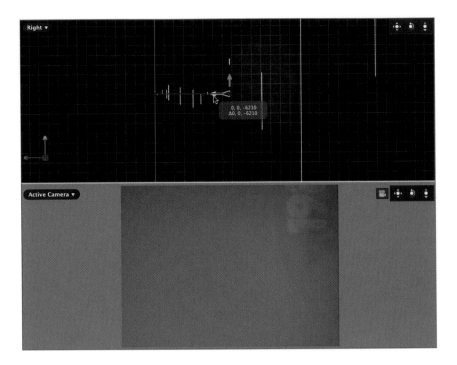

**NOTE** ▶ You see only the "last" photo in the Active Camera view, which will look like the first photo as the camera moves through it because the other pictures don't exist at the first frame of the project.

**NOTE** ▶ When you click in a viewport to make it active, the camera becomes deselected, so select it again to adjust it.

6   Now use the Properties tab to set the initial Z-rotation to -90 degrees.

Dragging the camera sets a keyframe for all three Position properties, but entering a value for Rotation sets a keyframe for only the Z-rotation. You may want to change the x-rotation and y-rotation at other frames, so let's also set keyframes for these two Rotation values at this frame.

7   Option-click the Animation menus for Rotation X and Rotation Y. The camera's position and rotation on all three axes are locked for the first frame and the marker frame, no matter what occurs between them.

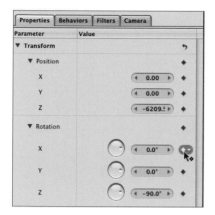

8   Make the Right view active and play the project. Then play the project with the Active Camera view active.

The camera makes a smooth backward dolly move as it rotates and settles on the DVD menu. You'd like it to emphasize the final landing, so set keyframes a little before the final landing to make the camera overshoot its target.

9   Move the playhead back 1.5 seconds to about 16;03.

10  With recording still turned on, in the Right view, drag the camera left to about 800 pixels. Then make the lower window active, and play the project.

The camera now overshoots the landing and comes back, but it's not the sudden landing you are looking for. To make the camera slam into the final position, let's adjust the keyframe's Bezier handles.

11  To make the adjusted curve fit in the Keyframe Editor window, click the "Fit visible curves in window" button.

12  Click the position Z keyframe at 16:03 to view the Bezier handles. Then drag the left handle out and down to create a sloping curve up into the keyframe. The camera will now start out very slowly and accelerate as it reaches this keyframe.

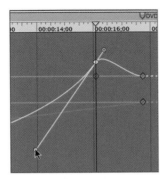

**13** Select the final position Z keyframe, and drag the Bezier handle straight upward to create a curve that ends pointing straight down into the keyframe.

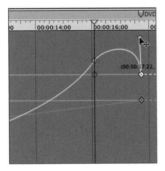

**14** Play the project in Active Camera view. The camera now slams into its final position. To make this animation look like the original camera animation, adjust the rotation curve and the initial keyframes.

**15** At 16:03, Option-click the Transform.Rotation.Z curve to add a keyframe, and adjust the Bezier handle to create a steeper curve through the keyframe.

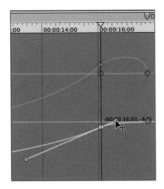

**16**  Finally, adjust the starting keyframes for both position and rotation to flatten out the start of the curve.

**17**  Play the project, adjust the keyframes if necessary, and save your work.

By using keyframes and adjusting the Bezier curves, you can create very precise camera moves.

## Using the Walk Camera Tool

Sometimes it can be faster and more intuitive to move the camera with the keyboard. The Walk Camera tool lets you manipulate the camera as you would in a first-person-shooter video game. Let's use it to replace the opening position keyframes and to create additional keyframes.

**1**  In the Keyframe Editor, drag a marquee around all of the keyframes at the beginning of the project and press Delete.

**2**  Select the Active Camera view. From the View Layouts pop-up menu, choose the single window layout. Select the *My Camera* layer, and move the playhead to the start of the project.

Once again, you want to push the camera deep into z-space, past all the graphics. Rather than using multiple windows, you can animate the camera directly in the Active Camera view using the Walk Camera tool.

**3**   In the Toolbar, select the Walk Camera tool.

**4**   With Recording still turned on, hold down the Up Arrow key to move the camera forward, stopping when you pass the last picture, at about -6200 pixels in the Inspector. The camera dollies forward as you tap or hold down the Up Arrow key, and a keyframe is set for the new position.

**5**   Try dragging around in the center of the Canvas, keeping an eye on the Rotation values in the Properties tab.

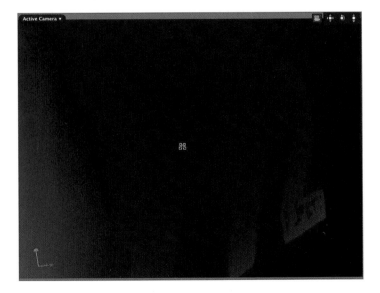

When the Walk Camera tool is active, dragging in the Canvas pivots the camera around its own x and y axes so that it can look in any direction. Here at the first frame, however, you want to rotate the camera on its z-axis.

**6**   Undo the rotation, and then, in the Rotation Z value field of the Properties tab, type *-90*.

**7**   Experiment with moving the playhead to the middle of the animation, drag in the Canvas to rotate the camera, and then press the Up, Down, Left, and Right Arrow keys to move the camera forward, backward, left, and right.

Because recording is still enabled, your changes set a keyframe at the playhead. When you drag in the Canvas with the Walk Camera tool, the camera pivots around its own body rather than around its focal point. You can see the difference more clearly in a view that shows the camera.

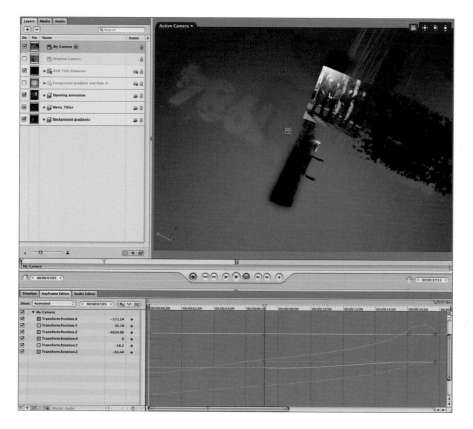

8   In the 3D View pop-up menu, return to a split-horizontal view. Set the upper window to the Right view and dolly in very close to the camera. Doing this deselects the Walk Camera tool. Notice that it is currently dimmed, so it can't be selected.

9   Click in the lower Active Camera view to make it the active window. You can now choose the Walk Camera tool, but the camera may no longer be selected.

10  Select the Camera; then choose the Walk Camera tool and drag in the Active Camera view. The camera pivots around its own body, as if you were holding the camera and turning to look around. Normally, the camera rotates around its focal plane.

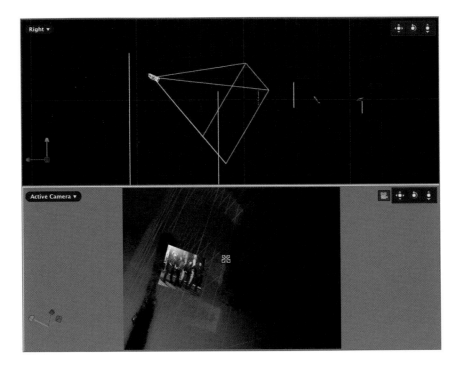

**NOTE** ▶ You have to drag in the Active Camera view for the Walk Camera tool to affect the camera.

11  In the Properties tab, drag in the Rotation X and Rotation Y value fields. The camera now rotates, or sweeps, around its focal plane, as if you were orbiting around the object while constantly facing it.

**TIP** ▶ You can use the Walk Camera tool to move and orient the camera by tapping or holding down the arrow keys, by dragging in the Canvas, or by dragging in the Position and Rotation value fields in the Properties tab.

12  In the View Layouts pop-up menu, return to the single-viewport layout of the Active Camera, and then move the playhead forward to a new frame of your choosing.

13  Experiment with moving the camera by pressing the arrow keys, dragging in the Canvas, and dragging in the Properties tab of the Inspector.

**14** Play the project, and adjust the interpolation of the keyframes as desired.

**15** Turn off recording, save your work, and close the project.

You've added a camera to a 3D scene, animated it with keyframes, adjusted the keyframe curves, and used the Walk Camera tool to move the camera and set additional keyframes.

## Using Advanced 3D Features

Motion has several other features that can create atmosphere and add more realism to your motion graphics. You can limit the camera's depth of field so that layers outside a set distance are blurred and layers within the distance are sharply in focus. You can animate the camera's focus to shift from one layer to another. You can make layers reflect other layers. You can add several kinds of lights to a scene, and those lights can cast shadows.

To finish this lesson, let's examine a completed project to learn how these advanced features work, how they can be adjusted, and how they can be enabled or disabled for export.

## Working with Depth of Field

By default, Motion's camera has infinite focus. By enabling Depth of Field, you can limit the focus distance and manipulate it in several ways.

**1**  Navigate to Motion4_Book_Files > Lessons > Lesson_16 and open the Advanced 3D Features Start project. This project includes a 3D scene containing the surfing videos.

**2**  Use the Camera menu or the Compass to display the Top view, and then use the 3D View tools to adjust the view to see how the videos and text graphics are placed at different distances from the camera.

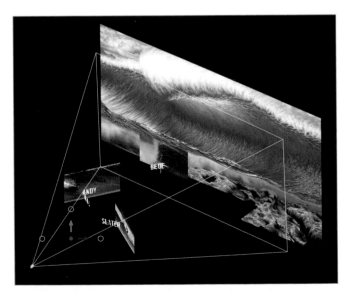

By limiting the camera's depth of field (DOF), you can focus the viewer's attention on a specific area of the frame.

3    Press Control-A to return to the Active Camera view, and then, from the Render pop-up menu at the top right of the Canvas, choose Depth of Field, or press Control-Option-D.

The front text and videos go out of focus, and the back video stays sharp, but not completely in. You can use a command to quickly focus the camera on any selected layer or group.

4    Select the *Kelly Slater* group, and then, from the Active Camera menu, choose Focus on Object, or press Control-F. The *Kelly Slater* group snaps into focus.

You can increase the blur on objects that are out of focus.

5    Select the camera. Press F4 to view the Camera tab of the Inspector. Open the Depth of Field section, and increase the DOF Blur Amount to about 25.

You can also use a behavior to animate the camera to shift its focus from one object to the next, a camera "move" called a *rack focus*.

**6**  In the Toolbar, click the Add Behavior icon. Choose Camera > Focus, trim the behavior's Out point to 2:00, drag the *Bede Durbidge* group to the well in the HUD, and play the first few seconds of the project. The focus shifts from the *Kelly* group to the *Bede* group.

Feel free to experiment with the other Depth of Field parameters.

## Turning On Reflections

Motion's layers can reflect other layers, and you can set this property on a layer-by-layer basis. The project has a large black rectangle that acts as a floor under the videos and can receive reflections.

**1**  From the Render pop-up menu, choose Depth of Field to disable it. Turning off DOF speeds up your workflow.

**2**  Reflections should already be selected in this menu. If not, select them now.

**3**  Open the *Floors for reflections* group and select the *floor black* layer.

**4**  In the Properties tab of the Inspector, select the Reflections checkbox, increase the Blur Amount to 3, and select the Falloff checkbox if it isn't selected. The videos now look as if they are hovering over a shiny black floor. A lighter floor can create a different look for the reflections.

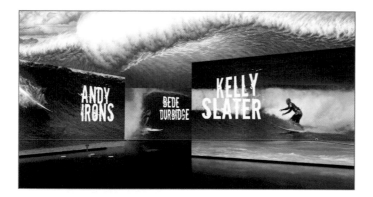

5    Turn on the *floor white* layer. Reflections have already been enabled for this layer.

6    Experiment with altering the other Reflection parameters, including the Falloff parameters and the Blend Mode.

> **TIP** ▶ Adding blur and falloff makes reflections look more realistic but also decreases playback performance and increases render times. You can set everything as you like, and then, to speed your workflow, turn off reflections in the Render pop-up menu.

## Using Lights and Shadows

Motion has four types of lights that you can add to your project, and each light can be adjusted to create visually striking effects. Certain lights can also cast shadows, and you can choose which layers cast shadows and which layers receive shadows.

1    Turn on and open the *Lights* group. This project contains five lights.

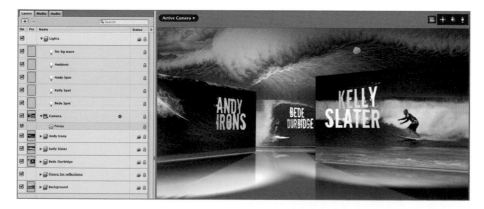

**2**    Select the *Ambient* light, and then turn off the visibility of the other four lights.

This light is an Ambient light type, as indicated in the HUD. Ambient light has no source and evenly lights everything in the scene. You can control only its color and intensity. It is here to add some overall light to the scene.

**3**    Select the *for bg wave* light and turn it on.

> **NOTE** ▸ Rendering lights, shadows, and reflections is processor and graphics card intensive. Allow some time for your Canvas to update when you turn these effects on and off.

This light is a Point light, which works much like a light bulb. It has a location and emits light in all directions. In the HUD, Shadows are enabled. This light adds some light to the wave graphic and casts shadows from the videos and text.

**4**    Select the *Andy Spot* light and turn on the rest of the lights.

These three lights are Spot light types as indicated in the HUD. They emit a cone of light that can be positioned, rotated, and adjusted in several ways. The spotlights are positioned to illuminate each of the videos and text graphics with a slight blue tint. You may wonder why the text graphics are not casting shadows onto the videos.

**5**    Open the *Kelly Slater* group, select the *Kelly Slater* video layer, and then, in the Properties tab of the Inspector, select the Receive Shadows checkbox. You can choose whether each layer will cast a shadow and if it will receive shadows. In this case, the video looks better without the shadow.

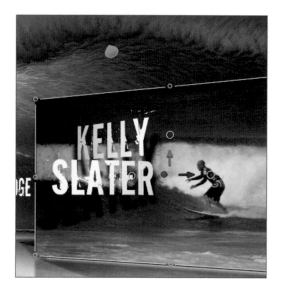

**6**  Deselect the Receive Shadows checkbox.

**7**  Select the *Kelly Spot* light, press F4 to view the Light tab of the Inspector, and open the Shadows section.

By deselecting the Uniform Softness checkbox, you can change the softness and color of a shadow, and make the shadow blurrier as it gets farther from the source object.

**NOTE** ▸ Increasing shadow softness and turning off Uniform Softness will decrease playback performance and increase render times.

**8**  Experiment with different Shadow settings for the lights, and try turning on Cast Shadows and Receive Shadows for different layers.

## Exporting Advanced 3D Features

After you have set up depth of field, reflections, lights, or shadows, you may want to turn them off in the Render pop-up menu to improve playback performance while you work. Even while they are turned off, you can choose which of these features you want to include in your final export.

1   Choose File > Export.

2   In the Export window, click the Options button.

3   In the Export Options dialog, click the Output tab. Here you can select which of the 3D features you want to include in the exported movie.

4   Deselect the "Use current project and canvas settings" checkbox, and then customize further to suit yourself.

You've built and arranged sets in 3D space; animated cameras through 3D space using both behaviors and keyframes; and used some advanced 3D features, including depth of field, reflections, lights, and shadows. Enjoy building your own 3D motion graphics with Motion!

# Lesson Review

1.  Name three of the Camera behaviors.

2.  Can the stacking order of Camera behaviors change the camera's animation?

3.  You've used a Framing behavior to frame a group. You then rotate the group 180 degrees around its y-axis and drag it down 1,000 pixels. How will this transformation affect the camera?

4.  What types of behaviors, besides Camera behaviors, can you use to animate a camera?

5.  You want to move a camera to a layer, and you also want to skew the camera angle, and push in closer than the layer's bounding box. Should you use behaviors or keyframes to do so?

6.  What tool lets you move the camera with the keyboard, and what keys do you use?

7.  How do you limit the camera's depth of field?

8.  How do you turn on reflections for a layer?

9.  You've added a light and turned on Shadows. Your text is throwing shadows onto the floor, which you want, but it is also throwing shadows onto another text layer, which you don't want. What do you do?

### Answers

1.  Framing, Sweep, Focus, Dolly, Zoom In/Out, Zoom Layer.

2.  Yes. For example, if the Framing behavior is on top of a Sweep behavior, it will force the camera to frame the target layer face-on, even if the Sweep tries to rotate it.

3.  The camera will also rotate 180 degrees and move down 1,000 pixels to properly frame the group.

4.  Basic Motion, Parameter, and Simulation behaviors—basically, any behaviors that work on a layer will work on a camera.

5.  You should use keyframes to set specific location and rotation values for the camera.

6.  The Walk Camera tool lets you move the camera forward, backward, left, and right by pressing the arrow keys.

7.  From the Render pop-up menu, choose Depth of Field.

8.  In the Properties tab of the Inspector, select the Reflections checkbox.

9.  Select the text layer that is receiving the shadows, and in the Properties tab, deselect the Receive Shadows checkbox.

## Keyboard Shortcuts

| | |
|---|---|
| **Option-L** | Turn on lights |
| **Control-Option-D** | Turn on limited depth of field |
| **Command-Shift-L** | Add a new light |
| **Control-Option-R** | Turn on reflections |
| **Control-Option-S** | Turn on shadows |
| **Command-Shift-' (apostrophe)** | Toggle 3D grid visibility |

# Glossary

**4:3**  The standard display aspect ratio of a traditional television set. See *aspect* ratio.

**8-bit**  For video, a bit depth at which color is sampled. Eight-bit color is common with DV and other standard-definition digital formats. Some high-definition acquisition formats can also record in 8-bit, but they usually record in 10-bit. Refers to 8 bits per color channel, making a total of 24 bits in an RGB image and 32 bits in an RGB image with an alpha channel.

**16:9**  The standard display aspect ratio of a high-definition television set. See *aspect ratio*.

**Action Safe**  The area inside a border that is 5 percent smaller than the overall size of the video frame. Some or all of the Canvas image beyond this border will be cropped by the video display monitor or television. How much is cropped varies among different TV manufacturers. See *Title Safe*.

**AIFF**  (Audio Interchange File Format) Apple's native uncompressed audio file format created for the Macintosh computer, commonly used for the storage and transmission of digitally sampled sound.

**alpha channel**  An image channel in addition to the R, G, and B color channels that is used to store transparency information for compositing. In Motion, black represents 100 percent transparent, and white represents 100 percent opaque.

**anamorphic**  An image shot in a wide-screen format and then squeezed into 4:3 frame size.

**anchor point**  In the Properties tab of the Inspector, the point that is used to center changes to a clip when using motion effects. A clip's anchor point does not have to be at its center.

**#**

**A**

**animation**   The process of changing any number of variables, such as color, audio levels, or other effects, over time using keyframes or behaviors. See *keyframe.*

**aspect ratio**   The ratio of the width of an image to its height on any viewing screen. Standard TV has an aspect ratio of 4:3; HDTV's is 16:9. See *high definition.*

**audio mixing**   The process of adjusting the volume levels of all audio clips in an edited sequence, including the production audio, music, sound effects, voice-overs, and additional background ambience, to turn all of these sounds into a harmonious whole.

**audio sample rate**   The rate or frequency at which a sound is sampled to digitize it. The standard sampling rate for digital audio is 48 kHz; CD audio is sampled at 44.1 kHz.

**audio waveform**   A graphical representation of the amplitude (loudness) of a sound over a period of time.

**AVI**   A PC-compatible standard for digital video no longer officially supported by Microsoft but still frequently used. AVI supports fewer codecs than Quick- Time. Some AVI codecs will not play back in QuickTime and will thus be inaccessible in Motion without prior format conversion.

**B**

**batch export**   The ability to export multiple clips and/or sequences with a single command by stacking them up in a queue. In Motion, the "Export using Compressor" option can be used to generate a batch export.

**Bezier handles**   The "control handles" attached to a Bezier curve that allow you to change the shape of the curve.

**black level**   The measurement of the black portion of the video signal. This level is represented by 7.5 IRE in the United States; Japan (NTSC) and PAL measurements are represented by 0 IRE. See *NTSC; PAL.*

**blanking**   The black border around the edges of a raw video image. This is the image created by the video camera CCDs—the photosensitive receptors that translate the lens image into digital information. The very edge of the picture is usually worthless. These black pixels should be cropped out of your image if you plan to composite it over the top of other footage.

**blend modes**  The methods used to combine overlapping elements. Blend modes use different mathematical formulas to combine the pixels, creating different effects between the elements.

**bluescreen**  A solid blue background placed behind a subject and photographed so that later the subject can be extracted and composited onto another image. See *greenscreen.*

**Broadcast Safe**  The range of color that can be broadcast free of distortion, according to the NTSC standards, with maximum allowable video at 100 IRE units and digital black at 0 IRE, or analog black at 7.5 IRE units.

**cache**  An area of the computer's memory (RAM) dedicated to storing still images and digital movies in preparation for real-time playback.

**C**

**Canvas**  The window in Motion in which you can view your edited sequence.

**center point**  Defines a clip's location in the X/Y coordinate space in the Canvas.

**chroma**  The color information contained in a video signal consisting of hue (the color itself) and saturation (intensity). See *hue; saturation.*

**chroma-keying**  Electronically matting or inserting an image from one camera into the picture produced by another. The subject to be inserted is shot against a solid color background, and signals from the two sources are then merged. See *keying.*

**clip**  A media file that may consist of video, audio, graphics, or any similar content that can be imported into Motion.

**clipping**  Distortion that occurs during the playback or recording of digital audio due to an overly high level.

**codec**  Short for *compression/decompression.* A program used to compress and decompress data such as audio and video files.

**color correction**  A process in which the color of objects is evened out so that all shots in a given scene match.

**color depth**   The possible range of colors that can be used in a movie or image. Higher color depths provide a wider range of colors but also require more disk space for a given image size. Broadcast video is generally 24-bit, with 8 bits of color information per channel. Motion works natively with 8 bits per channel of red, green, and blue.

**color matching**   Making the color of one shot correspond with that of another.

**component video**   A type of analog video signal where the luminance and chrominance signals are recorded separately, thereby providing better video quality. The signal can be recorded in an analog form (Y, R-Y, B-Y) as in a Beta SP, or in a digital form (Y, Cr, Cb), as in a Digital Betacam.

**composite**   The result of combining many different elements—some moving, some still. As a verb it refers to the process of combining these elements, or *layers;* as a noun it refers to the final resulting image. It's also sometimes referred to as a *comp.* In visual-effects work, the idea of a composite is to create a single image, which presents the illusion that all the elements were captured by a single camera filming the scene. In motion graphics, the concern isn't so much to convince the audience that everything was shot "in camera" as it is to present a stylistic and coherent blend of elements. See *layers.*

**composite video**   A type of analog video signal that combines all chroma and luma information into a single waveform running through a single pair of wires. This can result in analog "artifacts" affecting the quality of the video signal. See *chroma; luma.*

**compression**   The process by which video, graphics, and audio files are reduced in size. The reduction in the size of a video file through the removal of perceptually redundant image data is referred to as a *lossy* compression scheme. A *lossless* compression scheme uses a mathematical process and reduces the file size by consolidating redundant information without discarding it. Compression is irrelevant with clips imported into the Motion Canvas, since all clips are decoded into fully uncompressed frames before caching to system RAM. Compression is, however, a consideration in the final export of a composition to disk. See *codec.*

**contrast**   The difference between the lightest and darkest values in an image. High-contrast images have a large range of values from the darkest shadow to the lightest highlight. Low-contrast images have a narrower range of values, resulting in a "flatter" look.

**cut**  The simplest type of edit, where one clip ends and the next begins without any transition.

**cutaway**  A shot that is related to the current subject and occurs in the same time frame—for instance, an interviewer's reaction to what is being said in an interview or a shot to cover a technically bad moment.

**D**

**data rate**  The speed at which data can be transferred, often described in megabytes per second (MBps). The higher a video file's data rate, the higher quality it will be, but it will require more system resources (processor speed, hard-disk space, and performance). Some codecs allow you to specify a maximum data rate for a movie during render.

**decibel**  (dB) A unit of measure for the loudness of audio.

**decompression**  The process of creating a viewable image for playback from a compressed video, graphics, or audio file. Compare with *compression*.

**desaturate**  To remove color from a clip. Desaturation of 100 percent results in a grayscale image.

**dissolve**  A transition between two video clips in which the second one fades up over the top of the first one, eventually obscuring it.

**drop-frame timecode**  NTSC timecode that skips ahead in time by two frame numbers each minute, except for minutes ending in *0,* so that the end timecode total agrees with the actual elapsed clock time. Although timecode numbers are skipped, actual video frames are not skipped. See *timecode.*

**drop shadow**  An effect that creates an artificial shadow behind an image or text.

**dub**  To make a copy of an analog tape to the same type of format.

**DV**  (digital video) A standard for a specific digital video format created by a consortium of camcorder vendors, which uses Motion JPEG video at a 720 x 480 resolution at 29.97 frames per second (NTSC) or 720 x 546 resolution at 25 fps (PAL), stored at a bit rate of 25 MB per second at a compression of 4:1:1.

**DVCAM**   A standard-definition digital videotape recorder format that records an 8-bit, 5:1 compressed component video signal with 4:1:1 color sampling. Recorded using ¼-inch tape. Supports two tracks of audio with 16-bit, 48 kHz audio sampling, or four tracks of audio with 12-bit, 48 kHz audio sampling.

**DVCPRO**   Panasonic's native DV (digital video) component format that records an 8-bit, 5:1 compressed component video signal using 4:1:1 color sampling (PAL uses 4:2:0). This format supports two tracks of audio with 16-bit, 48 kHz audio sampling, or four tracks of audio with 12-bit, 48 kHz audio sampling. DVCPRO adds a longitudinal analog audio cue track and a control track to improve editing performance and user-friendliness in linear editing operations.

**dynamic range**   The difference, in decibels, between the loudest and softest parts of a recording.

**E**

**effects**   A general term used to describe filters and behaviors added to an object in Motion.

**envelope**   The visual curve of an audio waveform's pan or level. Essentially the same as a keyframe curve (the term *envelope* coming from the audio engineering world; the term *curve* coming from the digital animation world). See *pan*.

**F**

**fade**   The process of transitioning an object from fully transparent to fully opaque, or vice versa.

**favorite**   A custom effect that is used frequently. You can create favorites from any element or group of elements in your Layers tab.

**field**   Half of an *interlaced video* frame consisting of the odd or the even scan lines.

**FireWire**   Apple's trademark name for its implementation of the IEEE 1394 protocol used to connect external hard drives, cameras, and other digital devices to computers. It provides a fast interface to move large video and audio files to the computer's hard drive. FireWire exists as two standards: FireWire 400 and FireWire 800. FireWire 800 has twice the bandwidth of the traditional FireWire 400 and uses a different hardware connector.

**frame**   A single still image from either video or film. For video, each frame is made up of two interlaced fields. See *interlaced video.*

**frame blending**   A process of inserting blended frames in place of frames that have been duplicated in clips with slow motion, to make them play back more smoothly. Frame blending is available in the Scrub filter, part of the registration incentive pack of plug-ins.

**frame rate**   The speed at which the individual images making up a moving sequence play back. It's stated in terms of frames per second (fps). Film in 16mm or 35mm is usually shot at 24 fps; NTSC video is 29.97 fps; PAL video is 25 fps. HD can have several different frame rates.

**frequency**   The number of times a sound or signal vibrates each second, measured in cycles per second, or *hertz.* Audio recordings are made up of a vast collection of waveforms, using many different frequencies of sound. Each frequency in a recording is associated with an audio pitch. The frequencies of an audio recording can be changed to disguise a voice or to clean up an unwanted noise.

**gain**   In video, the level of white in a video picture; in audio, the loudness of an audio signal.

**G**

**gamma**   A curve that describes how the middle tones of an image appear. Gamma is a nonlinear function often confused with *brightness* or *contrast.* Changing the value of the gamma affects midtones while mostly leaving the whites and blacks of the image unaltered. Gamma adjustment is often used to compensate for differences between footage acquisition formats.

**garbage matte**   A matte that removes unwanted objects from an image.

**generators**   Clips that are synthesized (or generated) by Motion. Generators can be used as different kinds of backgrounds and elements for visual design.

**GPU**   (graphics processing unit) The central processor inside a modern computer graphics card.

**gradient**   A generated image that changes smoothly from one color to another across the image.

**grading**   The process of color-correcting footage to achieve a desired look.

**greenscreen**   A solid green background placed behind a subject and photographed so that later the subject can be extracted and composited into another image. See also *bluescreen*.

**H**

**Hi8**   A high-end consumer analog videotape format that has a quality between that of VHS and DV.

**high definition**   (HD) High definition was created to increase the amount of pixels onscreen (a higher definition) as well as to solve many of the frame rate and cadence problems between film and video. There are two main types of HD footage. The highest is 1080, with a native resolution of 1920x1080. The other is 720, which has a native resolution of 1280x720. Both formats can have different frame rates and can be either progressive or interlaced.

**high-key images**   Images that are made up of mostly light values.

**histogram**   A window that displays the relative strength of all luminance values in a video frame, from black to super white. It is useful for comparing two clips in order to match their brightness values more closely. Available in the Levels filter.

**hue**   A specific color or pigment, such as red.

**I**

**In point**   The first frame of an object to be displayed in the Canvas.

**Insert edit**   To insert a clip into an existing sequence into the Timeline, which automatically moves the other clips (or remaining frames of a clip) to the right to make room for it. An Insert edit does not replace existing material.

**interlaced video**   A video scanning method that first scans the odd picture lines (field 1) and then scans the even picture lines (field 2), which merges them into one single frame of video. Used in standard-definition video.

**J**

**jiggle**   To move a parameter away from its current value, then move it back to that original value. Used to force Motion to create a keyframe in Record Animation mode.

**jog**   To move forward or backward through your video one frame at a time.

**JPEG** (Joint Photographic Experts Group) A popular image file format that lets you create highly compressed graphics files. The amount of compression used can be varied. Less compression results in a higher-quality image.

**jump cut** A cut in which an abrupt change occurs between two shots, with no continuity from one to the other.

**keyframe** A point on the Timeline where a specific parameter value has been set. Motion interpolates between keyframes to create in-between frames.

**K**

**keying** The process of creating a mask (key) to eliminate a specific background area in order to composite foreground elements against a different background. See *chroma-keying*.

**layers** Containers that group several objects in a Motion project. Layers can be nested inside other layers. Filters and behaviors applied to a layer will affect all the elements contained within it. Known in other applications as *precompositions*.

**L**

**letterbox** Describes when video is displayed to fit within a standard 4:3 monitor, resulting in a black bar at the top and the bottom of the picture.

**linear editing** A video-editing style in which a program is edited together by copying shots from the original source tapes to a master tape, one by one. Because the assembly is linear, any changes made to an earlier point on the tape result in the rest of the edited tape having to be reassembled from that point forward. See *nonlinear editing*.

**low-key images** Images that are made up of mostly dark values.

**luma** Short for *luminance*. A value describing the brightness information of the video signal without color (chroma). Equivalent to a color television broadcast viewed on a black-and-white television set.

**Luma Key** A filter used to key out a luminance value, creating a matte based on the brightest or darkest area of an image. Keying out a luminance value works best when your clip has a large discrepancy in exposure between the areas you want to key out and the foreground images you want to preserve. See *keying* and *matte*.

**luminance** See *luma*.

**M**

**markers**   Indicators that can be placed on a clip or globally in a project to help you find a specific location while you edit. Can be used to sync action between two clips, identify beats of music, mark a reference word from a narrator, and so on.

**mask**   An image, clip, or shape used to define areas of transparency in another clip. Acts like an external *alpha channel*. A mask is an application of a matte.

**master shot**   A single, long shot of dramatic action from which shorter cuts, such as close-ups, and medium shots are taken in order to fill out the story.

**matte**   An effect that uses information in one layer of video to affect another layer. Mattes are useful when you want to use one clip to selectively hide or reveal part of another—for example, to reveal parts of a video layer with a round spotlight shape. Matte filters can be used by themselves to mask out areas of a clip, or to create alpha channel information for a clip in order to make a transparent border around the clip that can be composited against other layers. See *alpha channel*.

**media file**   A generic term for elements such as movies, sounds, and pictures.

**midtones**   The middle brightness range of an image. Not the very brightest part, not the very darkest part.

**mini-Timeline**   The small timeline at the base of the Canvas that solos the timing events for the selected object, filter, mask, or behavior.

**mono audio**   A type of sound in which audio channels are taken from a tape and mixed together into a single track, using equal amounts of audio channels 1 and 2.

**motion blur**   An effect that blurs any clip with keyframed motion applied to it, similar to blurred motion recorded by a camera.

**motion path**   A path that appears in the Canvas showing the path a clip will travel based on *keyframe* points that are applied to the clip.

**motion tracking**   A technique that involves selecting a particular region of an image and analyzing its motion over time.

**MPEG**   (Moving Picture Experts Group) A group of compression standards for video and audio, which includes MPEG-1, MPEG-2, and MPEG-4.

**MPEG-4**  A global multimedia standard based on the QuickTime file format, delivering scalable, high-quality audio and video streams over a wide range of bandwidths, ranging from cell phone to broadband, that also supports 3D objects, sprites, text, and other media types.

**nest**  To place a layer into another layer so that it effectively acts as a single object in the new layer.

**N**

**non–drop frame timecode**  NTSC timecode in which frames are numbered sequentially and run at 30 fps. NTSC's frame rate, however, is actually 29.97 fps; therefore, non–drop frame timecode is off by 3 seconds and 18 frames per hour in comparison to actual elapsed time.

**noninterlaced video**  The standard representation of images on a computer, also referred to as *progressive scan*. The monitor displays the image by drawing each line, continuously one after the other, from top to bottom.

**nonlinear editing**  A video-editing process that uses computer hard disks to random-access the media. It allows the editor to reorganize clips very quickly or make changes to sections without having to re-create the entire program.

**nonlinear editor**  (NLE) An editing platform (usually on a computer) used to perform nonlinear editing.

**nonsquare pixel**  A pixel whose height is different from its width. An NTSC pixel is taller than it is wide, and a PAL pixel is wider than it is tall.

**NTSC**  (National Television Systems Committee) The standard of color TV broadcasting used mainly in North America, Mexico, and Japan, consisting of 525 lines per frame, 29.97 frames per second, and 720x486 pixels per frame (720x480 for DV). See *PAL*.

**NTSC legal**  The range of color that can be broadcast free of distortion according to the NTSC standards, with maximum allowable video at 100 IRE units and black at 7.5 IRE units.

**offset tracking**  A tracking process that is used when your reference pattern becomes obscured. With offset tracking, the track point follows the same path, but a new search region/reference pattern is used to acquire the tracking data.

**O**

**opacity** The degree to which an image is transparent, allowing images behind to show through. An opacity of 0 percent means an object is invisible; an opacity of 100 percent means the object is completely opaque.

**Out point** The last frame of an object to be displayed in the Canvas.

**overscan** The part of the video frame that cannot be seen on a TV or video monitor. Broadcast video is an overscan medium, meaning that the recorded frame size is larger than the viewable area on a video monitor. The overscan part of the picture is usually hidden behind the plastic bezel on the edge of a television set.

**Overwrite edit** An edit where the clip being edited into a sequence replaces an existing clip. The duration of the sequence remains unchanged.

**P**

**PAL** (Phase Alternating Line) This system is the European color TV broadcasting standard, consisting of 625 lines per frame, running at 25 frames per second and 720x576 pixels per frame. See *NTSC*.

**pan** To rotate a camera left or right without changing its position. The term has been adapted in computer graphics to refer to the movement of individual video elements.

**PICT** The native still-image file format for Macintosh developed by Apple Computer.

**pixel** Short for *picture element*. One dot in a video or still image.

**pixel aspect ratio** The width-to-height ratio for the pixels that compose an image. Pixels on computer screens and in high-definition video signals are square (1:1 ratio). Pixels in standard-definition video signals are nonsquare.

**playhead** A navigational element on the scrubber bar that shows the current frame in the Timeline, Canvas, Keyframe Editor, or Audio Editor.

**postproduction** The phase of film, video, and audio editing that begins after all the footage is shot.

**premultiplication** The process of multiplying the RGB channels in an image by their alpha channel.

**preset**   A portion of a Motion project saved into the Favorites section of the Library.

**QuickTime**   Apple's cross-platform multimedia technology. Widely used for editing, compositing, CD-ROM, Web video, and more.

**Q**

**QuickTime streaming**   Apple's streaming-media addition to the QuickTime architecture. Used for viewing QuickTime content in real time on the Web.

**real time**   Refers to the ability to play back video content during preview at exactly the same frame rate as the final intended output. Can also refer to the ability to update parameters and instantly see the result of the change.

**R**

**redo**   To reverse an undo, which restores the last change made to a project.

**render**   The process by which the computer calculates final frames for a project. In Motion, the rendering takes place in the GPU of the graphics card.

**RGB**   An abbreviation for *red, green,* and *blue,* which are the three primary colors that make up a color video image.

**rotoscoping**   A frame-by-frame hand-painting technique to create imagery over time.

**safe zones**   The two sets of lines representing Action Safe and Title Safe areas in the Canvas. See *Action Safe*; *Title Safe*.

**S**

**sampling**   The process during which analog audio is converted into digital information. The sampling rate of an audio stream specifies how many samples are captured. Higher sample rates are able to reproduce higher-pitched sounds. Examples: 44.1 Kbytes, 48 Kbytes. Greater bit depths during sampling increase the dynamic range (changes in volume) of the audio.

**saturation**   The purity of color. As saturation is decreased, the color moves toward gray.

**scale**   An adjustable value that changes the overall size of a clip. The proportion of the image may or may not be maintained.

**scrub**  To move through a clip or sequence by dragging the playhead. Scrubbing is used to find a particular point or frame or to hear the audio.

**SECAM**  (Sequential Couleur Avec Memoir) The French television standard for playback. As with PAL, the playback rate is 25 fps and the frame size is 720x546. Primarily a broadcast medium; editing for SECAM broadcasts is still performed in PAL.

**sequence**  An edited assembly of video, audio, or graphics clips.

**SMPTE**  (Society of Motion Picture and Television Engineers) The organization responsible for establishing various broadcast video standards, like the SMPTE standard timecode for video playback.

**snapping**  The process by which the playhead or an object in the Canvas "snaps," or moves directly, to guides, markers, or edit points when it is moved close to them.

**solo**  The process of temporarily disabling all objects other than the selected objects in order to improve real-time performance.

**sound byte**  A short excerpt taken from an interview clip.

**square pixel**  A pixel that has the same height as width. Computer monitors have square pixels, but NTSC and PAL video do not.

**stabilization**  The process of selecting a particular region of an image and analyzing its motion over time. Once analyzed, the motion data is inverted and applied to the clip, causing it to become stable. Clips need to be stabilized for a variety of reasons, from weave created by an unsteady camera gate to a shaky camera move.

**standard definition**  The term used to differentiate traditional television broadcast signals from those of new high-definition formats. Standard-definition broadcast signals are usually 720x486 (for NTSC) or 720x576 (for PAL). See *high definition*.

**stereo audio**  Sound that is separated into two channels, one carrying the sounds for the right ear and one for the left ear. Stereo pairs are linked and are always edited together. Audio-level changes are automatically made to both channels at the same time.

**straight cut**    An edit in which both the video and audio tracks are cut together to the Timeline.

**streaming**    The delivery of media over an intranet or over the Internet.

**super black**    Black that is darker than the levels allowed by the CCIR 601 engineering standard for video. The CCIR 601 standard for black is 7.5 IRE in the United States and 0 IRE for PAL and NTSC in Japan.

**super white**    A value or degree of white that is brighter than the accepted normal value of 100 IRE allowed by the CCIR 601 standard.

**T**

**talent**    An actor in a clip.

**thumbnails**    Small square icons displaying a frame of the represented clip.

**TIFF**    (Tagged Image File Format) A widely used bitmapped graphics file format that handles monochrome, grayscale, and 8- and 24-bit color.

**tilt**    To pivot the camera up and down, which causes the image to move up or down in the frame.

**time remapping**    The process of changing the speed of playback of a clip over time. The equivalent of varying the crank of a film camera. Available in Motion via the Scrub filter, part of the registration incentive plug-in pack.

**timecode**    A unique numbering system of electronic signals laid onto each frame of videotape that is used to identify specific frames of video. Each frame of video is labeled with hours, minutes, seconds, and frames (01:00:00:00). Timecode can be drop frame, non–drop frame, time of day (TOD), or EBU (European Broadcast Union—for PAL projects).

**timecode gap**    An area of tape with no timecode at all. Timecode gaps usually signify the end of all recorded material on a tape, but they may occur due the starting and stopping of the camera or tape deck during recording.

**Timeline**    A window in Motion for displaying and editing the timing events for all objects, filters, and behaviors.

**Title Safe**   Part of the video image that is guaranteed to be visible on all televisions. The Title Safe area is the inner 80 percent of the screen. To prevent text in your video from being hidden by the edge of a TV set, you should restrict any titles or text to the Title Safe area.

**tracking**   The process of analyzing the motion of one clip and applying that motion to another clip.

**tracks**   Layers in the Timeline that contain the audio or video clips in a project.

**transfer modes**   Another term for *blend modes.*

**trimming**   To precisely add or subtract frames from the In or Out point of a clip. Trimming is used to fine-tune an edited sequence by carefully adjusting many edits in small ways.

**U**

**underscan**   To display video on a computer or video monitor with a black border around the edge, so that no part of the frame is hidden from the viewer (for example, the Action Safe area is not cropped out, as it would be on a normal television set). Computers display underscan video.

**undo**   A feature that allows you to cancel out the last change made.

**V**

**variable speed**   See *time remapping.*

**Vectorscope**   A window in Final Cut Pro that graphically displays the color components of a video signal, precisely showing the range of colors in the signal and measuring their intensity and hue. It can be used to calibrate the color in video signals being captured from videotape, as well as to compare two clips for purposes of color correction. Motion projects can be referenced in Final Cut Pro to take advantage of its Vectorscope.

**video-in-text effect**   When a video image is matted inside the shape of text.

**vignette**   A popular photographic effect in which the photo gradually darkens around the edges, usually in an oval shape.

**VTR / VCR**   (videotape recorder/videocassette recorder) A tape machine used for recording pictures and sound on videotape.

**VU meter**   (Volume Unit meter) An analog meter for monitoring audio levels.

**W**

**WAV**  A sound file format developed by Microsoft and IBM.

**white balance**   To make adjustments to a video signal being recorded in order to reproduce white as true white. For example, if the white in a shot is too green due to fluorescent lighting, white balancing adds enough magenta to make the white appear neutral.

**white level**   An analog video signal's amplitude for the lightest white in a picture, represented by IRE units.

**wide-screen**   A format for shooting and projecting a movie in theaters in which the original footage doesn't get cut off because of the 4:3 aspect ratio. With the advent of high-definition video, wide-screen 16:9 video is coming into more popular use. See *16:9*.

**wide-screen mask filter**   Adds black bars across the top and bottom of a 4:3 image that crop it to a 16:9 format.

**X**

**x-axis**   Refers to the *x* coordinate in Cartesian geometry. The *x* coordinate describes horizontal placement in motion effects.

**y-axis**   Refers to the *y* coordinate in Cartesian geometry. The *y* coordinate describes vertical placement in motion effects.

**Y**

**YUV**   The three-channel PAL video signal with one luminance (Y) and two chrominance color difference signals (UV). It is often misapplied to refer to NTSC video, which is YIQ.

**Z**

**z-axis**   Refers to the *z* coordinate in Cartesian geometry. The *z* coordinate describes perpendicular placement in motion effects.

**zoom**   To change the magnification of your Canvas or Timeline.

# Index

# Apple Certification
## Fuel your mind.
## Reach your potential.

Stand out from the crowd. Differentiate yourself and gain recognition for your expertise by earning Apple Certified Pro status to validate your Motion 4 skills.

This book prepares you to earn Apple Certified Pro—Motion 4 Level One. Level One certification attests to essential operational knowledge of the application. Level Two certification demonstrates mastery of advanced features and a deeper understanding of the application. Take it one step further and earn Master Pro certification in Final Cut Studio.

### Three Steps to Certification

1   Choose your certification path.
    More info: training.apple.com/certification.

2   Select a location:

    **Apple Authorized Training Centers** (AATCs) offer all exams (Mac OS X, Pro Apps, iLife, iWork, and Xsan). AATC locations: training.apple.com/locations

    **Prometric Testing Centers** (1-888-275-3926) offer all Mac OS X exams, and the Final Cut Pro Level One exam. Prometric centers: www.prometric.com/apple

3   Register for and take your exam(s).

*"Now when I go out to do corporate videos and I let them know that I'm certified, I get job after job after job."*

—Chip McAllister, Final Cut Pro Editor and
Winner of The Amazing Race 2004

### Reasons to Become an Apple Certified Pro

- **Raise your earning potential.** Studies show that certified professionals can earn more than their non-certified peers.

- **Distinguish yourself from others in your industry.** Proven mastery of an application helps you stand out from the crowd.

- **Display your Apple Certification logo.** Each certification provides a logo to display on business cards, resumes and websites.

- **Publicize your Certifications.** Publish your certifications on the Apple Certified Professionals Registry to connect with schools, clients and employers.

### Training Options

Apple's comprehensive curriculum addresses your needs, whether you're an IT or creative professional, educator, or service technician. Hands-on training is available through a worldwide network of Apple Authorized Training Centers (AATCs) or in a self-paced format through the Apple Training Series and Apple Pro Training Series. Learn more about Apple's curriculum and find an AATC near you at training.apple.com.

# The Apple Pro Training Series

Apple Certified

**The best way to learn Apple's professional digital video and audio software!**

The Apple Pro Training Series is the official training curriculum of the Apple Pro Training and Certification program. Upon completing the course material in these books, you can become an Apple Certified Pro by taking the certification exam at an Apple Authorized Training Center.

To find an Authorized Training Center near you, visit:

**www.apple.com/software/pro/training**

**Final Cut Pro 7**
0-321-63527-2 • $54.99

**Final Cut Pro 7 Advanced Editing**
0-321-64765-3 • $59.99

**Motion 4**
0-321-63529-9 • $54.99

**Sound Editing in Final Cut Studio**
0-321-64748-3 • $54.99

**Color Correction in Final Cut Studio**
0-321-63528-0 • $54.99

**DVD Studio Pro 4, Third Edition**
0-321-53409-3 • $54.99

**Logic Pro 9 and Logic Express 9**
0-321-63680-5 • $54.99

**Compressor 3.5**
0-321-64743-2 • $29.99

**Final Cut Server 1.5**
0-321-64765-3 • $54.99

**Final Cut Pro 7 Quick-Reference Guide**
0-321-69468-6 • $29.99

**Motion 4 Quick-Reference Guide**
0-321-63677-5 • $29.99

# The Apple Training Series

Apple Certified

**The best way to learn Apple's hardware, Mac OS X, and iLife applications.**

**iLife '09**
0-321-61850-5 • $39.99

**iWork '09**
0-321-61851-3 • $39.99

**GarageBand '09**
0-321-64852-8 • $39.99

**Mac OS X Support Essentials v10.6**
0-321-63534-5 • $59.99

**Mac OS X Server Essentials v10.6**
0-321-63533-7 • $64.99

**AppleScript 1-2-3**
0-321-14931-9 • $49.99

To order books or view the entire Apple Pro Training Series catalog , visit: **www.peachpit.com/appleprotraining**

# **Motion** Templates
*(with a flair for design)*

Creating professional-caliber motion graphics can be costly and time consuming. With Ripple Training's **Designer Templates**, you have access to title treatments, bumpers, and interstitials, created by the industry's top motion graphic designers.

Each template comes in 4 different color palettes, 13 different video resolutions and 2 hours of instructional videos that explain how to modify them in Final Cut Pro and Motion. Templates can be purchased separately or as a set.

Pleas visit www.rippletraining.com to order.

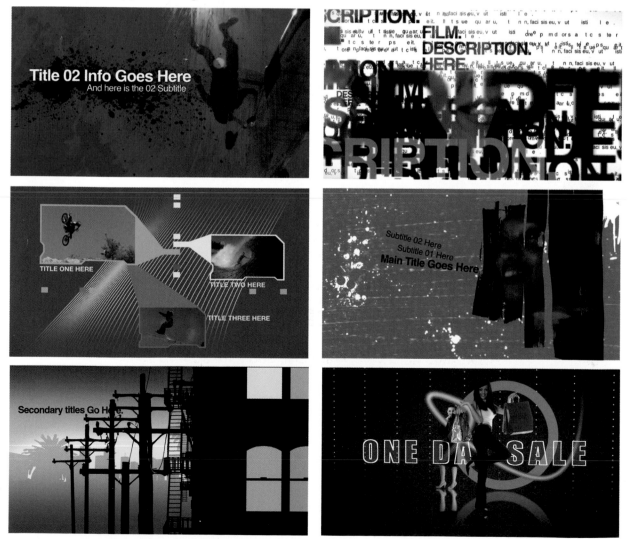